Performance on Behalf of the Environment

Performance on Behalf of the Environment

Edited by

Richard D. Besel and Jnan A. Blau

LEXINGTON BOOKS
Lanham • Boulder • New York • Toronto • Plymouth, UK

Published by Lexington Books
A wholly owned subsidiary of Rowman & Littlefield
4501 Forbes Boulevard, Suite 200, Lanham, Maryland 20706
www.rowman.com

10 Thornbury Road, Plymouth PL6 7PP, United Kingdom

British Library Cataloguing in Publication Information Available

Library of Congress Cataloging-in-Publication Data Available

ISBN 978-0-7391-7498-2 (cloth: alk. paper) – ISBN 978-0-7391-7499-9 (electronic)

♾™ The paper used in this publication meets the minimum requirements of American
National Standard for Information Sciences—Permanence of Paper for Printed Library
Materials, ANSI/NISO Z39.48-1992.

Printed in the United States of America

Contents

PART III: MATERIALS AND PROCESSES

Chapter One

Introduction:
Performance on Behalf of the Environment

Jnan A. Blau and Richard D. Besel

Human degradation of the environment has been documented by scholars across a range of disciplines: the global temperature of the planet continues to rise, abandoned industrial sites stain once vibrant communities, and questions about the purity of our water and foods linger. In the shadow of these material conditions, concerned citizens have reacted by issuing critiques against careless consumerism and excessive lifestyles. Their hope is to illustrate and inspire alternative ways of living. As part of such efforts and activism, some have turned to performance as a means to investigate matters further, pose challenges and questions, and enact new ways of being and thinking in a globalized world. Performance, as a generative method of inquiry, provides opportunities for both embodied practice and theoretical insight—with the two often very much intertwined. *Performance on Behalf of the Environment* is a collection of essays that explore critically the strengths, limitations, and processes of what can be termed environmental performances.

By "environmental performance," we do not mean to limit our focus with single, prescriptive definitions. Instead, we subscribe to broad understandings of both "environment" and "performance." As James Cantrill and Christine Oravec have argued, "the environment we experience and affect is largely a product of how we come to talk about the world," and thus, "environment" is a constantly contested and changing conception (2). Robert Cox concurs by noting that what people mean by "environment" is "highly *contingent*," shifting in various historical, ideological, cultural, and communicative contexts (39). "Performance," of course, is no easier to define than "environmental." However, seminal work by performance studies scholars can and does provide theoretical touchstones. Richard Schechner's now-famous notion that performance is/as "restored behavior" draws attention to the symbolic, theatrical, and transformative nature of human behaviors which take place on a continuum spanning—and blurring the lines between—everyday life, ritual, theatre, and culture. Here, the fields of anthropology and theatre studies (among others) cross-pollinate to reveal human activity as taking place within the widening concentric circles of *drama*, *script*, *theatre*, and *per-*

formance. Ronald Pelias and James VanOosting, for their part, note that the term encompasses *use, qualities,* and *effects* or *response*. Performance in/as *use* identifies instances of discourse or activity that "function aesthetically in the social and cultural life of various human communities" (220). To understand performance as a *quality* is to acknowledge, and to marshal, certain criteria—often referred to or understood as being "aesthetic" in nature—that frame the act as something "special," as a "heightened" communicative interaction, as phenomena somehow distinct, yet never really separable from, everyday communication (Bauman). Alternately, Pelias and VanOosting note that performance's constitutive elements are *text, event, performer,* and *audience*. The "performative turn" in recent multidisciplinary scholarship, in other words, renders *works* as *texts* and *products* as *processes* (see, e.g., HopKins; Cook; and Phelan and Lane), with "performance" becoming at once both a formally reflexive methodology and a means of communication.

To be sure, we are most keenly interested in the ways in which "environment" and "environmentalism" intersect with "performance," the term(s) interanimating, and mutually constituting, each other. We believe the collection of essays herein moves us toward understanding this intersection in important, even necessary, ways—and toward taking seriously the implications and injunctions of a sustained scholarship of "environmental performance."

Performance on Behalf of the Environment finds its conceptual origins in 2010, when we assembled an environmental performance panel for the National Communication Association Convention with the explicit aim of exploring the interconnections of environmental communication and performance studies scholarship. The panel was a success, and some of the revised papers from that panel are now included in this collection. Following the convention, we thought the area of environmental performance could benefit from a wider discussion involving voices beyond the Communication Studies discipline. Although one of us (Besel) had studied environmental communication and rhetoric for years and the other had a long-standing relationship with performance studies (Blau), it surprised both of us to discover that very little was published that put the two fields of study into conversation with one another. We issued a call for chapter proposals and are now delighted to present a collection that contains work grounded in an exciting array of perspectives and methods, addresses important subject matters, and illustrates the application of performance theory—all with an eye toward understanding and fostering dialogue about the environment.

The book is divided into three sections: Performers and Audiences; Places and Spaces; and Materials and Processes. Before briefly addressing the chapters included in each of these sections, a few comments about our choice to use these headings are in order. First, we do not wish to suggest that the study of environmental performances should be reduced to these three areas. We offer these divisions only as one of many possible assemblages available to researchers. Second, we also do not mean to suggest that the chapters in each section address issues included in that section alone. Indeed, rigorous analysis of any subject touches on a number of topical areas. We recognize that readers who may be interested in environmental performers may find material in a chapter included in the Places and Spaces section just as useful as one included in the Performers and Audiences section. Our decisions to place the chapters were based on our perceptions of what the chapters emphasized most, and on the ways in which the chapters within each section, taken together, make an interesting, important case.

Section 1, Performers and Audiences, contains four chapters that focus on performer-audience experiences and interactions. In "It's a Party, Not a Protest: Environmental Community Co-Incident Performance, and the San José Bike Party," authors David P. Terry and Anne Marie Todd investigate the San José Bike Party as "an embodied articulation" that both builds community and engages in the social construction of the urban environment. As a "performance of becoming," Terry and Todd's participation in a bike party via critical performance ethnography informs their understanding of how the event provides riders and bystanders a realistic alternative to fossil fuels-based transportation. In "Performing Nonhuman Liberation: How ALF and ELF Rupture the Political Imagination," Jason Del Gandio investigates the performances of the Animal Liberation Front and the Earth Liberation Front to argue that they "performatively rupture the political imagination and thus set conditions for the possibility of a different world" for audiences. Alison Bodkin, in "Eco-Comedy Performance: An Alchemy of Environmentalism and Humor," persuasively argues that environmentalists need not always embrace doom and gloom in their environmental messages. Using an array of examples, Bodkin contends eco-comedy performances have the potential to simultaneously advance environmentally friendly agendas while also resisting destructive, anthropocentric agendas by mimicking (perhaps even making fun of) the language of human-centered resourcist ideologies. Finally, Richard D. Besel uses theoretical concepts such as "perspective by incongruity" and "polysemy" to analyze the performances of self-proclaimed "vaga-bum" Daniel Suelo in "Embodied Perspective by Incongruity: Environmental Critique in an Age of Everyday Performance." Besel argues: "By juxtaposing Suelo's life with their own, audiences are confronted with an alternative way of seeing their relationship with the world." What all of these chapters have in common, despite the diversity of artifacts and approaches, is a focus on how performers encourage audiences to see their roles in the world in new and dynamic ways.

In section 2, Places and Spaces, the focus of the next four chapters shifts. While performers and audiences are certainly important to these chapters, *where* the performances take place or *where* space is defined is more prominently featured. Barbara Willard begins this section with her rhetorical and ethnographic study of community gardens in Chicago, titled "Reinhabiting the Land: From Vacant Lot to Garden Plot." Willard illustrates how these community gardens are "a performance of reinhabitation, as a way of reclaiming land cast aside as useless and separate from the productive life of the city." In "'Progress Fell Upon Us': Ecotourism, Culture, and Performance in the Peruvian Amazon," Jnan Blau draws on experiences from two trips to South America to offer an (auto)ethnographic analysis aimed at understanding "nature as phenomenal performative display," as a place "where the fate of human and nonhuman life on Earth is being worked out." Next, Julia Handschuh, in "'On Finding Ways of Being': Kinesthetic Empathy in Dance and Ecology," ruminates "on the kinesthetic relations between body and place." It is in the connections between performer and space that Handshuh argues we are best able to cultivate and understand how we are to "be" in/with the world. Finally, Leila Nadir and Cary Peppermint take us on a media-guided hike through urban areas in "*Indeterminate Hikes+*: Hiking Through the Urban Wilderness." Hikers in and around Denton, Texas, are asked to "rethink the remoteness and inaccessibility so often applied to 'nature' or 'wilderness,'" in favor of better appreciating the places and spaces that surround us in our everyday lives. Each of the chapters in section 2 invites readers to understand the influence environmental performances have in shaping our understanding of, and our relationship with, our surroundings.

The final section of the book consists of three chapters focusing on Materials and Processes. In "Indigenous Theatre in Global Times: Situated Knowledge and Ecological Communities in *Salmon is Everything* and

Burning Vision," Theresa J. May draws on her experiences with indigenous theater to illustrate how environmental performances, as a form of "ecodramaturgy," enable the process of "ecological healing" to take place. Ray Schultz and Jess Larson also investigate theatrical environmental performance in "Staging Sustainable Shakespeare: 'Greening' the Bard While Advancing Institutional Mission," but their emphasis is on the practical materials out of which performances emerge. Reporting on their experiences of sustainably presenting shows crafted from recycled materials, Schultz and Larson ask us to rethink the way we use the material world—as creative artists and, by extension, as reflexive citizens. Finally, Courtney Ryan, in "Puppet Planets and Spirit Soldiers: Staging Ecological Representations in *Baby Universe* and *Forgotten World*," asks whether or not "all human representations of nonhumans inevitably anthropomorphize, assimilate, or consume what they claim to represent." Each of these chapters investigates the material underpinnings of environmental representations, problematize processes, and point researchers in new directions.

As we end this brief introductory chapter, we realize that we do not have the final word on the nature of environmental performances. We wish for this diverse collection of topics and approaches to be another thread—hopefully a useful one—in the larger, ongoing conversation about performances on behalf of the environment. Indeed, we cannot wait to see what the next act will bring to the stage.

Works Cited

Bauman, Richard. "Performance." *Folklore, Cultural Performances, and Popular Entertainment: A Communication-Centered Handbook.* Ed. Richard Bauman. New York: Oxford UP, 1992. 41-49. Print.

Cantrill, James G., and Christine L. Oravec, eds. *The Symbolic Earth.* Lexington: U of Kentucky P, 1996. Print.

Cook, Nicholas. "Between Process and Product: Music and/as Performance." *Music Theory Online: The Online Journal of the Society for Music Theory* 7.2 Apr 2001. Society for Music Theory. Web. 4 May 2013.

Cox, Robert. *Environmental Communication and the Public Sphere.* Los Angeles: Sage, 2013. Print.

HopKins, Mary Frances. "The Performance Turn—And Toss." *Quarterly Journal of Speech* 81 (1995): 228-36. Print.

Pelias, Ronald J., and James VanOosting. "A Paradigm for Performance Studies." *Quarterly Journal of Speech* 73 (1987): 219-31. Print.

Phelan, Peggy, and Jill Lane, eds. *The Ends of Performance*. New York: New
     York UP, 1998. Print.
Schechner, Richard. *Between Theater and Anthropology*. Philadelphia: U of
     Pennsylvania P, 1985. Print.
Schechner, Richard. *Performance Theory*. New York: Routledge, 1998. Print.

Part I

PERFORMERS AND AUDIENCES

Chapter Two

It's a Party, Not a Protest: Environmental Community, Co-Incident Performance, and the San José Bike Party

David P. Terry and Anne Marie Todd

For twenty years, on the last Friday of every month, thousands of bicyclists have participated in Critical Mass, rolling through the streets of San Francisco and hundreds of other cities around the world, clogging commutes, and angering drivers—horrifyingly illustrated in Brazil, in February 2011, when a driver drove his car into a crowd of cyclists, injuring forty. Critical Mass rides are decentralized political actions, with varying goals of reclaiming space, promoting bicycle transportation, and protesting car culture. Similar rides with assorted degrees of affiliation have become regular events in cities all over the world. While the protest ethos of Critical Mass has played well in the city of San Francisco, cycling enthusiasts in Silicon Valley have rethought the protest as a party on wheels.

Beginning in October 2007 as a costumed pack of thirty riders, San José Bike Party is an organized monthly ride in San José, California, that attracts thousands of cyclists each month.[1] The monthly several-hour parade of bikes emphasizes a carnivalesque ethos over any political aims, seeking to "build community through bicycling." This community includes middle-aged activists on beach cruisers as well as aging fitness riders on the latest Gary Fishers, bands of teenagers on tricked-out fixies, well-to-do yuppies on sensible mountain-road bike hybrids, and hundreds of cyclists on "beater" bikes built from mismatched spare parts. The organization seeks to increase good-will towards cyclists on the part of motorists and city officials, promote sustainable transportation practices, create meaningful connections between various kinds of cyclists, and create an increased "local" awareness in a city known for its high-tech escapes and suburban bubbles. Every ride has a theme (World Cup, Anime, Space Cowboys, Rave, etc.) and a meticulously planned route through the streets of San José, in order to attract a diversity of riders on a tour through neighborhoods they might not otherwise visit.

When San José Bike Party's monthly rides seek/claim to be "one-half political party, one-half street party" they evoke a relationship between political efficacy and aesthetic expression that is, arguably, the raison d'être of performance studies (San José Bike Party, "Short Version" 2). Bike Party can be seen as both an expression and a re-enactment of San José and thus has practical and theoretical implications for understanding how performance informs our attitudes toward the spaces where we live, work, and play. Bike Party emerges from and re-sponds to a San José "hidden in the suburban sprawl," mobilizing people to "enjoy the South Bay, ride the streets, and make this place the active and exciting city we want it to be" (San José Bike Party, "About" 2). Bike Party's mobile street party is a "co-incident" performance of com-munity that has the potential to transform a city's very identity from an empty space to an active community (Terry 335).

As "co-incident," Bike Party is a "coming together in space about which the question of causality [and teleology] must remain suspended" (Terry 335). Bike Party is not a performance *by* a community of activists *for* an audience; it is, rather, an embodied articulation *of* diverse co-performers around the co-incidence of bicycling. Bike Party does not express the ideas of a given community of activists, but forges an as-yet-to-be-fully-defined community around multiple intersecting ways of rid-ing bikes. As a collective performance, Bike Party doesn't just "restore behavior" in time, it seeks to articulate new possibilities for co-being in space (Schechner 36). Thus, unlike other attempts at creating community that attempt to reason others into membership, this movement doesn't begin with a set of principles and move to practices, but begins with a performed practice and purposefully allows for multiple interpretations.

San José Bike Party is thus an important experiment in the perfor-mance of community and the social construction of environment, empha-sizing the way that the non- (or multi-) teleological practice of group cy-cling offers an open, but meaningfully articulated, identity. As a performance practice it gives flesh (and wheels) to Giorgio Agamben's abstract sense of a "coming community" (*Coming* 1). As the centerpiece for a "rolling community," cycling approaches what Agamben calls an "inessential commonality," a solidarity that is not a single essence (*Coming* 3). Bike Party moves towards a politics that is "neither of an end in itself nor of means subordinated to an end"; rolling through the streets of San José the cyclists approach "the sphere of a pure mediality without end intended" (Agamben, *Coming* 117). Bike Party is centered on the essentially complex and diverse activity of biking; it thus manages to bring people together in a way that gives greater credence to *togetherness itself* rather than to the ideological motivations for that togetherness. San José Bike Party performatively constructs community in a way that articulates a meaningful but nonessential identity of San José. In the midst of a disconnected, spread-out city, Bike Party creates a co-incidence, a locus for belonging that does not ask its constituent sub-groups to conform to one particular ideal.

These kinds of complex performances of becoming are particularly important for environmental movements because effective environmental activism must be able to not only critique existing relationships between humans and the broader environment but also offer positive, meaningful articulations of alternative modes of belonging. As a response to suburban sprawl, San José Bike Party is an environmental performance that seeks to change the relationship to the environment. And while most people riding in a given month are not likely to identify themselves or their participation in Bike Party as "environmentalist," sustainability is an explicit part of Bike Party's mission: "Bike Party rides aim to demonstrate a tangible alternative to car-based transportation and continue to provide a focal point for the local bike-friendly community for the long term. We aim to leave no trace behind except a good will towards cyclists in the areas we travel" (San José Bike Party, "About" 5). Indeed, the sustainability of Bike Party is what makes it interesting to study: Bike Party is a performance-centered environmental community and an environmentally centered performance community that articulates a way of belonging rather than striking a particular ideological (or particularly activist) stand.

In this essay, we discuss Bike Party as co-incident performance. We have engaged in critical performance ethnography with the monthly rides and rhetorical analysis of Bike Party's online discourse for over the course of a year and half (Madison). We understand our research is not just about reading texts, but about interacting both with and as living bodies. We understand ourselves not as disinterested researchers but as participant co-performers in the Bike Party movement. While astute readers may be able to distinguish the voices of two authors, we found that, as we relate to Bike Party, what unites our voices is of much greater significance than what divides us. The minor loss in specificity caused by the joined voice is, we hope, offset by significant gains in clarity and focus. This is not an *auto*ethnographic account about either of our individual subjectivities. We write, rather, in a "performative I" that recognizes our invested participation as researchers and our embeddedness within broader discourses in "a subjectivity defined by an ethics of sensuous coalition and a politics of errant possibility" (Pollock 239). We interweave the stories of our overlapping experiences within the matrix of overlapping performances that both create and are created by Bike Party.

We discuss four aspects of Bike Party to illustrate its performative qualities. We begin with two central aspects of the group ride: the call-and-response that expresses and extends a "Bike Party ethos" and the re-mapping of the cityscape enacted by the ride's circuitous routes. We then turn to the broader sense of co-incident identity that the rides perform, looking at the community enacted by the rides and the negotiation of conflicts that inevitably arise in such a diverse group. We conclude by discussing the implications of co-incident performance for environmental communication.

Hailing

Early one evening last summer, I sat down to do some writing—or procrastinate and avoid writing by engaging in some "social networking"—and was interrupted by what sounded like a group of undergraduates encouraging each other to take shots through boisterous yelling. It seemed a bit early for a keg party, but as I lived in an old building with thin walls in close proximity to many other such buildings, I had gotten used to sharing sonic space with my neighbors, and I did my best to tune it out. This particular din, however, was syncopated in a way that I couldn't quite place. It didn't slowly build to a crescendo; it got louder, then quieter, in inexplicably sudden bursts. As anyone who has shared a bed with a snorer can attest, the unpredictability of a sustained sound is often more of a nuisance than its pitch or volume.

After about thirty minutes of this, my annoyance and curiosity got the better of me and I left my desk to investigate. I looked up and down the street but could not determine the source of the sound. There were a few folks standing on the sidewalk, but no gathering nearly large enough to have produced the hubbub. Then, a light changed, auto traffic stopped, and I saw a steady stream of cyclists ride past: many colorfully decorated in Mexican, US, and Brazilian flags—this week's theme, I later learned, was "World Cup;" some towed makeshift trailers with massive speakers blasting music and/or companions who were unable to pedal for themselves; still others wove slowly on fixed-gear bikes ("fixies") in mint condition, being careful not to get grease stains on their skinny jeans; still others were clad in logo-laden spandex that, in my opinion, can only be excused by the fashion police in cases of serious feats of speed and endurance. Children rode beside their parents; bands of teenagers rode bikes rigged so low that their knees rose above their necks as they pedaled; a middle-aged woman who looked as though she might have gotten lost on her way to a knitting circle or a feline death support group gently reminded riders to "stay off the sidewalk."

As they passed by, many riders periodically yelled "Biiiiiiike Paaar-taaaaay!" At first I took the utterance to be part of a cultural performance: an expression of excess and joy to demonstrate that "this ride is not like other rides." While this is surely part of the call's function, it is far from an exhaustive account. I soon realized that most riders were not yelling *for* me as an audience; they were yelling *at* me as a potential co-performer: theirs was a performative utterance designed to hail me, to interpolate me into their caravan. I resisted for a while—I had an article to finish for an important journal. I was on a deadline. I didn't have time for this kind of a distraction—but was soon seduced by the sirens' call and ran behind my house to procure my sensible commuter bicycle and my cringe-inducing-grad-student-budget-Styrofoam helmet, and joined the parade.

Leaving my article unfinished, yet still caught up in the mindset of critical scholar, I recognized the "Bike Party!" hail as an effective rhetorical strategy (it had, after all, seduced me away from my writing) designed to "win the favor of this mass public by creating language that stimulates first consent and then identification" (Killingsworth and Palmer 25). The Bike Party hail works to "create valences, open links that attract individuals among the general public by realistically mirroring the experience of daily life without seriously challenging either the basic institutions and ideologies of American life or the values of consumer mentality" (Killingsworth and Palmer 25). Later, I saw this echoed in Bike Party's mission to be "empowering and inclusive: Riders of all ages, skills, and styles of bikes are welcome at Bike Party" (San José Bike Party, "About" 4). The diversity of this pedaling community is part of its siren call: I wasn't going to sign a petition, or hold a sign with my political affiliation; I was simply going to *ride*.

By the time I got out to the street, there were far fewer folks than I had seen from my window. Afraid I had missed the bulk of the party, I pedaled quickly in order to catch up with the group of what I assumed to be a few hundred riders. I'd been living in San José for almost a year and nothing remotely this interesting had happened during that time. I could feel the adrenaline, and was determined not to miss it. As I caught up to the pack, I had flashbacks to my first day at a new junior high school. I became acutely aware of my bike's many flaws: missing headlight, broken toe clips, milk crate secured by a bungee cord instead of a proper basket, grip tape replaced by pink duct tape. I overheard someone make fun of my helmet, and had an internal monologue about whether I should risk my safety to defend my street cred. I wished I had changed out of my sloppy writing outfit into something hipper. I wished I had stayed at home entirely. I fought the urge to turn back. Then, it happened: I saw a six-year-old child smiling at me from the side walk and then, almost involuntarily, I heard it escape my mouth: "Biiiiiiike Paaartaaaaay!" I heard an echo from behind me: "Biiiiiiike Paaartaaaaay!" It sounded like it came from the same person who had been making fun of my helmet. I turned around to confirm and she saw me looking at her. We made eye contact. I smiled awkwardly and wanted, for a brief second, to disappear. Before I sank again into a spiral of shame, I yelled it out again: "Biiiiiiike Paaartaaaaay!" and pedaled furiously away to avoid waiting for a response.

Route

I soon came to San José's City Hall, a hyper-futuristic building that I can see from my university office window and had come to exemplify everything I find problematic about my new city: it looks like a spaceship, it's trying too hard, it's all about the future but doesn't pay enough attention to the present, it's got huge empty space that must have been designed by architects for plastic models of people enjoying a brown bag lunch, but where, in actuality, people pass through, but seldom eat. And there, in this textbook case of urban planning gone wrong, I saw several thousand people racing, dancing, and jousting (yes, jousting) on their bikes.

As I took in the performances of gleeful cyclists, I reflected on these rhetorical actions as providing "some basis for identification, some grounding in the positive content of lived experience." On the grounds of City Hall, Bike Party demonstrated that "abstract forms of civic life have to be filled in with vernacular signs of social membership" (Hariman and Lucaites 25). The crowd pulsed with excitement, as beach cruisers jostled beater bikes, amid pockets of fixed-gear fanatics frolicking in their hipster credibility. Amid the festivities, City Hall gained new life. Was this what architects and city planners envisioned for this sprawling plaza? Perhaps not, one thing about the hundreds of citizens gathered here surely eluded their visions: everyone had a bike! The celebration of alternate transportation and the diversity of participants in this bike party felt different from, and certainly more exciting than, other political rallies I had attended.

I enjoyed the scene for a while and then left to go home to resume work on that all-important essay. As I pulled away, I noticed a steady stream of folks leaving the party together. In fact, what I had perceived as a static group of people on the capital grounds was a temporary pool formed by a much larger river of bodies. I heard the familiar Bike Party refrain as they rode away. Just as it called me from my apartment, it lured me now: I felt compelled to follow them. The ride was far from over. I followed the stream of riders thinking that any minute now it would fold back into a loop. It didn't.

And so I found myself exploring San José in a new way. As I rode along, familiar intersections and nearby trendy restaurants I had reviewed on Yelp! gave way to unfamiliar junctions, and a taste of the sprawl more familiar to South San José. The winding route was clearly purposive. Leaders and guides directed us turn by turn, and my fellow riders helped spread information down the pack of riders. "Bike Party rides explore different neighborhoods and streets of the San José area and with every ride it builds familiarity and connection with our proud city" (San José Bike Party, "About" 3). And while I rode unfamiliar streets, I became aware of a much larger San José than I knew before. Riding created a sense of possibility. Initially I rode *despite* not knowing where the pack was heading, as time past I continued to ride precisely *because* of this very uncertainty: not knowing imbued each block with a sense of discovery. At each turn, I felt a sense of expanse: I could feel my city growing larger and more interesting. Bike Party claims, "bicycling is the ultimate local transportation. . . a person on a bike will intimately know the streets she travels and easily explore diverse areas and encounter personal interactions everywhere" (San José Bike Party, "About" 3). The unconventional route didn't just show me which streets connect to which, it helped me to re-imagine a boring city as one full of life and possibility. My pedal pushes didn't just help me get from point A to point B, they formed a chain of cycling speech acts, which, like what Certeau has called "pedestrian speech acts," quite literally re-made the cityscape they traversed (97).

Over the next few hours I would hear "Biiiiiiike Paaartaaaaay!" — always with a nearly identical volume and inflection—used to inform car drivers that we were coming through and to encourage cops to look the other way in response to public drunkenness; to excuse sloppy riding and to punctuate silences; to cheer on speedy riders and to cheer up those stopped to fix flats. Most often I heard it as a call-and-response. I understood quickly that it is in poor form to hear another rider or spectator call out "Biiiiiiike Paaartaaaaay!" without returning the energy to the sender in some way. We weaved through streets that had clear bike lanes and many that did not. Bicycle Information Resource Directors (with winged badges reading "B.I.R.D.") helped us find the route when we lagged behind and the turns were less than obvious. It was dark at this point, and we rode through neighborhoods that I would have not ridden through alone at that hour. The trail ended at 11 p.m. in a shopping mall twelve miles from my house. I was too tired to join the revelry, so I turned in a direction I thought would take me back home. On my way, I rode back through the same "rough" neighborhood with a newfound confidence. I saw a child playing in her yard, up way past what I would hope to be her bedtime. Although I was alone, she called out to me: "Biiiiiiike Paaartaaaaay!" I returned the call, but before the ensuing involuntary smile had passed from my lips, I passed another house surrounded by four police cars, lights flashing, illuminating officers with guns drawn. I ogled for a few seconds before speeding past on my way home to pass out.

Bike Party routes re-map San José and create new possibilities for community by crossing typical urban boundaries and stitching together neighborhoods most often thought to be (and lived as) separate. In performing this tour of San José, Bike Party "takes us places and is a place, or destination, itself." Bike Party functions as a space for "forging connections between people and places, and (re)building communities"

(Pezzullo 233). The route defines and practices an alternate city from that which most riders experience in their daily commutes. Its collages of mobile sound create what Daniel Makagon has called a "mobile hetero-topia" that re-maps the cityscape by re-living it (223). The re-mapped/re-lived cityscape is full of possibilities for connection even as it exposes existing differences that are typically ignored and creates the possibility for future conflicts. Riding is a way of getting to know the city, but it is also a way of being known by and implicated in the messy realities of city life that one might otherwise ignore. Like those of any vibrant culture, the emergent articulations of Bike Party are defined by both centripetal and centrifugal forces, both pushing and pulling, creating possibilities for both community and conflict.

Community

This first ride piqued my interest. I started following Bike Party's activities online, and learned that the route into a new San José was the result of monthly planning. I learned that there was organization to this madness. B.I.R.D.s, for example, guide riders along the planned path, but also gently educate newer riders about best riding practices (wearing helmets, not riding on the sidewalk, use of turn signals, use of lights, maintaining a non-adversarial relationship with motorists, etc.). For most organizers, cycling is not just a means of transportation; it is a performative way of relating to the world. Thus, in addition to offering tips on how to survive the ride, participants try to recruit one another into particular ways of enjoying the ride. The B.I.R.D.s communicate organizational purpose and cultivate a sense of belonging by performing community. In contrast to Critical Mass, whose elusive Web presence and secretive, morphing route illustrate its decentralized nature, San José Bike Party exhibits purposeful organization, complete with ride counts, "how we ride" guidelines, and an extensive social media presence. When I learned that I was one of more than three thousand riders that night, I was even more enthused. The sense of community I felt on the ride was reiterated by online comments on the websites. I returned to the website periodically during that time, keeping my curiosity piqued until my next ride.

Months later, I finally rode in my second Bike Party (theme: "Lights!"). Starting out with friends this time, I again experienced an electric gathering at City Hall, but my ride was cut short by a flat tire. My attempts to fix the blowout, even with the myriad of folks who stopped to help, were in vain. I stood at an intersection taking some photographs, gearing up for the long walk home, when a Japanese American man in his seventies walked over from the senior center across the street to ask if I was okay. "I'm fine," I told him, just sorry to miss the party. "What is this? What is the point of this race?" he asked. I told him it wasn't really a race, but a party. As his English was limited and my Japanese nonexistent, I had a hard time conveying the point of the event. He did, however, perceive my disappointment at missing the ride. He spoke briefly in Japanese to the woman next to him before turning back to me: "You can borrow one of our bikes if you want."

I had to decline for a number of reasons, but I think of his kindness every time I pass that corner in Japantown. Perhaps the converse is even more important: I feel myself connected to his neighborhood when I remember his kindness. I have a physical memory of propelling myself from my front door to his. Remembering his kindness is not just about reaching back across time, it is about connecting across space. I have depended more than once on the kindness of strangers in getting to know the city of San José; what makes this particular experience memorable is the deceptively simple fact that I biked there (and walked home!). If you were to ask me how to get to the nearest shopping mall, I would think first of Google maps, then flash to my GPS screen. I'd tell you what freeways to get on and what times of day are best to avoid traffic. If you asked me how to get to Japantown, I would think of this man, engage my kinesthetic memory and, with a surprising degree of accuracy from almost any point in the city of San José, I could point you toward the intersection where he offered me his bike. As an act of performance, Bike Party is tied to an embodied epistemic: doing as a way of knowing; knowing as a way of doing.

In creating community through biking, San José Bike Party constructs a relationship between people and a relationship with the environment. "Community exists where people choose to make it so; making it so is work. That work of community constructs a relation between person and people, and between people and environment" (Rothenbuhler 169). Bike Party's response to San José's suburban sprawl is an articulation of an alternate city energized by community action. Bike Party invites riders to see San José and participate in city life in a new way:

"Everything looks better from the seat of a bike. You can feel the wind on your face, the rhythm of the ground in your legs; you can feel your heart pumping, and the energy of your surroundings encompassing your body. On a bicycle, you can see the city, talk to strangers, escape the insulated bubbles of cars and feel free from the confines of cubicles. A bicycle is freedom, a bicycle is friendly, and a bicycle is life. San José Bike Party is a place to ride bikes, make friends, and have a good time" (San José Bike Party, "About" 5). The perspective afforded by the view from the bicycle instills a new way of performing what it means to live in San José.

Bike Party enabled this meeting with an elderly man with whom I would have been unlikely to make a connection watching a World Cup match in a bar or passing on the street. Through Bike Party, I made connections with the people and places of San José. The feeling was liberating: "Bicycling frees people from costly fees, stuffy cars, sedentary lifestyles, and dreadful commutes. Bike Party rides aim to teach riders the street skills and confidence they need to become daily riders on all kinds of roads" (San José Bike Party, "About" 5). Because Bike Party removes us from our cars and from our neighborhood confines we are more likely to make connections within and across communities. "San José's a huge city with a lot going for it, but we often lack the sort of community gatherings, festivals, and events that other metro areas take for granted. That's where we come in. Bike Party is free to participants, open to all, and offers a great chance to explore our city's interesting neighborhoods while getting a bit of exercise and meeting hundreds of wonderful new friends" (San José Bike Party, "For Drivers," 1). Complaining about how much San José falls short of its potential as a place has, ironically, been one of the defining characteristics of life in the South Bay for some time. Bike Party thus offers a positive re-framing of the city.

In the afterglow of a recent ride, I was annoyed to read a blog post by a San Francisco Critical Mass veteran calling Bike Party a "rose by another name": a mere extension or watered-down version of the San Francisco original. My annoyance quickly turned to pride as I realized that the blogger was missing the point: "he's not *from* here, so he just doesn't get it." The very things that he wanted us to move past (i.e. waiting for lights) were those that made Bike Party meaningful for most participants. The very fact that this SF hipster didn't "get it" meant there was something to "get": with apologies to Gertrude Stein and the city of Oakland, there was a "there" here.

Bike Party's appeal is its performance of community, as experienced in its inclusive hail and geographic stitching together of diverse neighborhoods. This performance harnesses an untapped energy of many of San José's subcultures and performs a "way to San José"— a map toward identity. As the blogger (grudgingly?) wrote: "Given the participants in the ride, I doubt if the culture will remain the same for long. The youth culture in San José hasn't established its own voice in the Bay Area and it seems like the Bike Party might be a place where it could erupt" (Carlsson 12). The emerging empowered subcultures (youth and otherwise) will not have the same character as the relatively homogenous "white hipster" culture of Critical Mass. The "party" in Bike Party is not just a matter of putting a "fun" package on the idea of Critical Mass. The sense of inclusive play in the party is not a matter of marketing and representation: it is a productive force that brings together various constituencies. Play is always, at least partially, autotelic: much of the point of the party disappears into the "ambivalence" of a "carnival sense of the world" (Bakhtin 130). It may well be that, over time, one group takes control of the ride, but for now, the chief characteristic of the party is that anyone with a bike is invited. This is not to say that there are no conflicts; on the contrary, the party is vibrant precisely *because* it allows for productive conflict and doesn't collapse those conflicts into a single, dominant meaning.

Conflict

As Bike Party moves through San José, it performs San José: a city that suffers from an identity complex. Perennially less hip than San Francisco, less groovy than Berkeley, and less gritty than Oakland, San José is saddled with a reputation for sprawl, poor urban planning, and a dearth of good restaurants. Bike Party provides a new perspective, a way of seeing and enacting San José. Bike Party is an organized response to the city's lack of identity: "San José residents deserve alternative activities and a world-class bike ride provides the stepping stone to make the city a happier place to live. We love San José" (San José Bike Party, "About" 1). Bike Party doesn't just offer a way of branding San José so that people can feel more like they belong to the city; it offers an alternative *form* of belonging that is uniquely suited to the diversity and sprawl of the city, what Elspeth Probyn might call an "outside belonging," a connection that recognizes the essential fact of differences (Probyn 5). Bike Party is a mobilization: a movement about (and around) San José. For this reason, rolling community is not without its collisions.

The diversity of bikes and riders I encountered on my first ride, and every ride thereafter, created friction. Bike Party creates traffic. Bike Party is traffic. Thousands of riders pedal through miles of roads meant to hold a few lanes of cars. Red lights and stop signs regulate this flow so that hundreds of bicycles bunch up periodically, frequently surrounding unwitting motorists. The potential for collision exists throughout the ride. At the most basic level, different bikes are made for different kinds of riding. Commuter bikers can easily shift gears to slow down or speed up and stay in formation. Heavy beach cruisers have a hard time staying in a straight line. Racing bikes have a hard time moving slowly. Fixies don't have brakes at all. This is to say nothing of ten-foot-high bike-sculptures and unicycles. Even before accounting for the various skill levels, habits, and degrees of inebriation of their riders, the bikes of Bike Party are not really compatible. Being in the pack can feel empowering because it opens up new city streets, but it is also often scary. A small stutter from one cyclist can quickly cascade through the pack with unpredictable consequences. Furthermore, one quickly learns that, despite Bike Party organizers' attempts to inform "how we ride," it is not safe to assume that one's fellow riders know what they are doing, or have the same understanding of what ought to be done. Most riders are united by their sense that bike riding is cool, but riders' senses of what it actually means to ride are not the same. In support of its mission to educate cyclists about best biking practices, Bike Party publicizes "how we ride" guidelines, posting them online and passing out small flyers so that "Bike Party will be safe and a positive place for riders, drivers, pedestrians and the community" (San José Bike Party, "How We Ride" 1). Throughout the route, B.I.R.D.s help maintain awareness of rules: stay in the right lane, stop at red lights, ride predictably, ride sober. These guidelines work to both maintain and dampen the carnivalesque atmosphere of the rides.

As one might expect given the reputation of Critical Mass, conflict with cars presents itself at nearly every Bike Party. Invariably, cyclists surround cars waiting in left-turn lanes, stymie motorists trying to merge, and often, block intersections for extended bouts as thousands of cyclists stream through. Drivers register a spectrum of reactions from gaping awe at the number of cyclists to confused silence. From throwing out knowing "Bike Party!" yells and whoops of joy to cursing and mocking the riders. From short, rapidly sequenced honks of approval, to long sustained honks of frustration at being denied the right-of-way. Frustrated drivers frequently inch forward to block streams of cyclists. The "how we ride" guidelines advise cyclists to "Roll Past Conflict: If you see an angry driver or pedestrian, roll past it. Don't engage in shouting matches or violent people. Just enjoy your ride. If you see a fellow cyclist stopped in anger, remind them to 'Roll Past Conflict'" (San José Bike Party, "How We Ride"). B.I.R.D.s urge riders to give cars room, and often communicate directly with drivers to help them navigate away from the crowd of bicycles. While they are often successful at defusing conflict between cars and drivers, the process of doing so sometimes creates conflict between riders. Angry drivers visit Bike Party's website to comment on the ride. Detractors and supporters debate the effects of the ride, particularly the behavior of bicyclists, on traffic, on residential neighborhoods, on city life. On the Bike Party website is a letter addressed to drivers, explaining, "we're not out to make your life miserable or to cause a conflict, but sometimes inconveniences and worse do occur" (San José Bike Party, "For Drivers" 1). Bike Party's communicative practices highlight and address the friction between cyclists, drivers, pedestrians, and neighborhoods, and in promoting alternative means to navigate the city, Bike Party offers alternate ways of what it means to live in the city. Bike Party pushes against withdrawal by offering a positive articulation of diversity: enacting a sense of togetherness that doesn't so much eliminate conflicts as provide a meaning structure that makes working through them seem like a worthwhile endeavor.

Through the guidelines of and efforts by Bike Party to make riders and drivers aware of the rules, it aims to create a sense of community. An important part of this occurs in the communication about "how we ride." The Bike Party website acknowledges the social awkwardness of appearing to police others: "No one wants to be an authority figure but the only way to keep this ride going and safe is to be vocal about the rules of the road. A simple 'Stay to the right' is often enough to remind a rider that he or she is slipping. If you see a knucklehead throwing a bottle or littering simply boo that person. It's called community shaming. When everyone participates, it really works" (San José Bike Party, "How We Ride" 3). The communication of "how we ride" occurs in the performance of the shaming. This creates a sense of community: as riders make a choice to "boo" bad behavior, they perform the cultural mores of the community, and also address conflict with confrontation. These "boos" are as much invitation as injunction.

Bike Party offers a productive sense of "coming community" precisely because it allows for centrifugal as well as centripetal forces. The sense of conflict runs not just between cyclists and motorists or between one group of cyclists and another, but *inside* individual cyclists. During one ride, for example, several riders in front of me were verbally accosted by several occupants of a Hummer. Had I been a lone cyclist waiting at an intersection, I would have surely remained silent, fearful of escalating the conflict. Surrounded by an empowered mass is exhilarating, and the othering of and by motorists, particularly those driving Hummers, is undeniably pleasurable. Watching the drivers of the over-priced gas-guzzler being stopped by a bunch of inexpensive bikes was, in a word, awesome. When one of the passengers offered a vulgar sexist epithet, the hair on the back of my neck stood up. I physically felt my support of those who yelled vulgarities back at the motorists even as my sense of self-preservation wanted us to all "roll past" the conflict. I was equal parts "schoolmarm" wanting to end the conflict and (self-) righteous activist wanting to escalate it. My inner conflict reflected the friction engendered by Bike Party's co-incident performance, and exemplifies the power of "inessential commonality" as precisely what enables us to move beyond a single conception of ourselves and toward a sense of an emergent "we." Through encounters at intersections, in passing lanes, and across sidewalks, Bike Party pushes at the edges of San José's urban sprawl and creates connections, developing an emergent community dialogically and inductively rather than monologically and prescriptively.

Conclusion

Michel de Certeau might argue that the "practice" of interrupting traffic turns the over-determined place of the automobile intersection into a space of possibility (Certeau xi). Geographer Yi Fu Tuan might argue that my interaction with the generous man who offered me his bike was a "pause" in space that turned it into a meaningful place (Tuan 6). What both point to is the necessary relationship between embodied performance and the social construction of space and place. Before humans wrote ideas down in words, we "wrote" them on/with/as landscapes and on/with/as our bodies.

At a basic level, Bike Party is a "green" performance in its promotion of an environmentally friendly transportation, wherein the mode of transportation becomes, at the same time, a practice. At a more profound level, San José Bike Party is a performance of the local, and thus establishes a relationship between cyclists and their immediate environment. As a "green" performance, Bike Party works, at least in this instance, not because it requires or promotes some ideological vision of "the environment" that one is to save by driving less, but because it brings humans together in *undetermined* relationship to each other and their lived environment, allowing the rationality of space to emerge meaningfully, coincidentally. Bike Party helps to create environmental citizens precisely by leaving as open as possible the question of what being "environmental" is. It offers not a set of precepts, but a set of actions that can be performed with as-yet-to-be-determined reasons.

For Agamben, the inessential commonality of the coming community is defined by "whatever being" (*Coming* 1). By "whatever" he does not mean that it doesn't matter how the singular participates in the universal (how the specific cyclist relates to the categorical "Bike Party"), but, precisely, that the specificity of how one particular participates in the universal *always* matters. Whatever is thus not the *absence* of caring, but the very *condition of possibility* for meaningful connection. Being towards the other as "whatever" means accepting the other in the complexity of lived materiality, not through an ideological abstraction.

It is often noted that "carnivalesque" performances like the Bike Party can serve as a temporary reprieve that, in the long run, actually re-enforces the hegemonic status quo. This is an important critique that this essay does not dispute. However, to say that the party is not a *sufficient* part of social change does not imply that it is not *necessary*. In order to "think globally and act locally" one must first have a sense of what the "local" is in which one must act: "acting locally" first requires a performative enactment of locality. Forging meaningful articulations between the diverse and segmented suburban sprawl of the South Bay is not only a matter of defining a dominant sense of "us" and inviting the remaining "them" to join or move away. Convincing people to change their most basic habits in the face of grave environmental threats is not only a matter of persuasive PowerPoints. Both require the active cultivation of new forms of belonging. Bike Party illustrates the potential for co-incident environmental performance to forge meaningful but open relationships between living bodies and their environment. Bike Party re-performs San José, and its itinerant community and conflict, and in so doing cultivates a profound sense of local identity that is more dialogically responsive to its environment.

Notes

1. Ridership numbers and other details of Bike Party history are available: <http://wiki.sjbikeparty.org/>.

Works Cited

Agamben, Giorgio. *The Coming Community.* Trans. Michael Hardt. Minneapolis: U Of Minnesota P, 1993. Print.

———. *Means Without Ends: Notes On Politics.* Trans. Vincenzo Binetti and Cesare Casarino. Minneapolis: U Of Minnesota P, 2000. Print.

Bakhtin, Mikhail. *Problems of Dostoevsky's Poetics.* Trans Caryl Emerson, Minneapolis: U of Minnesota P, 1984. Print.

Carlsson, C. (2010, July 20). A Rose By Another Name: San José's Bike Party. Retrieved from <http://sf.streetsblog.org/2010/04/19/a-rose-by-another-name-san-joses-bike-party/>

Certeau, Michelle de. *The Practice Of Everyday Life.* Trans. S. Rendall. Berkeley: U Of California P, 1984. Print.

Hariman, Robert and John Lucaites. "Public Identity And Collective Memory in U.S. Iconic Photography: The Image Of 'Accidental Napalm'." *Quarterly Journal Of Speech* 20.1 (2003): 35-66. Print.

Killingsworth, Jimmie, and Jacqueline Palmer. *Ecospeak: Rhetoric And Environmental Politics In America.* Carbondale: Southern Illinois UP, 1992. Print.

Madison, D. Soyini. *Critical Ethnography: Method, Ethics, And Performance.* New York: Sage, 200. Print.

Makagon, Daniel "Sonic Earthquakes." *Communication and Critical/Cultural Studies* 3.3 (2006): 223-39. Print.

Pezzullo, Phedra. "Touring 'Cancer Alley,' Louisiana: Performances Of Community And Memory For Environmental Justice." *Text and Performance Quarterly* 23 (2003): 226-52. Print.
Pollock, Della. "The Performative 'I'." *Cultural Studies* <=> *Critical Methodologies* 7.3 (2007): 239-55. Print.
Probyn, Elspeth. *Outside Belongings*. New York: Routledge, 1996. Print.
Rothenbuhler, Eric W. "Revising Communication Research For Working On Community." *Communication and Community*. Eds. Gregory Shepherd and Eric W. Rothenbuhler. Mahwah, NJ: Erlbaum, 2001. 159-80. Print.
San José Bike Party. "For Drivers." <sjbikeparty.org> San José Bike Party, 20 August 2009. Web. 18 July, 2011.
———. "How We Ride." <sjbikeparty.org> San José Bike Party, Jan 7 2009. Web. 18 July 2011.
———. "About Bike Party." <sjbikeparty.org> San José Bike Party, 2011. Web. 18 July 2011
———. "The Short Version of Everything You Want to Know." <sjbikeparty.org> San José Bike Party, 2011. Web. 18 July 2011
Schechner, Richard. *Between Theater And Anthropology*. Philadelphia: U Of Pennsylvania P, 1985. Print.
Terry, David. "Global Co-Incidence: 'Ontos' Poetics Of The Worldwide." *Text and Performance Quarterly* 30.4 (2010): 335-55. Print.
Tuan, Yi Fu. *Space and Place: The Perspective Of Experience*. Minneapolis: U Of Minnesota P, 1977. Print.

Chapter Three

Performing Nonhuman Liberation: How the ALF and ELF Rupture the Political Imagination

Jason Del Gandio

Those who believe that the purposes of animal liberationists are unjust would appear to inherit the burden of proof. After all, there is little dissension concerning the liberation of slaves, Indians, and Afghans. The objective of freeing groups of individuals from a repressive regime so that they can live autonomous lives hardly seems in need of vindication. Thus, the anti-liberationist bears the onus of showing why the animal liberation movement is relevantly different from these other lauded campaigns. Effectively, he or she needs to demonstrate why, although improving the plight of oppressed human animals is a good, taking measures to try to enhance the lot of nonhuman animals is not.

—Philosopher Mark Bernstein (95)

We embrace social and deep ecology as a practical resistance movement. We have to show the enemy that we are serious about defending what is sacred. Together we have teeth and claws to match our dreams. Our greatest weapons are imagination and the ability to strike when least expected.

—ELF Communiqué (Best and Nocella, "Appendix" 408-09)

Each evening American television viewers witness endless depictions of abuse, exploitation, and oppression of nonhuman life. These depictions rarely educate or critically document the abuses of nature, the environment, or animals. Instead, these depictions act as "innocent" forms of entertainment that allow us to "veg-out" (pun intended) after a hard day's work. But such "innocence" masks serious consequences.

The History Channel's *Ax Men* dramatizes the daily activities of the logging industry—an industry that contributes to deforestation, destruction of natural habitats, and loss of biodiversity. Discovery Channel follows suit not only with *American Loggers* and *Swamp Loggers*, but with *Deadliest Catch*, which showcases the crabbing industry without addressing issues of sustainability, overfishing, and pollution. Discovery

also airs *Build it Bigger*, a show that depicts massive, breathtaking feats
of engineering. This show—as a discursive phenomenon—subtly contributes to the masculine, patriarchal, and even quasi-imperialistic practices of "bigger is better" and "expansion is progress." It also ignores
issues of population displacement and the extinction of indigenous practices and knowledges caused by urban sprawl. The Travel Channel's
Man vs. Food transforms extreme, even grotesque acts of eating into
competitive sporting events. Food (and by extension, nature) is to be
confronted and conquered. Individuals who cannot fully consume are
weak and feeble while those who can *over*-consume are heroic and courageous. And the Food Channel and Cooking Channel *are* performative
gestures of conspicuous consumption. The editing, camera angles, cine-
matography, and narratives do not necessarily highlight the artistry of
cooking, but instead, deify food and the consumerist impulse. Such pro-
gramming is equivalent to food fetishism, or, as a good friend often says,
"food porn."

This brief list does not invalidate other, more conscientious pro-
gramming. *Planet Earth* by Discovery and *Human Planet* by
BBC/Discovery are both entertaining *and* educational; and Animal Planet's *Whale Wars* follows longtime radical animal liberationist Paul Watson (to be discussed below) as he confronts illegal Japanese whaling.[1]
But I agree with Noël Sturgeon when she argues that the environmentalisms commonly found in popular culture often act as narrative frameworks that "legitimate certain aspects of U.S. consumerism, family values, global military power, and American history. The implications of
these popular narratives about nature cut two ways: they become a way
of explaining U.S. power and dominant cultural practices; and they become a way of promoting mainstream environmentalisms" (6). Such
mainstream environmentalisms may raise awareness about, but do not
sufficiently tackle the root causes of, environmental problems. Recycling, bicycling, reusable products (like bottles and bags), and more en-
ergy-efficient appliances are necessary lifestyle choices that lead to a
more eco-friendly society. But oil-based economies, wasteful transportation practices, inflated military operations, and the global production of
meat and other foods overshadow personal habits. Undergirding each of
these issues is free-market capitalism and its logic of private profit. We
live in a society in which personal gain outweighs collective benefit. It is
thus obvious that popular culture, while implicated within this critique, is
not solely responsible for animal abuse, environmental degradation, or
overconsumption. The corporate-State complex is *far more* responsible;

it actually institutionalizes the exploitation and oppression of nonhuman life in its will-to-profit-and-power. Thinking critically about both popular culture *and* the corporate-State complex reveals the ubiquity of the problem: American society produces, participates in, and profits from the exploitation of nonhuman life and the natural environment.

Most people are open and receptive to these critiques, but very few people are willing to actively change such conditions. That's not true for everyone, of course. Nonhuman liberationists like the Animal Liberation Front (ALF) and Earth Liberation Front (ELF) seek direct and immediate intervention. These groups are best known for executing clandestine, often illegal actions to save and protect the natural environment and nonhuman animals and to inhibit and even damage exploitative industries. Their repertoire of actions includes but is not limited to releasing and/or rescuing animals from factory farms, laboratories, and vivisection facilities; destroying animal research compounds; squatting in and spiking trees in order to discourage and/or halt logging and deforestation; blockading roads and construction sites; dismantling cell phone and radio towers; sabotaging dam projects; vandalizing luxury housing developments; monkeywrenching tractors and other heavy machinery; and even torching SUV dealerships.[2]

These radical actions are far beyond the comfort zones of most people. Protests, sit-ins, and even building occupations are semi-acceptable to the average person; vandalism, sabotage, and arson are not. But it should be noted that no human has ever been killed during any ALF or ELF action. Both groups publicly condemn harming any life (human or otherwise) and take excruciating precautions to avoid such consequences—they will scout a site for weeks or even months, thoroughly search facilities before executing an action, and even postpone an action if safety is not ensured. ALF and ELF members target systems, industries, profit, and property rather than people and lives. Nonhuman liberationists support their actions by arguing that property damage is not violence. Acts of sabotage and arson may be illegal, but are not, according to nonhuman liberationists, violent. Violence is perpetrated against living beings, not inanimate objects. The ALF and ELF thus identify as nonviolent freedom fighters following in the traditions of Gandhi, Dr. Martin Luther King, Jr., the Underground Railroad, and even the Boston Tea Party.

The following pages are divided into two main sections. The first section provides an overview of the ALF and ELF. These are two of the most radical and perhaps "notorious" nonhuman liberationist groups. But unlike other well-know organizations such as Greenpeace, PETA, and, to a lesser extent, Earth First!, very few people are familiar with the ALF and ELF. I thus cover some of the histories, controversies, and philosophies of these two groups. This provides the necessary background for the second section in which I argue that nonhuman liberationists like the ALF and ELF performatively rupture the political imagination and thus set conditions for the possibility of a different world. Not everyone will agree or even sympathize with their nonhuman liberationist performances (and perhaps for good reason). But I contend that the mere existence of these groups undermines the hegemonic hold of particular discourses and thereby expands our understandings of what is and is not possible in terms of social and political change. We can and should debate the philosophies and consequences of ALF and ELF actions. But their immediate, uncompromising embodiment of nonhuman liberation is valuable for what it suggests: that we are capable of manifesting a radically different and presumably better world right here and now.

Before moving forward, I feel obligated to position myself. Although I enjoy the outdoors and am a quasi-vegetarian (technically a pescetarian, since I eat fish), I am not a nonhuman liberationist. I have never been a member or committed any action in the name of the Animal or Earth Liberation Front. I am not even an environmentalist or animal rights activist. But I have been intimately involved with radical politics for more than a decade. Radicalism, generally speaking, goes to the root of social and political problems, overturns those root problems, and lays groundwork for a better world. My radical politics began with the Global Justice Movement of the late 1990s/early 2000s. Since then I have worked on issues of free/fair trade, sweatshop labor, and Latin American solidarity; have worked on pro-peace and antiwar campaigns; traveled to Venezuela to observe and report upon the Bolivarian revolution; participated in the Occupy Wall Street Movement; and regularly conduct talks and workshops for activists and organizers. These experiences have familiarized me with the practices and philosophies of nonhuman liberation. I do not fully condone *or* condemn the more radical factions of these movements. Instead, I seek to understand them in the hopes of becoming a more ethical and politically conscientious human being. Intellectually, I understand and even sympathize with their overall cause (liberation for *all* life). But I do not have the same emotional attachment to nonhuman species. I am thus called to reflection. Am *I* emotionally stunted? Is *my* political framework limited? Is *my* worldview too narrow? Should *I* be more alarmed and outraged by the systematic exploitation and destruction of nonhuman life? These unsettling politico-existential questions influence my orientation to the subject matter of this essay.

Nonhuman Liberation: An Overview

You are sitting down to watch the evening news when a special report airs about a new domestic terrorist threat. To your surprise it is not an offshoot of al Qaeda, but instead, animal and earth liberationists. A succession of images begins flashing across the television screen. People clad in black ski masks and one-piece jumpers are sabotaging research facilities and fast-food chains. Some swing sledgehammers; others wield crowbars; and still others use industrial-strength wire cutters to dismantle chain-link fences. Fast-paced, heart-thumping techno music plays in the background. Clips of busted computers, broken doors, smashed windows, and even burning buildings are interspliced with voiceovers and interviews representing competing perspectives. Both sides are angry and inflammatory. One side argues that these people are "special interest terrorists" who use violence, fear, and property damage to intimidate hard-working Americans and well-respected industries. The other side screams hypocrite. How can nonhuman liberationists be considered terrorists when they target property, not people? Isn't it more accurate to apply the terrorist label to the corporate industries that kill and murder in the name of profit? This special news report eventually ends with images of "ALF" and "ELF" spray painted across various brick buildings and a voiceover announcing, "This is the new face of homegrown terrorism."

Nonhuman liberation is not necessarily new. It traces back to at least nineteenth century British society and the rise of industrialism (Best and Nocella, "A Fire" 10). People's relationship to both the environment and animals began to change as the Industrial Revolution took hold. Nonhuman species were then being commodified en masse and became more readily objectified and exploited. Oppositional organizations sprung up across Britain during this time period. One early group was the Royal Society for the Prevention of Cruelty to Animals (Best and Nocella, "Behind" 19). Members of the RSPCA eventually broke off and created the Bands of Mercy—a militant group that fought British hunting practices. Other people focused on the relationship between humans and the environment. Such well-known individuals as "William Blake, William Wordsworth, Samuel Taylor Coleridge, John Keats, and others observed with alarm how both outer and inner worlds were threatened by mecha-

nistic science, the technological onslaught, and the ruthless commodification of nature and human relations" (Best and Nocella, "A Fire" 11).
Industrialism and its discourses of progress, expansion, and conquest co-
arrived with opposition, resistance, and liberationist practices.

Today's nonhuman liberation movements began in the 1960s and
1970s. This era of radicalism gave rise to not only civil rights, women's
rights, gay liberation, and antiwar movements, but also to environmental
and animal rights movements. The Hunt Saboteurs Association was
founded in 1963 in order to aggressively contest British hunting practices. By the early 1970s members of the HAS broke off and established a
more militant, clandestine operation. Reviving and acknowledging the
spirit of the earlier organization, they named themselves Band of Mercy
and engaged in acts of sabotage, equipment and property damage, and
animal rescues. Then, in 1974, organizational leaders Ronnie Lee and
Cliff Goodman were arrested and sent to prison. Upon release Goodman
became a police informant while Lee created a new organization—the
Animal Liberation Front (Best and Nocella, "Behind" 20).[3]

The ALF migrated from England to the United States at some point
during the late seventies or early eighties. It is difficult to pinpoint an
exact history since the ALF is a clandestine operation with no official
organizational structure. Anyone can act in the name of the ALF by
simply adhering to the official guidelines: "to inflict economic damage to
those who profit from the misery and exploitation of animals"; "to reveal
the horror and atrocities committed against animals behind locked doors,
by performing nonviolent actions and liberations"; and "to take all necessary precautions against harming any animal, human and nonhuman."
The guidelines also state that "Any group of people who are vegetarians
or vegans and who carry out actions according to ALF guidelines have
the right to regard themselves as part of the ALF" (Best and Nocella,
"Animal Liberation" 8).

This open structure serves at least three purposes. First, it reflects a
general antiauthoritarian sentiment held by most if not all ALF members.
They fight not only for nonhuman liberation, but also for an alternative
world of bottom-up, nonhierarchical social relations. They believe that
everyone should have direct, immediate, and equal participation in the
decisions that affect their lives. This directly contests our current systems
of leaders and followers, bosses and workers, teachers and students, police and prisoners, politicians and voters. Second, this open structure
strengthens the ALF's political efforts. Traditional social movements
have used media-savvy leaders to act as the interface between the masses

and the movement's constituency (think of Malcolm X and Dr. King, for instance). But movements can easily disintegrate if the leaders are imprisoned, assassinated, or simply step down. A decentered, leaderless movement avoids this possible pitfall. And third, an open structure safeguards against arrest and prosecution. If anyone can participate, then there is no single individual to target. The point is to keep ALF members out of prison so they can continue liberating the animals.[4]

This open structure is not without consequences. Someone acting in the name of the ALF might commit an action that harms or even kills another human being, thus bringing a firestorm of negative attention and criticism. But ALF participants are prepared to readily distance themselves from such circumstances since harming other humans obviously violates the basic tenet of nonviolence. An open structure may have its flaws, but it is rational and practical.

The Earth Liberation Front has a separate yet interconnected history. Today's environmental movement began taking shape during the 1960s when organizations like Friends of the Earth and the Environmental Defense Fund were being founded. Other organizations such as the Sierra Club and the Wilderness Society, though founded decades earlier, suddenly exploded in size and reputation. These organizations lobbied Congress, fought for policies, and educated the public. But radical factions of the environmental movement became frustrated with the direction of these organizations. These factions argued that such organizations were too appeasing, reformist, bureaucratic, and careerist; that few differences existed between these organizations and the larger corporate-political system; and that direct and immediate action must be taken now, not later.

Greenpeace, founded in the early 1970s and long known for its radical environmentalism, was even too moderate for some. Canadian Paul Watson (mentioned at the beginning of this essay) was actually expelled from Greenpeace for his militancy and confrontational tactics. This incident symbolized the tension between moderately radical and extremely radical environmentalists. Watson went on to establish the Sea Shepherd Conservation Society—a militant, direct-action organization dedicated to defending marine wildlife. Then, in 1980, Earth First! emerged under the banner of "No Compromise in Defense of Mother Earth!" Seeking to build upon but also eclipse the creative/performative protest tactics of Greenpeace, Earth First! incorporated more militant civil disobedience. Their first major action unraveled a fake three-hundred-foot crack in the Glen Canyon Dam, intended to symbolize the end of industrial expan-

sionism. Since then Earth First! has organized demonstrations, street performances, and political satires, as well as blockades, tree spikes, sit-ins,
and occupations.[5]

Earth First! spread to Britain in 1991 and became so popular that
some members felt that they should publicly distance themselves from
the illegal ecotage (ecology and sabotage) tactics that were being linked
to their movement. Debates ensued and a proposal was soon reached:
Earth First! would continue concentrating on mass demonstrations and
civil disobedience while anyone carrying out more militant ecotage actions would operate under a new name—the Earth Liberation Front
(Molland 49). This name was no coincidence as the newly founded ELF
wanted to emulate and promote similar politics, actions, and organizational structures as those of the ALF. The ELF's guidelines are almost
identical: "to inflict economic damage on those profiting from the destruction and exploitation of the natural environment"; "to reveal and
educate the public on the atrocities committed against the earth [sic] and
all species that populate it"; and "to take all necessary precautions
against harming any animal, human or otherwise" (Best and Nocella,
"Appendix" 407).

The ELF migrated to Canada and the United States by the mid-
1990s. Up to this point there had been no coordinated actions between
the ELF and ALF. But that changed in 1997 when a series of West Coast
actions—including tree spikes, animal releases, and a firebombing—
occurred within an eight-month time frame. In each case the ELF and
ALF claimed joint responsibility (Molland 56). Other joint actions continued throughout the late 1990s and early 2000s, thus forging a political
link between the two groups.

Such activities have motivated the FBI to place the ALF and ELF on
the official domestic terrorism watch list. The FBI refers to them as "eco-
terrorists" and pursues and prosecutes them under such legislation as the
2006 Animal Enterprise Terrorism Act ("Putting"). Congress passed this
bill in order to "provide the Department of Justice the necessary authority to apprehend, prosecute, and convict individuals committing animal
enterprise terror" (United States Cong.). Though officially passed in
2006, the AETA had been in the works since the early 1980s. The rise of
the ALF and Earth First! caught the attention of private industry, particularly Ron Arnold, who is the Executive Vice President of the Center for
Defense of Free Enterprise. Arnold first coined the term "ecoterrorism"
in 1983 and has publicly stated that he wants to "destroy environmentalists by taking their money and their members" (Smith 545). He and his

associates have continuously lobbied for anti-ecoterrorism legislation for almost thirty years. An earlier version of the AETA was passed by Congress in 1992. Private industry thought it would be advantageous to revisit and update the bill in light of the 2001 terrorist attacks. Then, five months after 9/11, members of the FBI testified before Congress that the ELF and ALF had caused more than $43 million in property damage since 1996 (Smith 553). These two groups were thus declared the top priority in domestic terrorism, with four out of the eight most wanted suspects being ALF and/or ELF affiliates ("Most Wanted"). The FBI officially defines ecoterrorism as "the use or threatened use of violence of a criminal nature against innocent victims or property by an environmentally-oriented subnational group for environmental-political reasons, or aimed at an audience beyond the target often of a symbolic nature" (Smith 553; Wagner 26). This definition strategically constructs terrorism as any action that is environmentally motivated and involves the *mere* threat of violence against *inanimate objects*, even if no property damage actually occurs.[6]

Some people may agree with the FBI and argue that nonhuman liberationists are rash, chaotic, misplaced, and even illogical. But nonhuman liberationism is actually supported by sound (though obviously debatable) philosophical principles. The ALF argues, for instance, that too many humans are besieged by speciesism, which is "the belief that nonhuman species exist to serve the needs of the human species, that animals are in various senses inferior to human beings, and therefore that one can favor human over nonhuman interests according to species status alone" (Best and Nocella, "Behind" 13). Speciesism is underwritten by a common binary logic that funds various oppressions: white/black, man/woman, rich/poor, boss/worker, heterosexual/homosexual, and, in this case, human/animal and human/nature. In each example an oppression is constituted by assigning values to differences and then ranking those differences hierarchically, with some differences being superior and others inferior. Oppressing the "inferior side" is then rationalized as natural and normal.[7] This is often the case when people argue, for instance, that animals are here for human consumption. This claim cannot be wholeheartedly proven or disproven. But, like most claims, it is supported by a larger cultural framework: most people eat meat and the overwhelming majority of authoritative texts (like legal documents, spiritual scriptures, and mass-mediated images) suggest that eating and exploiting animals is morally, politically, and/or economically justified. This claim is then presumed to be a God-given fact when it is actually a socially constructed fiction subject to scrutiny and contestation. This cultural presumption then produces material consequences.

- 25 million animals are used every year for the researching and testing of cosmetic and household products. Such tests are conducted not only on mice, but also on dogs, rabbits, and chimpanzees ("Issues," Humanesociety.org).
- Scientists, military personnel, and medical and veterinary students conduct experiments on goats, sheep, and numerous other animals. Such experiments involve operations on both deceased *and* living animals, the latter of which receive no pain medication in order to test stress levels.
- 90,000 cows and calves are killed every 24 hours in the United States for food consumption. Another 14,000 chickens are killed every minute. Overall, approximately 10 billion food animals (not including marine animals) are killed each year in the United States ("What's Wrong").
- Much of this food production revolves around factory farming, which is both inhumane and unsustainable. Factory farms neglect and abuse animals, force animals into undersized cages that are filled with their own excrement and that severely restrict natural and necessary movement. These unsanitary conditions expose humans to increased possibility of disease and illness: e.g., an estimated 89 percent of US beef patties contain traces of E. coli; approximately 650,000 Americans are sickened by salmonella-tainted eggs each year; and more than 5,000 people contract food poisoning, the primary source of which is contaminated chicken flesh.
- Factory farms also devastate the environment. According to the Food and Agriculture Organization of the United Nations, animal agriculture is responsible for 18 percent of human-induced greenhouse gas emissions. This occurs because the production of eggs, milk, and meat involves the production of grain to feed the animals; the production of fertilizer to maintain the soil; and the use of water, gas, and electricity to run operations and transport animals and goods.
- 90 percent of US forests have been cleared over the last 400 years. An area of rainforest the size of a football field is cut down every second. And 56,000 square miles of total forest are lost every year.

- Worldwide there are 405 "ocean dead zones"—large areas of ocean in which nothing can live due to fertilizer runoff and sewage dumping in coastal areas ("Issues," Takepart.com).
- Statistically speaking, each person in the United States generates about 4.6 pounds of trash every day, and 80 percent of what Americans throw away is recyclable.

It is this kind of grand-scale devastation that motivates nonhuman liberationists. They argue, for instance, that modern civilization is tending toward omnicide; that we are destroying our living habitat and thereby destroying the very conditions of our own existence; and only by adopting biocentric (life-centered) and ecocentric (ecologically centered) ways of life can we avoid such catastrophe. As one liberationist argues:

> I do not think I have overestimated the urgency of the environmental cause. I maintain that something radical needs to be done while there is something left to save. We cannot continue to dig for oil in sensitive areas and build large tracts of unplanned suburban housing, and expect that future generations won't suffer the consequences. We also should not continue to pretend that negotiating with powerful groups—whose only concern is short-term monetary profit—has gotten us somewhere. Acts of vandalism against specific targets is an effective way to take away the profit motive that drives the exploitation of the environment. The radical environmental movement values life over property and carries this priority to its logical conclusion. Our vision is a world where human beings recognize that everything, including their own species, is a part of the environment. (Wade 282-83)

Nonhuman liberation is often undergirded by a philosophical combination of deep and social ecology. Deep ecology was first developed by Norwegian philosopher Arne Naess and then further developed by American thinkers like Bill Devall and George Sessions (Garland 59-61). Deep ecology seeks to develop harmonious relations with nature in every imaginable context—housing, clothing, farming, consumption, technology, transportation, etc. Such an ecological orientation is rooted in the belief that all species are equally and intrinsically valuable. The living environment as a whole thus has a *right* to live and flourish according to *its own natural progression*. We are not separate from but rather part of nature and must live in accordance *with* nature.

Social ecology was developed by American anarchist Murray Bookchin as a response to deep ecology. Bookchin, though highly sympathetic to nonhuman liberation, argues that environmental problems are rooted in our current modes of social organization. Our society is based on hierarchical institutions of racism, sexism, classism, patriarchy, the State, and, most of all, capitalism. Not until we dismantle these and other such institutions will we achieve more bio- and eco-centric ways of life. Bookchin thus argues for decentralized, autonomous, and community-based modes of social organization that undercut the very possibility of top-down power relations. Bookchin theorizes that human beings are less likely to destroy their habitats (and each other) if each person equally participates in the decision-making processes that affect their immediate lives, environments, and social and political relations. In this sense, then, nonhuman liberation is based on the antiauthoritarian philosophy of social ecology and the environmental philosophy of deep ecology.

Rupturing the Political Imagination.

I argue that nonhuman liberationists like the ALF and ELF performatively rupture the political imagination. I define the political imagination as the shared capacity for collectively understanding our personal-and-social relations of the past, present, and/or future. The hyphens between the personal-and-social signify the inherent reflexivity and interdependency of the individual and the collective. That reflexivity and interdependence generate the productive tension and conflict that perpetually alter human existence. The ALF and ELF rupture this imagination because there is no common conceptual framework for understanding nonhuman liberation. Although both animals and the environment have basic legal rights, they are not perceived as autonomous subjects on equal footing with human beings. In this sense, then, liberating animals and/or the environment is as incomprehensible as liberating rocks.

My analysis focuses on the *performance* of nonhuman liberation. By performance, I mean the interplay between the body and the production of meaning. On one hand, there is the body's actions, gestures, and comportments. On the other hand, there are the signs, meanings, and symbolic constructions of those actions, gestures, and comportments. The body is perpetually signifying and being signified, and there is no signification without a body. Embodiment-and-signification are therefore two poles of the same phenomenon—i.e., performance.

Rehearsal and craft are part of the performative process. It is commonly understood, for instance, that staged actors rehearse and craft their lines, gestures, movements, and scripts. This helps actors communicate particular meanings to specific audiences. But rehearsal and craft are part and parcel of all human activity. Something as simple as walking down the street has been rehearsed and crafted since we were young children. Our childhood caregivers first instructed us how to walk. We then rehearsed it over and over until it became habituated within our bodies and we "got it right." At that point we developed our own style of walking, and each style evokes a unique system of meaning (slow, sexy, burly, lumbering, awkward, funny, speedy, etc.). This type of performative accomplishment even applies to bodies that use wheelchairs, walkers, crutches, and canes, or to bodies that cannot walk at all. Each of these examples is an embodied production of meaning that is rehearsed and crafted, and that constructs and is constructed by systems of interpretation and understanding.

These examples also point to the ideological implications and material consequences of our performances. Each performance is uniquely different, and some performances are privileged while others are marginalized. This occurs because every performance exists within, gives rise to, perpetuates, and/or contests, "wider regimes of power." Such regimes are constituted through time and repetition. For example, a group of people may repeatedly enact certain gestures and meanings over an extended period of time. These gestures and meanings eventually become habitual and naturalized—i.e., people no longer recognize the origins and/or implications of the gestures/meanings. This naturalization is not necessarily good or bad, but it *does* establish conditions for the *possibility* of unknowingly enacting oppressive gestures/meanings. For instance, enactments of homophobia, racism, sexism, classism, and, in this case, speciesism, are often rendered "invisible" because people have little impetus to question, let alone challenge and change, such performances. It is difficult to challenge that which one does not see. Such blindness both produces and is produced by naturalization.

Naturalization also delimits our range of possibilities. For example, my present and future choices to enact particular gestures and to graft particular meanings are conditioned—but never determined—by previous choices. Walking *this way* will increase the likelihood that I will walk *this way* again in the future, and walking *this way* means that I am not walking *that way*. Naturalization is therefore a process of inclusion-and-exclusion, which establishes systems of implications and consequences. But we are never fully trapped within these systems because every performance is *both* subjected *and* resistant to wider regimes of power. Subjection and resistance exist together, always. We cannot be subjected if there is no possibility of resistance, and we cannot resist if we are not subjected to someone or something. Our embodied productions of meanings therefore exist within various grids of relations and possibilities.[8]

This theoretical framework helps explain the unsettling effects of nonhuman liberation: the nonhuman liberationist performance calls attention to interconnectedness that can never be completely ignored or denied. Liberating people from another country, or even of a different socio-cultural group, can be perceived as a distant concern. But we are all members of this Earth and we all interact in some way and to some degree with nonhuman species. Witnessing and learning about ALF and ELF actions thus calls us to conscience: How, and to what degree, am I implicated in the systems and habits that they critique?

The nonhuman liberationist performance poses this question not necessarily as a linguistic utterance, but rather, as an embodied action that seeks an embodied response. For instance, rescuing minks from fur farms and sabotaging dam and logging projects are concrete physical actions. Those actions suggest that anyone associated with or benefiting from such operations should cease any and all implicit and/or explicit support—find other work, create different solutions, boycott particular companies and products, etc. Such a tacit, unspoken "bodily dialogue" is perhaps one reason why the ALF and ELF are so anxiety-producing: they force us to recognize (either implicitly or explicitly) the radical uncertainty of our world-creating activities. It may be common practice to eat the flesh of other animals and to act upon the environment as if it were an endless resource for our own taking. But these practices are nothing more than sedimented patterns of behavior inscribed and justified through various discourses, traditions, structures, and legalities. Each of these could be inverted, thus recasting nonhuman liberationists as bona fide freedom fighters and the rest of us (including me) as criminals or even terrorists.

The nonhuman liberationist performance may seem more sensible—or at least more comprehensible—when outlined in such a logical fashion. But the initial witnessing of a nonhuman liberationist action does not lend itself to intellectual reflection and slow, methodical analysis. It is experienced, instead, as a wicked jolt of "radical uncertainty." The world is suddenly thrown into relief, and we are unnerved and vulnerable. This is because the nonhuman liberationist performance—and its unspoken call to conscience—does not fit into the preestablished frameworks of traditional political activities (such as voting, lobbying, or debating on well-defined stages with well-behaved audiences). The intelligibility of the action is then rendered mute and invisible. The experience of psycho-existential drama blinds us to the logic of the deed. But this blindness is discursively produced rather than inherently given. As Michel Foucault states: "We know perfectly well that we are not free to say just anything, that we cannot simply speak of anything, when we like or where we like; not just anyone, finally, may speak of just anything." And why is that? Because "in every society the production of discourse is at once controlled, selected, organized and redistributed according to a certain number of procedures, whose role is to avert its powers and its dangers, to cope with chance events, to evade its ponderous, awesome materiality" ("Discourse" 216).

Some of those discourses that might inhibit our ability and willingness to understand nonhuman liberation include: that humans have divine dominion over the Earth and all of its inhabitants; that nonhuman animals are inferior; that humanity and nature are fundamentally separate; that expansion is progress; that technology can solve all of our problems; that those who govern should direct the course of history; and that social/political change is slow and incremental. Such discourses, when taken together as a whole and repeated and reified through our daily practices, work to exclude the very possibility of nonhuman liberation. But, ironically, this is the very same reason why nonhuman liberationists rupture the political imagination: because their actions exceed and eclipse the discursive mechanisms that work to silence their conceivability. If animal and Earth liberationists are assumed to be unfathomable, then their mere existence ruptures the confines of what we can and cannot imagine.

Such rupture, in and of itself, may not appear to be "political." But this is only true if we restrict ourselves to representational politics and legislative processes. The ALF and ELF obviously contest this conception of politics and follow, instead, a long tradition of non-institutionalized, extra-legislative social change. Some of those groups and movements include, but are not limited to, Luddites, anarchists, Autonomist Marxists, hippies and Yippies, the Black Panthers, the Situationist International, the Women's Liberation Movement, the Gay Liberation Front, the Zapatistas, the Global Justice Movement, and most recently, Occupy Wall Street.

For the purposes of this essay, I want to focus on one common thread that runs throughout this tradition, which is the practice of *radical immediacy*: i.e., the immediate evocation of one's desired world.[9] For instance, the ALF and ELF obviously seek a future world void of nonhuman oppression. But rather than patiently waiting for that world, they are immediately evoking it in the here and now. Their actions *are* the revolution. That revolution is no doubt imperfect, incomplete, and uncertain. But that is the case for all revolutions (and all life, in general). Most modern nation-states were founded on revolutions that occurred hundreds of years ago. One would think that a few hundred years would be enough time to settle any debates, mishaps, and/or inconsistencies. But these nations—including the United States—are a long way off from such utopian dreams. Slavery, civil wars, suffrage rights, worker rights, marriage rights, political scandals, and numerous other upheavals and contestations have been and surely will continue to be part of the ongoing revolutionary project that *is* "the modern nation-state." Why should nonhuman liberation (or any other radical movement) be any different?

Rhetorical scholar Robert E. Terrill makes a similar point when discussing the political significance of Malcolm X. Terrill acknowledges that Malcolm is a historically transformative figure. But, strangely enough, Malcolm never directly orchestrated any traditional political action. According to Terrill, Malcolm:

> never led his followers in large-scale collective action, never organized a mass protest march, and never was associated with the passage of any piece of legislation designed to improve the condition of African Americans . . . . What Malcolm did do was talk, and his talk often was criticized as taking the place of real political action. The hundreds of speeches and statements and interviews and newspaper columns that Malcolm produced, a flood of words augmented by his radio and television appearances that has few rivals in either its vehemence or in its sheer volume, often was—and is—dismissed as mere verbal swagger. (1-2)

But how can this be true? How can Malcolm be so historically impactful without directly engaging concrete political processes? Terrill argues that Malcolm's public address "*was* social change [original emphasis]; his words are his deeds. It is through his public discourse that members of his audiences are made to see the limits imposed upon them by the dominant white culture and are shown attitudes and strategies that invite them to transgress against those limits" (6). According to Terrill, Malcolm's rhetoric and politics cannot be separated; each helps to inform and constitute the other. Malcolm's speeches did not lead to liberation, but instead, *were* liberation. His rhetorical labors—i.e., *his performativity*—evoked and manifested the reality of Black defiance and resistance. Malcolm's rhetorical performance *was* the insurrection and *that* is why he is so historically significant.[10]

I believe that this practice of radical immediacy speaks back to a common criticism: that radical tactics can often hinder rather than help one's political cause. There is no doubt some truth to this criticism. Most people are turned off by the tactics of sabotage, arson, and property damage. This is a very understandable response, but the overall criticism does not sufficiently consider the value of radical immediacy.[11] Nonhuman liberationists prove in no uncertain terms that future dreams and alternatives can be evoked and manifested right now. Radical immediacy is therefore the "art of the impossible." As the London-based artist/activist collective "Laboratory of Insurrectionary Imagination" states in its *A Users Guide to Demanding the Impossible*:

> But there is another story to art. This is the one where it escapes the prisons of the art world, forgets its name, drops its starlit ego and becomes a collective movement of creativity applied to the material of everyday life. In such moments, art enters other relationships, other kinds of making take place. Liberated from the demands of the market it begins to remake the life that lies between us. Transforming the way we relate and make art, the way we refuse and rebel, the way we love and eat. When this is done in the cauldron of struggle, an occupation, a social movement, a protest—new friendships are woven, new forms of living become possible. This kind of culture brings us together rather than separates us, it allows us to find each other amongst the ruins. Such moments re-produce the feelings and excite the senses which used to bear the name "art," and yet they build different desires and worlds, perhaps even ones that some people once dared to call impossible. This is the art that does not show the world to us, but changes it. This art of social movement has its own secret history of rebellious performances, subtle images, insurrectionary inventions and seductive sounds. Our challenge today is not only to remember (literally—put back together) this secret history of art, but to discover and create tendencies in the present which provide alternative paths out of the current crisis. (4)

This approach to art and social change underscores the value of the nonhuman liberationist performance: its radical immediacy ruptures a political imagination that is not only colonized by speciesism and omnicide, but also by capitalism, two-party systems, free-market fetishism, American exceptionalism, brands, logos, patriotism, advertising, and the belief that the current world is the best that we can do. In this sense, then, nonhuman liberationists not only defend animals and the living environment, but actually undermine various bedrocks of contemporary society. Fissures are created within the public mind that enable the possibility of alternative thoughts and practices.

My argument can be supported by looking at the political value and efficacy of radical street performance. Tony Perucci, in "What the Fuck is That?: The Poetics of Ruptural Performance," addresses the interventions, happenings, culture jams, and agit-pop activities conducted by the Yes Men, Billionaires for Bush, Reverend Billy and the Church of Stop Shopping, Brazil's *Opovoempé* ("People on their Feet"), and Russia's *Voina* ("War"). He argues that most people have very little understanding of the messages or philosophies behind these performances and thus commonly respond with "what the fuck is that?" Performances that evoke such responses could be judged as failures. But that is only true if our criteria for evaluation and judgment are based on a strict paradigm of intention-and-interpretation: performer intends X; passersby interpret the performance as either X or not X; the performance is successful if, and only if, passersby properly interpret it as X. These criteria for evaluation and judgment may be helpful in some instances, but they are insufficient for understanding radical street performance. Perucci argues that such performances are politically valuable because they disrupt the experience of everyday life (3). Our mass-mediated consumer society is so ritualized that we tend to move through the day without critically engaging our actions or thoughts. Calling attention to mechanized behavior, if even only momentarily, ruptures the taken for granted activities of daily living. Such rupturing may not bring about grand social change, but it *is* an effective mode of political action that intervenes into the tiny capillaries of the social body. It is the action of radical street performance, rather than the specific message or philosophy thereof, that people experience, remember, and are affected by.

I believe that Perucci's argument applies to not only the physical actions of street performance, but also to the imagistic actions of printed and/or digital performance. For instance, the ALF commonly circulates a particular image of itself: ALF members are wearing their typical black ski masks and jumpers and are adorned with such accessories as tool belts, backpacks, and headsets (for communication purposes); they are standing in nondescript locations (perhaps a forest, open field, or empty warehouse) while affectionately cradling rescued animals, usually bunny rabbits, beagles, baby lambs, abused dogs, or meek and bandaged baby monkeys.[12] This image is a heterogeneous assemblage of signifiers: the ski masks and jumpers signify thief, villain, guerrilla, terrorist, and saboteur; the animals signify innocence, helplessness, and harmlessness; and the affectionate cradling of those animals signifies hero, savior, rescuer, and shepherd. These contrasting signifiers transform ALF members into militant shepherds of innocence and uncompromising defenders of animals and nature. This imagistic performance casts the ALF as provocateurs of a bio/ecocentric revolution.

This performance also issues an invitation: The faceless and featureless black ski masks invite observes to project themselves *onto* that image and, consequently, *into* that situation, action, position, relationship, and/or movement. Some folks might be attracted to this image and thus take up the invitation, while others might be repulsed by the image and therefore reject the invitation. But either way the implication is intimated: *anyone* can act in the name of nonhuman liberation. As an official ELF press release states: "Because involved individuals are anonymous, they could be anyone from any community. Parents, teachers, church volunteers, your neighbor, or even your partner could be involved. The exploitation and destruction of the environment affects all of us—some people enough to take direct action in defense of the Earth" (Best and Nocella, "Appendix" 406). Such a rhetorically ambiguous yet politically specific performance no doubt evokes the "WTF?" response. But it does so not simply because it is incomprehensible or unintelligible, but rather, because it indicates an insurrectionary intelligence that challenges dominant discourses: nonhuman animals are not commodities to be bought, sold, and consumed at will; the value of nature precedes and exceeds capitalistic logics; industrialism is neither the beginning nor sole purpose of civilization; nonhuman liberationists are not just radical and scary but also ethical and heroic; and the world is not static and certain, but instead, processual, ever-changing, and up for grabs. This insurrectionary intelligence also suggests the legitimacy and value of radical immediacy: nonhuman liberationists undercut and bypass the bureaucratic maze of legislative activism and choose, instead, to manifest alternative realities right here, right now.

There is much to be debated about the serious controversies surrounding the ALF and ELF. But if nothing else, I believe that the nonhuman liberationist performance ruptures and therefore expands the collective imagination. The radically immediate now is a stage without walls; it is a space of action that is as expansive as the Earth itself; it is a rehearsal process that is always in motion. The script is never completed and there are no spectators, only actors. We are thus called to attention: What kind of lives do we want to live and what kinds of worlds do we want to create? One does not have to participate in or even sympathize with nonhuman liberationist movements to appreciate the political and existential implications of such (embodied) questioning.

Notes

1. See Besel and Besel for an interesting critique of *Whale Wars*. In brief, they argue that the structure of reality television masks the ethical issues of illegal whaling.

2. Tree squatting is the occupation of a tree—the occupant usually sits or lies down near the top of the tree for an indefinite period of time. Spiking involves the insertion of a hard material (usually metal or ceramic) into a tree trunk in order to damage axes and saw blades. Monkeywrenching refers to small-scale property damage.

3. It is important to note Peter Singer's contribution to this history. His book *Animal Liberation* (originally published in 1975) applied the utilitarian principle of "the greatest good for the greatest number" to nonhuman animals, which allowed him to argue that *all animals* are equal and thus deserve just treatment. Despite Singer's importance, his work follows a different trajectory than that of the ALF. Singer's arguments and audiences are more moderate and mainstream while the ALF's are much more radical and clandestine.

4. For more details on antiauthoritarian social movements, see Amster et al.; Day; and Sitrin.

5. For detailed descriptions and analyses of Greenpeace and Earth First!, see Deluca (2009; 1999).

6. For detailed analysis of the AETA, see Lovitz and Potter.

7. The lineage of thinkers that contribute to this analysis of "binary logic and oppression" is far too complex to outline here. For more information, see Derrida's concept of logocentrism (*Of Grammatology*) and Butler's use of phallogocentrism (*Gender Trouble*).

8. My account of performance is heavily influenced by Judith Butler and Michel Foucault. See, for instance, Butler's notions of performativity and subjectivization (*Gender Trouble*; *Psychic Life of Power*) and Foucault's notion

of biopolitics (*History of Sexuality*) and his understanding of "the self as a practice of freedom" ("Afterword" and "The Ethics").

9. I am coining this phrase for the purpose of this essay. Related concepts might include prefigurative politics, which is a widely discussed practice in anti-authoritarian movements that can be easily researched online, and Hakim Bey's immediatism, cited at the end of this essay.

10. Some people might question the equivalence between the *speech* of Malcolm and the *action* of nonhuman liberationists. But I argue that speech is action, and that action is a form of speech. My argument is supported by Austin's speech acts (*How to Do Things*) and Butler's performativity (*Gender Trouble*).

11. For a related discussion within performance scholarship, see the debate about the benefits and drawbacks of carnivalesque street protest (Bruner; Chvasta; and Shepard, Bogad, and Duncombe). In brief, the debate addresses whether or not carnivalesque protest is capable of bringing about significant, long lasting social change.

12. Doing an online search for "Animal Liberation Front images" should provide plenty of examples of what I am describing.

Works Cited

Amster, Randall, et al. *Contemporary Anarchist Studies: An Introductory Anthology of Anarchy in the Academy.* New York: Routledge, 2009. Print.

Austin, J. L. *How to Do Things with Words.* Eds. J. O. Urmson and Marina Sbisà. Cambridge: Harvard UP, 1975. Print.

Bernstein, Mark. "Legitimizing Liberation." *Terrorists or Freedom Fighters?: Reflections on the Liberation of Animals.* Eds. Steven Best and Anthony Nocella. New York: Lantern, 2004. 93-105. Print.

Besel, Richard D., and Renee S. Besel. "Whale Wars and the Public Screen: Mediating Animal Ethics in Violent Times." *Arguments About Animal Ethics.* Eds. Greg Goodale and Jason Edward Black. Lanham: Lexington, 2010. 163-77. Print.

Best, Steven, and Anthony Nocella. "A Fire in the Belly of the Beast: The Emergence of Revolutionary Environmentalism." *Igniting a Revolution: Voices in Defense of the Earth.* Eds. Steven Best and Anthony Nocella. Oakland: AK Press, 2006. 8-29. Print.

———. "Animal Liberation Guidelines." *Terrorists or Freedom Fighters?: Reflections on the Liberation of Animals.* Eds. Steven Best and Anthony Nocella. New York: Lantern, 2004. 8. Print.

———. "Appendix: Earth Liberation Front Communiqués." *Igniting a Revolution: Voices in Defense of the Earth.* Eds. Steven Best and Anthony Nocella. Oakland: AK Press, 2006. 406-17. Print.

——. "Behind the Mask: Uncovering the Animal Liberation Front." *Terrorists or Freedom Fighters?: Reflections on the Liberation of Animals.* Eds. Steven Best and Anthony Nocella. New York: Lantern, 2004. 9-63. Print.

Bey, Hakim. *Immediatism.* San Francisco: AK Press, 1994. Print.

Bruner, M. Lane. "Carnivalesque Protest and the Humorless State." *Text and Performance Quarterly* 25.2 (2005): 136-55. Print.

Butler, Judith. *Gender Trouble: Feminism and the Subversion of Identity.* New York: Routledge, 1999. Print.

——. *The Psychic Life of Power: Theories in Subjection.* Stanford: Stanford UP, 1997. Print.

Chvasta, Marcyrose. "Anger, Irony, and Protest: Confronting the Issue of Efficacy, Again." *Text and Performance Quarterly* 26.1 (2006): 5-16. Print.

Day, Richard J.F. *Gramsci is Dead: Anarchist Currents in the Newest Social Movements.* London: Pluto, 2005. Print.

Deluca, Kevin Michael. "Praxis: Interview. Greenpeace International Media Analyst Reflects on Communicating Climate Change." *Environmental Communication* 3.2 (2009): 263-69. Print.

——. *Image Politics: The New Rhetoric of Environmental Activism.* New York: Guilford P, 1999. Print.

Derrida, Jacques. *Of Grammatology.* Trans. Gaytari Chakravorty Spivak. Baltimore: John Hopkins UP, 1997. Print.

Foucault, Michel. "The Ethics of the Concern of the Self as a Practice of Freedom." *Ethics: Subjectivity and Truth.* Ed. P. Rabinow. Trans. P. Aranov and D. McGrawth. New York: New Haven P, 1997. 281-301. Print.

——. *The History of Sexuality: An Introduction, Vol. 1.* Trans. Robert Hurely. New York: Vintage books, 1990. Print.

——. "Afterword: The Subject and Power." *Michel Foucault: Beyond Structuralism and Hermeneutics.* Eds. H. L. Dreyfus and P. Rabinow. Chicago: Chicago UP, 1982. 208-26. Print.

——. "Discourse on Language." *Archaeology of Knowledge.* Trans. R. Hurley. New York: Pantheon, 1972. 215-37. Print.

Garland, Davey. "To Cast a Giant Shadow: Revolutionary Ecology and Its Practical Implementation Through the Earth Liberation Front." *Igniting a Revolution: Voices in Defense of the Earth.* Eds. Steven Best and Anthony Nocella. Oakland: AK Press, 2006. 59-70. Print.

"Issues." <Humanesociety.org/issues>. The Humane Society of the United States, n.d. Web. 23 July 2011.

"Issues." <Takepart.com/foodinc>. Take Part, n.d. Web. 23 July 2011.

Laboratory of Insurrectionary Imagination. *A Users Guide to Demanding the Impossible.* London: Laboratory of Insurrectionary Imagination, 2010. Print.

Lovitz, Dara. *Muzzling a Movement: The Effects of Anti-Terrorism Law, Money and Politics on Animal Activism.* New York: Lantern, 2010. Print.

Molland, Noel. "A Spark that Ignited a Flame: The Evolution of the Earth Liberation Front." *Igniting a Revolution: Voices in Defense of the Earth.*

Eds. Steven Best and Anthony Nocella. Oakland: AK Press, 2006. 47-58. Print.

"Most Wanted, Domestic Terrorism." <Fbi.gov>. Federal Bureau of Investigation, n.d. Web. 23 July 2011.

Perucci, Tony. "What the Fuck is That?: The Poetics of Ruptural Performance." *Liminalities: A Journal of Performance Studies* 5.3 (2009): 1-18. Web. 23 July 2011.

Potter, William. <Greenisthenewred.com/blog>. Green is the New Red, n.d. Web. 23 July 2011.

"Putting the Intel to Work: Against ELF and ALF Terrorists." *Fbi.gov*. Federal Bureau of Investigation, 30 June 2008. Web. 23 July 2011.

Shepard, Benjamin, L.M. Bogad, and Stephan Duncombe. "Performing vs. the Insurmountable: Theatrics, Activism, and Social Movements." *Liminalities: A Journal of Performance Studies* 4.3 (2008):1-30. Web. 23 July 2011.

Singer, Peter. *Animal Liberation*. New York: HarperCollins, 1990. Print.

Sitirn, Marina, ed. *Horizontalism: Voices of Popular Power in Argentina*. Oakland: AK Press, 2006. Print.

Smith, Rebecca K. "'Ecoterrorism'?: A Critical Analysis of the Vilification of Radical Environmental Activists as Terrorists." *Environmental Law, Lewis and Clark Law School* 38.2: 537-76. Print.

Sturgeon, Noël. *Environmentalism in Popular Culture: Gender, Race, Sexuality, and the Politics of the Natural*. Tucson, AZ: U of Arizona P, 2009. Print.

Terrill, Robert E. *Malcolm X: Inventing Radical Judgment*. East Lansing, MI: Michigan State UP, 2004. Print.

United States. Cong. *Animal Enterprise Terrorism Act*. 109th Cong., 2nd sess. S. 3880. Washington: GPO, 2006. Print.

Wade, John. "Radical Environmentalism: Is There Any Other Kind?" *Igniting a Revolution: Voices in Defense of the Earth*. Eds. Steven Best and Anthony Nocella. Oakland: AK Press, 2006. 280-83. Print.

Wagner, Travis. "Reframing Ecotage as Ecoterrorism: News and the Discourse of Fear." *Environmental Communication* 2.1 (2008): 25-39. Print.

"What's Wrong with Factory Farming?" <Centerforfoodsafety.org>. The Center for Food and Safety, n.d. Web. 23 July 2011.

Chapter Four

Eco-Comedy Performance:
An Alchemy of Environmentalism and Humor

Alison Bodkin

In 2005, the executive producer of HBO's show *Curb Your Enthusiasm* and producer of the documentary *An Inconvenient Truth*, Laurie David, wanted to prove that environmentalists are funny. To do this, she rallied Jason Alexander, Steve Martin, Larry David, Ben Stiller, Wanda Sykes, Jack Black, Will Ferrell, and other comedians in Las Vegas for two and a half hours of environmental consciousness-raising in a live show entitled, *Earth to America!* The show was recorded and has since been televised on HBO and TBS every year since then (Ruckman para 6). Laurie David explained the intention of the show in a National Public Radio interview: "I see environmentalists as something other than all doom-and-gloom. . . yes, that's part of being an environmentalist, but that doesn't mean we don't know how to have fun" (para 6). Opening the show is a tape of Larry David clad in Minute Man costuming as Paul Revere riding a horse down the strip in Las Vegas while waving a lantern and screaming, "Global warming is coming!" His revision of the midnight ride was clever, from the flailing of his sustainable light source to the terrified look on his face as his horse urgently galloped to Caesars Palace.

David parodies the stigma that environmentalists are alarmists who peddle visions of the apocalypse. His warning was clear: the enemy of global warming was upon us. Michael Janofsky, of *The New York Times*, did not share the same reading. His review of the show was guided by the question, "Do comedy and global warming really mix?" (para 2). Janofsky insinuates that environmental advocacy is serious, and not comedy's fodder. Ice caps are melting. Oceans are rising. Global warming is serious stuff. So serious that Al Gore charted the dire consequences that abound if we fail to take it seriously. The broad, general principles of environmentalism become prescriptive codes with hortatory and rigid standards for "the everyday performance of environmentalists." Indeed, complex ethical tensions, tactical political commitments, and moral ambiguities are inextricably caught up in the act of performing (Conquergood, "Moral Act" 4). In an age when the president of the United States makes and circulates YouTube videos, and television shows on Comedy Central pose some of the most pointed political criticisms, we must seek ways to account for and re-imagine the intersections between persuasion and pleasure, politics and aesthetics, citizenship and entertainment, and activism and art (Gencarella and Pezzullo 1). Such intersections between ideology and action, and between description and prescription, are not strangers to performance studies. "The movement from stage performances to broad claims about the politics of self-performance is a dialectic under constant negotiation" (Bell, "Toward" 106-7). Every time I watch David's parody I smugly grin and remember that "pleasure has always been the bedrock of performance studies" (Bell, "Toward" 99).

Schechner characterizes performance as a continuum, that is dependent on contexts and functions, that moves between efficacy (ritual) and entertainment (theatre). "When efficacy dominates, performances are universalistic, allegorical, ritualized, tied to a stable established order. . . When entertainment dominates, performances are class-oriented, individualized, show business, constantly adjusting to the tastes of fickle audiences" (123). Yet, the idea that comedic performances are unsuitable forms for environmental advocacy hinges on the belief that for any political agenda to be taken seriously, the person with the agenda must be serious at all times. Success requires unwavering attention to the environmental goal—any diversion becomes an obstacle.

The intersection between rhetoric and performance is the idea that the world is constantly in an open and unfixed process of social transformation, rather than a static state of being with a determined outcome (Gencarella and Pezzullo 2). Ursula Heise observes: "a steady drumbeat of gloom-and-doom rhetoric is liable to discourage and alienate individuals more than incite them to action" (142). Heise also reminds us that, conversely, "too much normalization of crisis might lead to an implicit acquiescence to the environmental status quo" (142). Indeed, the expectation to perform the role of sincere environmentalist all the time is an overly simplistic and reductionist Band-Aid we slap on. We hope it conceals and heals what's beneath.

But can we be serious and utilize the performance of environmentalists—the one about not being all doom and gloom—that Laurie David suggests is politically useful? What happens when an environmentalist re-reads a serious environmental script with a big, toothy grin while donning a vintage 1950s housedress and apron? How about when another environmentalist spouts dire consequences while parodying Paul Revere? Can both performances be read with the environmental intentions of such messages while simultaneously nudging knowingly at more subtle nuances?

I believe that the fluid nature of performance of comedy is precisely what makes it promising to the acculturated performances we put on in our everyday environmentalism. Eco-comedy is a way to subvert the standard doom-and-gloom environmentalism that David and Heise refer to. I define eco-comedy as comedic performances (i.e., deliberate jokes) that purport environmentalist agendas or debunk anthropocentric agendas that support "the belief that humans are above any other aspect in nature" (Foreman 29).

In this chapter, I argue that comedic performance is a viable method that matches the messages of environmentalism. This kind of performance becomes a kind of discursive biomimicry that mirrors, as a predator does a prey, the language of anthropocentrism. Since performing comedy is dependent on contradiction and juxtaposition, it becomes an adequate tool for calling the bluff of anti-environmental agendas that are based on illogical claims that sound ecologically savvy (e.g., clean coal). Eco-comedy becomes "a language of possibility that is capable of thinking risky thoughts, that engages a project of hope, and points to the horizon of the 'not yet'" (Giroux 52). In what follows, then, I first explain how humor is productive for everyday performances of environmentalism. Second, I articulate how environmental melodrama has worked in the past, as well as the language characteristics and agendas of the anthropocentric resourcist ideology (hereafter, ARI). Finally, I make a case for comedy's ability to reveal the truths that ARI tries to conceal.

Everyday Performances of Biomimicry

Environmentalists are accustomed to using the rhetorical appeals of guilt and sacrifice to advocate for our agendas (Lertzman; Maniates and Meyer; Verhoeven). While these appeals have been relatively effective at bringing about individual change (e.g., recycling), the motivations of guilt and sacrifice do not mirror the goals of sustainability. Nor are these appeals self-sustaining in everyday life. Erving Goffman sees performance as the deliberate roles constructed and embodied in the "presentation of self in everyday life." With that in mind, I argue that an ethics of performance necessitates asking questions about our assumptions of the dynamic of personalizing the politics and publicizing one's personal life. Similar to Foucault's notion of *Askesis*, "not a disclosure of the secret self but a remembering. . . performing exercises in which the subject puts himself in a situation in which he can verify whether he can confront events and use the discourses with which he is armed" (238-39). A Foucauldian ethos demands that one is "engaging the present, taking responsibility for oneself and the world" (Taylor and Vintges 4). These techniques can be important strategies for environmentalism. Therefore, environmentalism is "strengthened not by the assertion of a single, homogeneous identity but rather through a dedicated, contextual, and critical engagement with itself and the world" (4). In this sense, performance is a means to display the intentions of sustainability, sustainably.

I would argue that the work of planetary sustainability makes it especially necessary to be in touch with the irony of the everyday. After all, when an environmentalist starts to think about how all of her daily choices have environmental consequences her own existence can feel hypocritical. With irony, she can still take environmental issues seriously, but not feel as implicated by her daily choices. Regina Barreca, in her work about humor's role in feminism, mentioned feeling implicated "just by existing." This feeling that "this world was not made by or for your kind" is so pervasive, she seems to imply, that it can only be handled with humor (18-19). Our everyday performances of environmentalism need to be sustainable for our own sakes as environmentalists. Accordingly, such performances should employ a kind of biomimicry so that our method matches our message. The word biomimicry comes from the Greek word bios (life) and mimesis (imitation). In short, biomimicry is comprised of imitations of nature. Biomimicry is the mirroring (i.e., technological, structural) of biological processes to solve modern problems and dependencies on natural resources.

The three primary areas of biomimicry include using nature as: a model, a standard of measure, and as a mentor. Take for example, Velcro, created in the image of seed hooks, Velcro fastens onto objects when it brushes up against them (Reed 24). Another example is the German corporation, Isbo, wanted to rework architectural skyscraper designs that were aesthetically beautiful but terribly high maintenance, since they require life-threatening window washing and carbon-guzzling aircrafts that soap-spray large buildings about twice a year (Benyus 202). They considered these conundrums and asked, "what in nature has to keep itself clean?" The answer: leaves. Leaves must photosynthesize and cannot do so if their surfaces are dirty. Isbo designed an external layer that mimicked a lotus leaf, so that now when it rains the building cleans itself (202). The foundational belief under biomimicry is that humans have very much to learn from the processes of natural selection, whether it's how to make a wing more aerodynamic, a city more resilient, or an electronic display more vibrant (Vanderbilt 50). Biomimicry has spawned the creation of bat-inspired ultrasonic canes for the blind, synthetic sheets that collect water from mist and fog as desert beetles do, and paint that self-cleans like a lotus leaf (Lovins 49). Essentially, our everyday choices about self-presentation of environmentalism would be guided by the question: "what would nature do?"

Discursive biomimicry might look at the standard doom-and-gloom environmental advocacy and ask about its sustainability—just how does nature deal with despair? Well, nature would reconcile, adapt, and work for balance. Many of us are inclined to perform comedy for the same reasons. For example, you may not understand an issue and use self-deprecating humor, or you might tell a joke to relieve a tense situation. All of these defense mechanisms are reconciliations and adaptations to disparities between our understanding or orientation and the status quo.

We reconcile, adapt, and work for balance when we try to get people to laugh with us; we have won them over, however, briefly, to our side. We have created a climate of consensus, a moment of agreement when everyone is in sync; our humor functions as a social cement, especially in tense or oppositional situations. Comedy can create a situation where individuals who might have opposite views on an environmental issue can at least share a moment where their perspectives align. Everyday environmentalism can be seen as a reflection of Michel de Certeau's claim that "discourses are not abstract ideas; they are performed, and they are often used for rhetorical purposes" (139). Rather than take the opportunities we are given on a day-to-day basis to describe environmental degradation, explain its causes and consequences, and present strategies for preservation, we are inclined to think of our daily performances of environmentalism as political commitments to nature's value and to intellectual critique.

For example, suppose you are at a city council meeting and you are at odds with another city resident about an environmental ordinance, let's say composting. He thinks that composting should be illegal within city limits because it's disgusting, while you believe that composting should be encouraged by the city because it is ecological. He appears unmovable about his position and the allotted time to discuss composting is almost up. As you grab your notes, you make a joke about how the meeting format has been around since the toilet and has yet to work for an entire agenda of a city council meeting. Your opponent laughs for a moment, and even if it's only for a moment, you've shared something. You've indicated a harmless scapegoat—the format of meetings—and both of you agree on how awful it is without compromising either of your positions. You give the format of the city council meeting a significance it otherwise would not have, and by exaggerating its poor design, you draw fire away from the issue where you and your opponent are divided, although you still make an implicit point concerning the importance of rewarding efficiency and effectiveness (thanks to the toilet). No doubt, you'll return and do battle over this issue again, but your use of humor indicates that you intend to keep a reasonable perspective on the matter, as well as subtly indicating that you expect him to do the same. Your slice-of-life humor shows that you expect him to be able to switch from an antagonistic mode into a friendly one without losing a beat, as you've obviously been able to do. When proposing any kind of societal change, an environmentalist needs to prove that he is working for balance, or equilibrium. A surefire way to show such an intention is to be approachable and good-humored.

Our everyday performative displays of environmentalism need to be infused with a great deal of kairos, the rhetorical concept that denotes a right and opportune moment to speak in a situation. Arguably, some of the best comedy is an interpretation of a situation. Paul Lewis argues that more than any other performance mode, comedy functions as zeitgeist; "it speaks to our culture right now" (22); and right now environmentalism is "in." T-shirts have saucy slogans such as "I'm hotter than I should be;" screen savers show the kids of the animated television comedy *South Park* as endangered aquatic life, and videos of gas-mask-wearing hedgehogs can be found on YouTube.

Moreover, right now the academic culture of environmental studies, as an inter-discipline, arises at a moment of crisis, that is "defined in not insignificant ways by human-caused threats to both biological systems and human communities, and also by the continuing failure of societal institutions to sufficiently engage these pressures" (Cox, "Crisis" 7). Much like the trans-disciplines of conservation and biology, communication strives to illustrate and explain the biological elements and human causes of ecological collapse, in an attempt to both halt and reverse this collapse. Richard Rogers believes that environmental scholars have an ethical duty to try to explain environmental problems and help change the society that has caused ecological collapse by not responding adequately to environmental crises.

Environmental Melodrama
and Anthropocentric-Resourcist Ideology

Consider this: What if Mother Nature was paid for her services, like decomposition? What if the people who fostered environments for optimal decomposition were the richest? What would that look like? Compost piles would become enviable, boast-worthy yard centerpieces. We would brag to our neighbors about how our piles smell and what we put in it. People with the biggest decomposing dumps would be in public office, economic gurus on Saturday morning news programs (touting, "It takes a lot of green to be green"), and religious leaders (How should the farmer who used pesticides pay for his sins?).

This imaginary situation emphasizes the way in which the cultural norms of environmental ambivalence create performative rules to suit the powers that be—rules derived from an anthropocentric-resourcist ideology (ARI) that justifies "the continued human control and domination of nature solely as a benefit for humans" (Cox, *Environmental Communication* 149). Attention to individual performances allows us to posit and to explore cultural rules surrounding the performance of environmentalism, often unexamined and unarticulated, manifested in performance expectations and evaluated as "cultural competence," with a Victor Turner sensibility. Turner argues that cultural performances that do not meet our expectations should not be dismissed as moments of incompetence. Rather, these performances should be "the focus of postmodern analytical attention" (77).

Environmentalist and anthropocentric debates typically rely on four antagonisms, each of which features an ecological virtue pitted against an anthropocentric value. These antagonisms are: 1) preservation/conservation versus exploitation; 2) human health versus economic growth; 3) environmental justice versus nature as a place apart from the places where people live, work, and play; and 4) global communities versus economic globalization (Cox, *Environmental Communication* 40). Societal assumptions regarding the environment are framed, shaped, and created to reflect an anthropocentric-resourcist ideology (ARI), as in the latter half of each binary (Rampton and Stauber). These oversimplifications tend to erase and marginalize not just those who fall into the former half of each binary, but also those who fall outside the two limited choices.

Raymie McKerrow argues for challenging rigid binary thinking through "embodied rhetoric" to recognize when such binaries are predicated on the existence of each other (324). For example, it is hard to define nature without comparing it to culture. In addition, today nature needs people to change culture to protect nature, and culture needs nature to exist. Embodied rhetoric is useful to complicate the dualisms that divide the world into falsely rigid binaries by interrogating rhetorical constructions into realized, embodied performances.

According to Steven Schwarze, environmentalists have had relative success addressing blatant anthropocentrism with Burke's melodramatic frame because it "re-moralizes situations that are demoralized by inaccuracy, displaying concerns that have been obscured by the reassuring rhetoric of anthropocentrism" (248). Melodrama is effective because environmentalists do not argue against an anthropocentric concept, but against the people purporting it. The melodramatic frame draws sharp, polarizing distinctions between evil and virtue; a performance that invites simple solutions and denies the complexity of controversial situations.

In the melodramatic frame, environmental activists are expected to perform both "impending catastrophe and future redemption," discourses characterized by a simultaneous warning of a coming "cataclysm while holding out hope of a millennial future" (Ellis 141). Essentially, Ellis's observation is an apt description of the stereotypical performance of environmentalism; hence the reason why many advocates have historically used the melodramatic frame to expose anti-environmental agendas. For example, the Sierra Club's Grassroots Training Manual teaches its members to use an explicitly melodramatic frame when constructing communication strategies for campaigns:

> To be compelling, stories must have the following core elements: a problem, a victim, a villain who is responsible and should be held accountable (This can be a group of people, such as the city council or a corporation, or an individual such as one politician), a hero (presumably the public who can make a difference by getting involved. . .), [and] a successful resolution. (Bsumek 84)

Environmentalists have exploited the stories that had these core elements. The melodramatic frame uses artificial polarities like "good and evil" or "truth and falsehood" to persuade and to clarify obscurities about environmental problems. The performances of antagonisms in the melodramatic frame ask the audience to choose to elevate one side and diminish the other. The performances of ARI typically gloss over environmental issues in strictly scientific or economic terms. Such performances reassure citizens about human technological control of natural phenomena, whereas the melodramatic frame foregrounds the moral dimensions of environmental virtues. For example, the melodramatic frame cuts through a global warming debate with images of hurricane refugees, drowned polar bears, and mothers' demands for clean water. ARI gets debunked in the melodramatic frame.

"Dramatizing communication creates social reality for groups of people" and provides an outsider "with a way to examine messages for insights into the group's culture, motivation, emotional style, and cohesion" (Bormann 396). Environmentalists are expected to perform our politics as a kind of "performance competence ... a descriptive and evaluative term for the performer's responsibilities" (Bauman 11). That is, the performer "assumes accountability to an audience for the way in which communication is carried out, above and beyond its referential content" (11). For the audience, "the performer is marked as subject to evaluation for the relative skill and effectiveness of the performer's display of competence" (11).

Paul and Anne Ehrlich described contradictory environmental practices as "aggressive mimicry" (16). Jennifer Peeples saw this mimicry in Wise Use's environmental politics and practices; Wise Use sounds like a genuine environmental or scientific public interest group, but in reality, it works against the interests implied in the name Wise Use. In the 1970s, Wise Use's founder, Ron Arnold, was a member of Sierra Club when he became disillusioned with the tactics of the environmental movement. He began creating media presentations for timber firms and industrial clients (Switzer). "A former environmentalist explains what you should know about the environmentalists, why the forest industry has lost so many battles, and how to fight environmentalists more effectively" (Arnold 22). The answer is "If you can't beat them, become them."

Aggressive mimicry can be seen in a spider's behavior. A spider would imitate an insect that is her intended prey. In this way, the spider can gain control over her prey's behavior. In aggressive mimicry, a predator provides the insect, its prey, with a signal. But in this instance, "the predator attempts to elicit a response that benefits itself and not the prey" (Jackson para 7). Thus, the audience of the mimicking behavior is always the victim because the goal of the aggressor is to control its prey's behavior. To environmentalists, the rhetoric of ARI is not unlike that of the spiders. When confronting the false dilemmas of ARI, many environmentalists feel cornered into justifying the virtue of nature and the intentions of our discourse; we respond to what we perceive as threats to our politics. What is deceptive about ARI's appropriation of environmental-ist rhetoric is that the mimic's goal is to permanently assume an envi-ronmentally virtuous identity.

The more environmentalists know about ARI and how it is covertly used in language, the better we can adapt our own messages to counter it. Americans are inundated with political phrases and buzzwords that re-flect an anthropocentric agenda, such as: energy security, clean coal, al-ternative fuels, and fuel efficiency. So, in a sense, terms operate on the same binaristic principle as antagonisms. Essentially, these phrases rely on a "both/and" logic. Such a logic appeals to both sides of an antago-nism. These phrases invert commonly understood concepts and enable politicians to never have to know or even explain a specific policy, per-petuating their ubiquity all the while lulling us into believing that it's for the best.

Statements like: "we're taking another look at the science associated with the problem" and "we want to make decisions based on sound sci-ence" have an obtuse quality that welcomes a kind of helplessness or enslavement to science for societal solutions. Such statements perpetuate the obscurity of environmental issues, making us believe that compre-hending such issues is constantly out of reach—we are still waiting on the sound science, as if it were food from a drive-thru window. These statements are insults to the intelligence of the mass public and "they blatantly disregard democratic concern," assuaging us to believe that car-ing for the environment is not our job to begin with (Gore 63). At the same time, these statements usually pander to corporate interests instead of those of American citizens.

ARI language reassures us that science and policy are working on the solutions, and everyone else should keep quiet. The language of ARI is intended not only to assert enthusiasm for making progress on environ-mental problems, but also to cast doubt on the motives or mental capaci-ties of anyone with criticizing or opposing views. For example: "We should regulate based on science, not emotion" (Inhofe 27).

The language of ARI creates a complicated, cross-pollinated field of understanding. Manipulative in strategy, anthropocentric appropriations soothe the public concerns about environmental problems while quietly acting to implement changes that weaken environmental protection (Gore 44). Many Americans become besieged by linguistic power and never think to question the perversity of environmental realities. Ultimately, anthropocentric appropriations are what many environmentalists call "AstroTurf" because it is neither "green" nor "grass" roots (Brick).

The phrases themselves are relatively innocent; but the duplicity behind their use is problematic. Such a covert propaganda uses ecologically savvy rhetoric to promote an agenda that is devoid of ecological concern. In other words, an anthropocentric appropriation of environmental discourse is a wolf dressed in sheep's clothing. Language no longer reflects meaning as much as it deflects meaning (Burke *Language and Symbolic Action*, chapter 3).

ARI's contradictions can be viewed as unproductive on one end of the spectrum and as capitalistic deceptions at the other end of the spectrum. Most likely, they are deceptions from one of two strands: epistemological filibustering or scientific "manufactroversy." Marcus Paroske refers to "epistemological filibusters" as appeals to uncertainty in order to delay policy implementation. Such filibusters sustain the status quo of societal uncertainty about environmental issues. For example, I recently attended a local community meet-up between stakeholders (read: anyone who was interested) to discuss the implications and effects of mountaintop removal in the community. One stakeholder (a fiscal benefactor to be more precise) put our dialogue on pause by mentioning "clean coal." For the remainder of our discussion we debated what constitutes "clean coal" rather than discussing what we were there to discuss.

"Manufactroversies," or manufactured scientific controversies (Ceccarelli), are rhetorical traps set around environmental issues that exploit the democratic ideal of deliberation. For example, at a congressional hearing about global warming in which Congress discussed carbon offsets, attention was diverted to the legitimacy of climate change. Discussion about carbon offsets gets co-opted by the appeal to fairness; deliberations about fair representation of "science" trump the overwhelming scientific consensus that says global warming is a crisis we needed to address yesterday.

These two different strands of deception are so pervasive in environmental talk that we cannot assume that ARI's contradictions are based on misunderstandings. Nor can we assume that public figures and policymakers are consistently going to utilize responsible rhetorical choices. There has to be a clear line between real and unreal. These contradictions must be treated as failures to communicate intentions properly. However, the idea to separate language from action in an attempt to argue that words are not linked to deeds is an all-too-easy assumption to make with environmentalism. Bronislaw Szerszynski deflates this argument:

> [t]he persistence of unsustainability is due not simply to the ignorance
> or duplicity of individuals, or even to the mere logic of the capitalist

system, but also to a crisis in political meaning. . . The solution to this
crisis is not to be found in a simple restoration of political language's
reference to a reality outside language, as if language is a flapping sail
that can simply be re-secured to its mast. (338)

In other words, a serious or sincere environmentalism is problematic not
just because it is out of step with the postmodern tendency toward irrev-
erence and questioning; it's problematic because it assumes that we can
solve ecological problems simply by swapping out corporate, capitalist
"untruths" for environmentalist "Truth." In an era of multiple, competing
truths, this assumption seems naïve.

Comedic performance is productive in blurring the line between real
and unreal. Actually, it's one of the only rhetorical and performative
modes where the blurring of real and unreal is necessary. ARI uses contradictions to obscure communication, whereas comedy relies on contradictions for jokes to work. The distinction between the two motives can
best be seen in Burke's perspective of incongruity, which relies on the
recognition that one's way of seeing something is also inevitably "a way
of not seeing" (*Permanence* 49). By turning the argument on its head, we
see that the "obvious" is really just a disguise for the convenient. After
reviewing the sometimes arbitrary ways that performing ARI have become the norm I next discuss how troubling the norm through performances of eco-comedy may create social change.

Comedy Calls ARI's Bluff

Comedy thrives on the same competencies as ARI: contradictions, in-
congruities, and juxtapositions. To understand a joke, we have to be able
to think of comedy in more than one dimension (Berger 60). Contradictions are not problematic, but a necessary feature in comedy. In order to
find something amusing, someone usually has to turn things upside down
or present something in more than one frame at the same time (22-30).
As cultural performances of environmentalism, jokes depend on efficacious enactments of conventions and scripts, "performance consciousness of the performers, deliberate manipulation of time and space, and
the imposition of the frames of belief and play" (Bell, "Weddings" 185).
Performance, in this sense, is much like Noam Chomsky's concept of
"performance"—with its genesis in structural linguistics and generative
grammar, performance here is the manifestation of deep structures of
language, that Chomsky called "linguistic competence" (9-12). In this

usage, performance is riddled with mistakes, flaws, and imperfections. Seen this way, performance is "a site of transformation and even a paradigm for cultural resistance" (Pollock 657), or a performance that can be defined as "an activity which generates transformations" (Sayre 103).

Take for example, the joke that stand-up comic Greg Malone gave at the 2006 Natural Resources Defense Council annual gala: "Today with sunscreen, bottled water, air conditioners and oxygen masks, we don't need the environment as much as our ancestors did. We're more modern, sophisticated people; we can live on bus fumes" (Nordhaus and Shellenberger 62). Malone's joke asks: where does nature stop and where does culture begin? If we ask it carefully enough, examining our physical dependence on the world in something as simple as breathing, we find no place where we can do anything but arbitrarily say, here the environment stops and here I begin. His joke highlights the antagonism of environmental justice versus nature as a place apart from where people live, work, and play. Malone's joke is an interpretation of how dismissive and adaptable humans have become to nature. Adaptability has become a way to no longer need anything natural because as a species, humans are post-nature. Malone critiques the business-as-usual, industry-must-prevail mentality that has submerged America into a state of denial. The arrogance that humans are without nature, or do not need nature to survive, let alone thrive, is exposed in Malone's joke. This kind of comedy holds ARI up to ridicule. Malone proves that through absurdity, like living off bus fumes, we can gain new insights—ones that we cannot reach, or ones that might be difficult to reach with reason and logic alone (Brigham). He interpreted ARI as the cocky, arrogant, self-absorbed, mono-cultured ideology that it is. All the while, Malone reaffirmed for the members of NRDC that considering nature is what environmentalism is all about and illustrated that comedy is a viable way to reorient us to the common everyday assumptions about the environment.

Eco-comedy can reveal such an agenda and challenge the notion that humans are above nature. Performing eco-comedy in a situation is like lateral thinking—it allows you to see things from a new angle. It is at once a "perceptual intervention" to the rhetorical appeals to guilt and sacrifice, with a wink to ARI and a nudge at remaking social realities. In this light, eco-comedy subverts ARI and sustains environmentalism (Apple).[1] For example, Greenpeace Canada has been involved in the debates about developments of nuclear plants in Ontario and Toronto for the past six or seven years, according to David Murray. This movement started as a response to Ontario Premier Dalton McGuinty's obscure rationale:

"We are not embracing nuclear energy, we are merely experimenting" (Crawford para 1). "Lately, safety is the biggest concern at the hearings, especially in the wake of the Fukushima disaster" (Murray). Greenpeace has also been arguing dollars and cents—touting that each nuclear plant will cost the country $10 billion. And that figure does not include any effective solution for dealing with the nuclear waste that would be pro- duced. After months of petitioning, leafleting, and speaking at hearings, Greenpeace members decided that they had nothing to lose, so why not focus on the ridiculousness of this "debate?" Greenpeace set up a faux nuclear movement on the website, www.ilove-nukes.ca. The website fea- tured a petition to name a nuclear reactor after McGuinty. Their response was a video of pro-nuclear protesters waving signs that said, "Chernobyl was a fluke, let's go nuke" (Crawford para 3). They flipped McGuinty's logic by holding it up to ridicule. McGuinty relies on and masks contra- diction, and Greenpeace revealed this contradiction by ridiculing the il- logical premise of "not embracing" but "experimenting" with nuclear energy.

This kind of humor brings energy to dissent against ARI rhetoric. The faux nuclear movement website, www.ilove-nukes.ca, started as Greenpeace Canada's mockery of its government's blatant display of ARI. "Chernobyl was a fluke, let's go nuke," was a witty way to translate truth to power. While the Canadian government may have thought nucle- ar power was just an experiment, Greenpeace was able to translate the absurdity of a nuclear venture. The sarcastic "Chernobyl was a fluke" was in reference to the twenty-year anniversary of one of the worst nu- clear disasters in world history. When the Canadian government failed to respond to the organization's dissent, Greenpeace launched a calendar campaign of "365 near misses." The calendar has been the highest- grossing revenue-raising campaign for Greenpeace Canada in the past thirty years (Crawford para 2). The popularity proves that nothing un- dermines the status quo quite like holding it up to ridicule. Such perfor- mances point to comedy's potential to show the relationship between actual environmentalists and perceptions of environmentalism, old con- cepts and new, the past and the future, and unjust actions and just. Our individual and collective performances of environmentalism—even if they maintain the status quo through unerring reflections of socio- political values—are always threatened by the potential for radical and reflexive ways of performing anew (Bell, "Weddings" 190).

Performance is at the intersection of the individual and the social, two terms that quickly collapse under the larger term, politics. "Responsibility exists in discourses that offer tools and vocabularies that persons can utilize in creating themselves as responsible, ethical, and political—but always discursive—subjects" (Taylor and Vintges 3). Margaret McLaren writes about Foucault's later work: "it articulates a connection between self-transformation and social transformation and practices of freedom open up space for both individual creativity and social innovation" (239). Both are important for a biomimic refashioning of the world. Bell reminds us that performance studies has long been a space for individual creativity and social innovation, "doing the work of returning bodies to theories" and materiality to ideology ("Sex Acts" 212). This kind of performance places the emphasis not on performance consciousness, or on audience evaluation, but on representation (Bell, "Weddings" 188). The way each environmentalist chooses to perform his or her politics becomes collective political work. The politics of the everyday engagement with (and in regard to) nature that occurs on "the shifting middle ground of those things which may or may not be important in the long run, which are crucial to one person and inconsequential to the next, which seem essential and life-sustaining one day and downright stupid the next" (Schoemperlen 145).

A challenge to eco-comedy is the humor used by opponents. All socio-political performances reflect implicit and explicit socio-political values and are opportunities for reflexivity regarding those same values (Bell, "Weddings" 181). Like humor that is misogynist or racist, anti-environmentalist punch lines usually appeal to the lowest common denominator. Anthropocentric jokesters put on blast their complaints because they do not disturb or inconvenience others (well, except for abstract ideals like health and nature). But when environmentalists complain, we are not being "universal," we are inconvenient nuisances who want to save forests and marry trees. Anthropocentric jokes appear as crises of human existential conflicts; whereas environmentalist jokes appear misanthropic. In other words, the environmentalist or anthropocentric performances position the "joking matter" differently, vis-à-vis the wider socio-political context. Environmentalist complaints aren't seen as being about people—they're seen as being about polar bears and forest preserves that most people will never even see in real life. Conversely, the difference between performing eco-comedy and performing anthropocentric comedy seems to be the difference between resistance and revolution. The former includes digs at environmental conventions and pokes fun at the status quo, but without the truly "humankind has always been preeminent" edge that characterizes the latter. Eco-comedy calls into question the largest issues; it questions the way the world is put together with an ethic that does not position the performer as humbled by and in combat with the dominant ARI. It is a performance that does not guiltily succumb to charges of selfishness, privilege, and appropriation; a transformation that does not bemoan binaries but revels in their tensions; a theory-in-the-making that does not excuse itself from practice. In short, this is not your garden-variety self-deprecating humor.

The performance of eco-comedy presents us with a choice: take it seriously and it dies; fail to take it seriously and it might kill. E. B. White quipped, "humor can be dissected, as a frog can, but the thing dies in the process and the innards are discouraging to any but the scientific mind" (303). Throughout this chapter, I have taken comedy seriously by dissecting it, and therefore probably rendering my examples no longer funny. Nevertheless, White's observation is applicable to the choice that the performance of eco-comedy presents us: take it seriously and it dies; fail to take it seriously and it might kill. While my examples of eco-comedic performance do not explain environmental science, they do make environmental issues more accessible than the doom-and-gloom rhetoric of melodrama, which works just fine—as former vice president Al Gore proved when he won an Academy Award for showing us the "inconvenient" consequences of our inaction. What I am proposing is that we cannot solely rely on the threat or possibility of an apocalypse. Instead, to consider how "performance flourishes in the liminal, contested, and re-creative space between deconstruction and reconstruction, and crisis and redress" (Bell, "Weddings" 176). We must ask ourselves how our day-to-day performances of environmentalism (be they melodrama or eco-comedy or both) "reproduce, enable, sustain, challenge, subvert, critique, and naturalize ideology" (be it anthropocentric-resourcist or environmentalist) (Conquergood, "Rethinking Ethnography" 190). Remember, also, that performance is a means to display the intentions of sustainability, sustainably.

Ultimately, the characterizations of Greenpeace's performance as a kind of faking, and Malone's joke as a kind of breaking, are claims about utility as theorists attempt to answer the question, "What does performance do?" (Bell, "Weddings" 176). Performance studies, according to Elizabeth Bell, is "long familiar with negotiating binaries of local/historical, self-conscious/unconscious, and theory/practice," making it well positioned to explore the continuum of effects and social meanings that fall between anthropocentrism and environmentalism ("Sex Acts" 206). This particular kind of comedic performance is adept at

showing how the present mechanisms allow the status quo to go unchecked, rather than trying to explain why something happens. Postmodern theorists emphasize performances that check, or break, those structures and roles (Bell, "Weddings" 176)—reminders of the performative
rules that underlie and constitute identity, in turn re-making the multitude
of identities of environmentalism and anthropocentricism.

By way of an unwelcome but rhetorically useful coincidence, according to the Center for Biological Informatics of the U.S. Ecological
Survey, the same frogs White compared to comedy "are in decline in
many areas of the world. In cities and the countryside, in rainforests and
wetlands, countless areas which previously hosted a range of healthy
amphibian population now have fewer—and even no frogs, toads, or sal-
amanders" (31). Scientists who administered this survey suspect the population decline is due to environmental changes such as industrial pollution, UV radiation, habitat loss, and global climate change.

As evidence has accumulated over the past several decades, the possibility that we are in the midst of global climate change has struck environmentalists as presenting us with a similar choice: take it seriously and
act accordingly, or fail to take it seriously and suffer the consequences. If
we take the threat seriously, we can improve the quality of life on Earth.
If we fail to take it seriously, as I noted with Schwarze's work, the melodramatic forecasts of apocalypse authored by Al Gore and others are
likely to become realities. Even with the margins of error, these predic-
tions are probably conservative. In other words, if we fail to take the
threat seriously, the state of the world may be worse than Gore's predic-
tions.

Comedy's fluidity can be seen as a biomimicry of ecosystem equilibrium that resituates environmentalism as a response to crisis, and not
necessarily about crisis. It can simultaneously be an effective tool to subvert the performance of crisis and, at the same time, reaffirm environmentalist beliefs. Environmentalists do not want to spout off at the mouth
and waste energy in addressing techno-jargoned anthropocentric rhetoric.
Most environmentalists think the way we do because we believe in a future (Merchant). Why should our rhetorical strategies be anything different? At the same time, environmentalists should not abandon the doom-
and-gloom rhetoric because environmental concerns oftentimes warrant
the rhetoric of melodrama and apocalypse. Instead, environmentalists
should look to nature and employ an eco-effective rhetoric that is designed with a future in mind.

Environmentalists can conceive of our daily performances like a dark comedian would, combining ruthless assault on the current categorization of environmental antagonisms with a joyful juggling of categories. Performances that have an emphasis in rhetorical studies on invention and the emphasis in performance studies on disruption of power relations that privilege only the few and marginalize the many bear the potential to advance critical interventions that would promote a more inclusive and pluralistic public culture. In this conception, comedy can attract more environmentalists, and make environmentalism more engaging for all of us involved. Like Emma Goldman, who demanded there be dancing during an anarchist revolution, I demand there be room for humor in the struggle for planetary salvation. If not, then I am going to pack up my freestanding tent, GORE-TEX outerwear, and designer rucksack, and go home and wait for the apocalypse.

Notes

1. Jacki Apple argues that perceptual interventions are necessary conditions for performance art.

Works Cited

Apple, Jacki. "Performance Art is Dead: Long Live Performance Art!" *High Performance* 66 (1994): 54-9. Lexis Nexis Academic. Web. 13 Feb. 2013.
Arnold, Ronald. "Score: Environmentalists 6 Industry 2." *Logging Management* (1979): 22-7. Lexis Nexis Academic. Web. 11 Oct. 2012.
Barreca, Regina. *They Used to Call Me Snow White . . . But I Drifted.* New York: Penguin, 1963. Print.
Bauman, Richard. *Verbal Art as Performance.* Prospect Heights: Waveland, 1984. Print.
Bell, Elizabeth. "Operationalizing Feminism: Two Challenges for Feminist Research." *Women & Language* 33 (2010): 97-102. Lexis Nexis Academic. Web. 13 Feb. 2013.
———. "Sex Acts Beyond Boundaries and Binaries: A Feminist Challenge for Self Care in Performance Studies." *Text and Performance Quarterly* 25 (2005): 187-219. Lexis Nexis Academic. Web. 13 Feb. 2013.
———. "Toward a Pleasure-Centered Economy: Wondering a Feminist Aesthetic of Performance." *Text and Performance Quarterly* 15 (1995): 99-121. Lexis Nexis Academic. Web. 13 Feb. 2013.

———. "Weddings and Pornography: The Cultural Performance of Sex." *Text and Performance Quarterly* 19 (1999): 173-95. Lexis Nexis Academic. Web. 13 Feb. 2013.

Benyus, Janine M. *Biomimicry: Innovation Inspired by Nature.* New York: Harper Perennial, 2002. Print.

Berger, Peter L. *Redeeming Laughter: Comic Dimension of Human Experience.* New York: Walter de Gruyter & Co, 1997. Print.

Bormann, Ernest G. "Fantasy and Rhetorical Vision: The Rhetorical Criticism of Social Reality." *Quarterly Journal of Speech* 58 (1972): 396-407. Print.

Brick, Phil. "Determined Opposition: The Wise Use Movement Challenges Environmentalism." *Environment* 37 (1995): 17-42. Print.

Brigham, Stephen. *Limitations of Reason and Liberation of Absurdity: Reason and Absurdity as Means of Personal and Social Change. Case Study: Psychotherapy.* Wollongong, NSW: U of Wollongong, 2005. Print.

Bsumek, Peter K. "Kairos: Time to Get Down to It (Should Have been Done Long Ago)." *Environmental Communication: A Journal of Nature and Culture* 2 (2008): 81-90. Print.

Burke, Kenneth. *Language and Symbolic Action: Essays on Life, Literature and Method.* Berkeley: U of California P, 1966. Print.

———. *Permanence and Change: An Anatomy of Purpose.* Third Edition. Berkeley: U of California P, 1984. Print.

Ceccarelli, Leah. "Manufactured Scientific Controversy: Science, Rhetoric, and Public Debate." *Rhetoric and Public Affairs* 14 (2011): 195-228. Print.

Chomsky, Noam. *Topics in the Theory of Generative Grammar.* Paris: The Hague, 1966. Print.

Conquergood, Dwight. "Performing as a Moral Act: Ethical Dimensions of the Ethnography of Performance." *Literature in Performance* 5 (1985): 1-13. Lexis Nexis Academic. Web. 13 Feb. 2013.

———. "Rethinking Ethnography: Towards a Critical Cultural Politics." *Communication Monographs* 58 (1991): 179-94. Lexis Nexis Academic. Web. 13 Feb. 2013.

Cox, Robert. *Environmental Communication and the Public Sphere.* Thousand Oaks: Sage, 2013. Print.

———. "Nature's 'Crisis Discipline': Does Environmental Communication Have an Ethical Duty?" *Environmental Communication* 1.1 (2007): 5-20. Print.

Crawford, Trish. "Environmentalists Know How to Take a Joke." *Sierra Club Canada.* 9 June 2007: 2. Lexis Nexis Academic. Web. 2 Feb. 2013.

de Certeau, Michel. *The Practice of Everyday Life.* Trans. Steven Rendall. Berkeley: U of California P, 1984. Print.

Ehrlich, Paul, and Anne H. Ehrlich. *Betrayal of Science and Reason: How Anti-Environmental Rhetoric Threatens Our Future.* Washington D.C.: Island Press, 1998.

Ellis, Richard J. *American Political Cultures.* New York: Oxford UP, 1996. Print.

Faderman, Lillian. "Queer." *Exploring Language.* Ed. Gary Goshgarian. New York: Addison-Wesley, 2001. 482-85. Print.

Foreman, Dave. *Confessions of an Eco-Warrior.* New York: Crown, 1991. Print.

Foucault, Michel. "Technologies of the Self." *Ethics: Subjectivity and Truth: The Essential Works of Michel Foucault.* Vol. 1. Ed Paul Rabinow. Trans. Robert Hurley, et al. New York: New P, 1994. 223-51. Print.

Gencarella, Stephen Oblrys, and Phaedra Pezzullo, Eds. "Introduction." *Readings on Rhetoric and Performance.* State College, PA: Strata, 2010. Print.

Giroux, Henry A., ed. *Postmodernism, Feminism, and Cultural Politics: Redrawing Educational Boundaries.* Albany: State U of New York P, 1991. Print.

Goffman, Erving. *The Presentation of Self in Everyday Life.* Garden City: Doubleday Anchor, 1959. Print.

Gore, Al. *The Assault on Reason.* New York: Penguin, 2008. Print.

Greenpeace. 2005. I Love Nukes! 8 May 2009. <http://www.ilovenukes.ca> Lexis Nexis Academic Search. Web. 12 Feb 2013.

Heise, Ursula. *Sense of Place and Sense of Planet: The Environmental Imagination of the Global.* New York: Oxford UP, 2008. Print.

Inhofe, James. *A Skeptic's Guide to Debunking Global Warming Alarmism.* 8 December 2006. *U.S. Senate Committee on Environment & Public Works.* <http://epw.senate.gov/public/index>. Lexis Nexis Academic Search. Web. 19 Feb, 2013.

Jackson, Robert. "Eight-Legged Tricksters." *Bioscience* 42 (1992): 590-9. Lexis Nexis Academic Search. Web. 13 Feb. 2013.

Janofsky, Michael. "Preserving the Earth One Joke at a Time." nytimes.com. *The New York Times.* 19 November 2005. Web. 23 April 2012.

Lertzman, Renee. "Psychoanalysis, Culture, Society and Our Biotic Relations: Introducing an Ongoing Theme on Environment and Sustainability." *Psychoanalysis, Culture & Society* 15.2 (2010): 113-6. Print.

Lewis, Paul. *Cracking Up: American Humor in Time of Conflict.* Chicago: U of Chicago P, 2006. Print.

Litfin, Karen. "Articulating the Sacred in the Politics of Sacrifice" *International Studies Association Conference 2006.* EBSCO Academic Search. Web. 2 February 2013.

Lovins, Amory. "Janine Benyus." *Time International* 29 Oct. 2007: 49. Print.

Maniates, Michael and John Meyer, Eds. *The Environmental Politics of Sacrifice.* Cambridge: MIT Press, 2010. Print.

McKerrow, Raymie. "Corporeality and Cultural Rhetoric: A Site for Rhetoric's Future." *Southern Communication Journal* 63 (1998): 315-28. Print.

McLaren, Margaret A. "Foucault and Feminism: Power, Resistance, and Freedom." *Feminism and the Final Foucault.* Ed. Dianna Taylor and Karen Vintges. Urbana: U of Illinois P, 2004. 214-34. Print.

Merchant, Carolyn. *Reinventing Eden: The Fate of Nature in Western Culture.* New York: Routledge, 2004. Print.

Murray, David. "The Fallout Continues—23 Years After Chernobyl Became a Byword for Nuclear Disaster, the Number of Victims Continues to Grow." *The Sunday Mail* 26 Apr. 2009. Lexis Nexis Search. Web. 11 Feb. 2013.

National Biological Information Infrastructure. 2005. "FrogWeb: Amphibian Declines." 20 January 2009. <http:frogweb.nbii.gov/declines/> Web. 18 Feb, 2013.

National Public Radio: Environment. 2005. "Environment in the Comedy Arts: An Interview with Laurie David." 17 pars. 8 February 2008. <http://www.npr. org/templates/topics/topic.php?topicId=1025> Web. 19 Feb. 2013.

Naylor, Gloria. "Nigger: The Meaning of a Word." *Exploring Language.* Ed. Gary Goshgarian. New York: Addison-Wesley, 2001. 459-62. Print.

Nordhaus, Ted, and Michael Shellenberger. *Break Through: From the Death of Environmentalism to the Politics of Possibility.* New York: Houghton Mifflin, 2007. Print.

Paroske Marcus. "Deliberating International Science Policy Controversies: Uncertainty and AIDS in South Africa" *Quarterly Journal of Speech* 95 (2009): 148-70. Print.

Peeples, Jennifer. "Aggressive Mimicry: The Rhetoric of Wise Use and the Environmental Movement." *The Environmental Communication Yearbook* (2005): 1-17. Print.

Pollock, Della. "Performativity." *The Oxford Companion to Women's Writing in the United States.* Eds. Cathy N. Davidson and Linda Wagner-Martin. Oxford: Oxford UP, 1995. 657-58. Print.

Rampton, Sheldon, and John Stauber. *Toxic Sludge is Good For You!: Lies, Damn Lies and The Public Relations Industry.* Monroe: Center for Media & Democracy, 1995. Print.

Reed, Philip. "A Paradigm Shift: Biomimicry." *Technology Teacher* 63 (2004): 23-27. Lexis Nexis Academic Search. Web, 3 Feb. 2013.

Romm, Joseph. *Hell and High Water: Global Warming—the Solution, the Politics—and What We Should Do.* New York: Harper Collins, 2007. Print.

Ruckman, Justin. "Earth to America, Space to Earth." Centripetal Notion. 2006. 28 February 2008. <http://centripetalnotion.com/2005/11/23/02:00:28/> Web. 13 Feb. 2013.

Sayre, Henry. "Performance." *Critical Terms for Literary Study.* Eds. Frank Lentricchia and Thomas McLaughlin. Chicago: U of Chicago P, 1990. 92-104. Print.

Schechner, Richard. *Performance Theory.* Rev. 2nd ed. New York: Routledge, 1988.

Schoemperlen, Diane. *In the Language of Love: A Novel in 100 Chapters.* New York: Viking, 1994. Print.

Schwarze, Steven. "Environmental Melodrama." *Quarterly Journal of Speech* 92 (2006): 239-61. Print.
Switzer, Jacqueline Vaughn. *Green Backlash: The History and Politics of Environmental Opposition in the U.S.* Boulder: Lynne Rienner, 1997. Print.
Szerszynski, Bronislaw. *Nature, Technology and the Sacred.* Malden: Wiley-Blackwell, 2005. Print.
Taylor, Dianna, and Karen Vintges. "Introduction: Engaging the Present." *Feminism and the Final Foucault.* Ed. Taylor and Vintges. Urbana: U of Illinois P, 2004. 1-11. Print.
Turner, Victor. *The Anthropology of Performance.* New York: PAJ, 1988. Print.
Verhoeven, Betsy. "New York Times Environmental Rhetoric: Constituting Artists of Living." *Rhetoric Review* 30 (1): 2011, 19-36. Print.
White, E. B., Ed. Preface. "Some Remarks on Humor." *A Subtreasury of American Humor.* Ed. Katherine S. White. New York: Coward-McCann, 1941. Print.

Chapter Five

Embodied Perspective by Incongruity: Environmental Critique in an Age of Everyday Performance

Richard D. Besel

More than ten years ago, self-proclaimed "vaga-bum" Daniel Suelo stopped using money (Suelo, "Living Without"). Living in a cave an hour outside of Moab, Utah, Suelo's personal decision to abandon the world of material consumption has been met with looks of both admiration and disdain. Some believe him to be an environmental prophet while others believe him to be mentally unbalanced—judgments the generally cheerful ascetic often uses to his advantage. According to Suelo, "I've been totally without cents since Autumn of 2000 (except for a couple months in 2001). I don't use or accept money or conscious barter—don't take food stamps or other government dole" ("Moneyless World"). Although the humorous homonym ("cents" versus "sense") might suggest Suelo sees his lifestyle decisions in a lighthearted manner, the point he attempts to make is anything but trivial. Environmentally aware, philosophically informed, and deeply spiritual, Suelo notes: "When I lived with money, I was always lacking. Money represents lack. Money represents things in the past (debt) and things in the future (credit), but money never represents what is present" (qtd. in Osborne). Daniel Suelo's rejection of capitalism combined with a devout mindfulness of the "here and now" not only have earned him local celebrity status in eastern Utah, but it garnered "him national media attention and a growing list of internet admirers" (Mills 35).

Although Suelo's decision might be read as one of personal choice, it is also simultaneously a performative critique of mainstream society's obsessions with consumption, excess, and waste. While many environmental communication studies have addressed "high-profile environmental controversies," activist and environmental performance scholar Dave Horton argues, "environmentalism is also about the everyday" (63). Suelo's lifestyle choices thus act as an important case study that allows us to explore the microphysics of power as they function in response to a complex assemblage of hegemonic discourses, a part of everyday life that Horton argues is "an important, and frequently overlooked, part of contemporary environmentalism" (63). Drawing primarily on the works of Michel de Certeau and Kenneth Burke, I contend Suelo's persuasion does not function by forcing observers to confront an individual who simply *uses* tactics of resistance in his "everyday life," but instead, it functions because his everyday life *is* a tactic. By juxtaposing Suelo's life with their own, audiences are confronted with an alternative way of seeing their relationship with the world. In other words, Suelo's lifestyle choices become an embodied "perspective by incongruity" (Burke, *Permanence*).

In the following analysis, I first explore the theoretical connections between the concepts of performance, "everyday life," and "perspective by incongruity." This is followed by an analysis of Suelo's rhetoric and performances found in interviews, on his website, and on his blog. After analyzing these texts, implications for understanding the rhetoric of everyday life and environmental performance as a means of producing new, alternative worldviews are discussed.

Performance and Perspective

In recent years, studies across a variety of fields have recognized the importance of methodological approaches that allow for the exploration of performance. As a result, according to Nigel Clark, the "growing interest in the performative dimensions of human existence amongst certain sectors of the social sciences and humanities has served to accentuate the 'doing' side of social life as opposed to the 'being' or givenness of particular social identities or categories" (165). However, the notion of performance can be understood from a variety of theoretical and practical perspectives. Performance studies scholars Elizabeth Bell and Stacy Holman Jones have argued there are at least three "metaphorical stages" from which one can view performance: the theatrical stage, the streets as global stage, and the stage of the everyday (199). In the first two metaphorical stages, performance was traditionally viewed as a discrete event, one that had a clear beginning and end. A theatrical performance often began at a predetermined time and often ended once the script had been articulated in a particular context. Likewise, a protest that was organized to begin at a predetermined time could also come to an end once the protesters had dispersed. Mary Frances HopKins captures this view of the first two stages in her observations about the performative turn taking place across disciplinary lines: performance "once referred to an event somehow set apart from everyday actions, an event that might be separated, or bracketed, from what the audience perceived as 'everyday life'" (229). This chapter subscribes to a broader view of performance, one that does not see performance as only a matter of special, discrete events, but one that emphasizes what Bell and Jones would say fits onto the third stage—the stage of "everyday life." Doing so allows and encourages scholarly understanding that reaches beyond the limited spaces of special and often isolated performances.

According to rhetoric scholar Philip Wander, in his introduction to Henri Lefebvre's book *Everyday Life in the Modern World*: "'Everyday life' refers to dull routine, the ongoing go-to-work, pay-the-bills, homeward trudge of daily existence. It indicates a sense of being in the world beyond philosophy, virtually beyond the capacity of language to describe, that we know simply as the grey reality enveloping all we do" (vii-viii). It is in this "grey reality" that people find themselves the targets of systems of power. The everyday is not just something we live; it is something that is actively created. Influenced by the pessimistic assessment of capitalism articulated by Marx, Lefebvre trenchantly argues that "the everyday is a *product*," one that "constitutes the platform upon which the bureaucratic society of controlled consumerism is erected" (9). In other words, Lefebvre follows Marx's pessimism in vilifying capitalistic influence—our everyday interactions involve the articulation, maintenance, and support of systems that promote false consciousness. Equally pessimistic, Michel Foucault's work on disciplinarity suggests everyday life is vulnerable to the exercise of external systems of power, especially through hierarchical observation, normalization, and examination (170-194). As society shifted from an age where humans were controlled through public display (punishing bodies in stocks or public executions) to one where humans were controlled through other more subtle means (self-policing and surveillance), power structures tightened their grips on the everyday actions of individuals. For cultural studies critic John Bolton, "This pessimism [in Foucault] is tied to a view of everyday life as a passive field waiting to be dominated by disciplinary structures. The lines of influence are all one-way. Thus it would only be a small step from the argument that discipline creates individuals to the argument that it also creates the everyday" (328). But this pessimism may be an oversimplification of lived experience. Is it not possible to find acts of resistance in the everyday? Although Foucault does not rule out this possibility, it is left largely undeveloped. In a well-worn quote, Foucault notes that, "Where there is power, there is resistance" (95). Foucault under-

stood that concluding the everyday offers no room for individual agency
would be a mistake. This is precisely where the work of Michel de Certeau becomes pertinent.

Michel de Certeau explicitly engages Foucault's pessimism and offers a slightly more optimistic understanding of the everyday. For Certeau, everyday life constantly "invents itself by poaching" on instruments
of power and processes of control (xii). In other words, individuals make
use of existing structures in ways that were not intended by the very
forces that attempt to control those individuals. The institutions and assemblages of power noted by Foucault make use of what Certeau calls
"strategies" in "the calculus of force-relationships" that enable the exercise of power (xix). The use of strategies can be challenged by subjects
through the use of "tactics." Tactics are "the ingenious ways in which the
weak make use of the strong, thus lend[ing] a political dimension to everyday practices" (xvii). People are often finding unique and improvisational ways to manipulate, undermine, and take advantage of the very
discourses forced upon them. Although Certeau's work is often interpreted as a "corrective" to Foucault's, both perspectives have much to offer.
Foucault can be appreciated for highlighting the use of power by systems
and institutions, while Certeau can be appreciated for underscoring the
creative means by which individuals resist those systems and institutions
in their everyday art of making do.

A simple example Certeau offers to explain the difference between a
tactic and a strategy can be observed in the French example of *la per-
ruque*, or, the "wig." The "wig" "is the worker's own work disguised as
work for his employer" (25). One can imagine typing a personal email at
work as a kind of poaching, a use of a tactic, a small act of resistance
against the dominant powers attempting to control you to keep you producing in a docile, compliant manner. Although this example is prosaic,
there are a range of other examples one can imagine as a kind of poaching in a variety of contexts. However, Suelo's performative resistance
does not blend seamlessly into Certeau's strategy/tactic dichotomy. It
seems clear Suleo is resisting the strategies employed by capitalism, but
it is not so clear that Suelo is relegated to the use of tactics in his everyday life. What makes Seulo's use of tactics significantly different from
examples such as the "wig" is that Suelo's life is openly observable to
others. One who poaches often attempts to fly under the radar of those in
power. It is through making his life visible to others that audiences are
able to juxtapose their own lives with Suelo's life. In this sense, Kenneth
Burke's explication of perspective by incongruity becomes salient.

According to Burke, each of us has an expectation of—an orientation toward—"how things were, how they are, and how they may be" (*Permanence* 14). When one's expectations are violated through a juxtaposition of things that to do not fit together—an incongruity—the perspective on how things were, are, and will be has the potential to change. Words and ideas—as well as habits and behaviors—that do not ordinarily go together are bonded just as those that do ordinarily go together are divorced. Perspective by incongruity serves as an "'opening wedge' that unbalances our understanding of how the world does and ought to function" (Whedbee 48). However, to fully understand Burke's notion of perspective by incongruity, that is, how expectations can be violated to enact change, one must also explore what Burke means by "piety."

Following Spanish poet and philosopher George Santayana, Burke sees piety as a "loyalty to the sources of our being" (*Permanence* 71). In other words, "Piety is *the sense of what properly goes with what*" (*Permanence* 74). Piety is thus not limited to the religious sphere: "where you discern the symptoms of great devotion to any kind of endeavor, you are in the realm of piety" (*Permanence* 83). Perspective by incongruity is impious "insofar as it attacks the kinds of linkage already established" (*Permanence* 87). But this is precisely what makes perspective by incongruity such a potent rhetorical tool. According to Naomi R. Rockler, "Perspective by incongruity is powerful because, if successful, it jars people into new perceptions about the way reality can be constructed and may encourage people to question their pieties" (38). Burke's perspective by incongruity meshes with Certeau's theoretical perspective in the sense that pieties are "beliefs and values people have come to accept and expect in everyday life" (Besel and Besel 56). For Suelo, everyday performance provides the perspective through which he can expose people to impious actions, actions that challenge what he believes to be the corruptive hegemony of late capitalism.

Suelo's Everyday Life

Daniel Suelo was not always environmentally sensitive and spiritually aware. An anthropology major who graduated from the University of Colorado, Suelo was once like any other "normal" person subject to the pressures and constraints of capitalism. He had a job. He had money. He had credit. But then something changed. The turning point in his life came in 1987, when he joined the Peace Corps and was sent to an Ecuadorian village in the Andes to offer basic medical services (teaching first aid and handing out medicine) to the people who lived there. Despite being removed from the everyday interactions of modern North America, Suelo noticed that as the local populations became increasingly wealthy, their cultural values and health practices began to change. He recalls: "It looked like money was impoverishing them." (Ketcham 66). Although it was his two years abroad that allowed Suelo to reconsider his place in American culture, it was not until 2000 that he decided to reject the use of money and retreat to an economically spare, but highly natural, lifestyle.

For the last five years Suelo has taken up residency in a cave outside Moab, and he has done so with very few modern amenities. According to Christopher Ketchum, a journalist who made the trek to the cave for his interview with Suelo: "From the outside, the place looks like a hollowed teardrop, about the size of a cello case. Inside it's as wide as an Amtrak bathroom, with enough space for a few pots that hang from the ceiling, a stove under a stone eave, big buckets full of beans and rice, a bed of blankets in the dirt, and not much else" (66). From his refusal to participate in modern economic systems to his choice of where to sleep, Suelo appears to be practicing what he preaches: how we choose to live our everyday lives matters for the development of the human spirit, the wasteful consumption of material, and the persuasive potential to influence others.

Wild Nature and Spirited Sharing

The spiritual antecedents of Suelo's philosophy on life began in his early childhood and were further strengthened by his travels. According to Mills, Suelo "was raised in a strict evangelical family." He often "wondered why so few Christians who considered themselves devout were not prepared to adopt the ascetic lifestyle espoused by Jesus" (35). Trips to places such as India and Thailand later exposed him to the teachings of Tibetan Buddhism and the Hindu sadhus, "the holy men who wander the country without money or possessions. Suelo began to wonder if he could become an American sadhu – a wandering ascetic in 'one of the most materialistic money-worshipping nations on earth . . . to be a vagabond, a bum, and make an art of it'" (Mills 35). According to Suelo, "this idea enchanted me" (Mills 35). This spiritual theme saturates much of Suelo's rhetoric and performances and animates his willingness to share all that he has, because as Suelo would argue, the items he shared were never really his to begin with. After all, "ownership is but an illusion" (Suelo, "Moneyless World").

For Suelo, the idea that one does not ever truly own possessions is rooted in an understanding that humans are a part of nature. As such:

> Wild Nature, outside commercial civilization, runs on gift economy: "freely give, freely receive." Thus it is balanced. Commercial civiliza- tion runs on consciousness of credit and debt (knowledge of good & evil); thus it is imbalanced. What nation can even balance its own budget or environment? Gift Economy is Faith, Grace, Love – the core message of every religion. The proof is inside you: Wild Nature is your True Nature, crucified by commercial civilization. ("Living Without")

In this excerpt, Suelo makes use of the well-worn environmental trope of "balance." The simple binary of associating a life outside commercial civilization as being balanced forces those who hear him and see how he lives to reconsider their own lives: "Am I upsetting the natural balance?" Additionally, the last portion of this excerpt allows for an introspective understanding: Suelo seems to suggest that we do not necessarily have to engage in large-scale environmental policymaking to combat the envi- ronmental consequences of capitalism because the answers are "inside" each of us. The religious allusions are unmistakable. However, this in- ward turning for answers about how we should remain in "balance" with nature is not a onetime event—it is a constant questioning and unending process. Through his actions and introspective lifestyle, Suelo illustrates the performative power of everyday decisions. By calling for a new per- spective through his everyday life, Suelo denaturalizes one's assump- tions about everyday lifestyle choices. For Suelo, this constant and re- peated questioning is "the essence of all life. That's what doesn't end and what we can every day cultivate within ourselves" ("Moneyless World"). Following Foucault and Certeau, Suelo's actions may be read as an at- tempt to free individuals from policing themselves in a world obsessed with excessive consumption. It is at the level of individual action and performance where one can make meaningful change.

Suelo's everyday practices exemplify the religious foundations of his beliefs. By turning inward, Suelo concluded his "possessions" were not really his; so he gave them away and used only what was readily availa- ble. However, he claims this was not done for attention or congratula- tions:

We must wake up and realize that sharing is no act of goodness, nothing that deserves reward or praise, but simply a natural act like breathing free air in and out, or a natural act like the sun sharing its energy on ALL life forms, expecting nothing in return! Working with no thought of reward or ownership is a constant theme of the Bible, the Baghavad Gita, the Quran, the Buddhist Sutras, the Tao Te Ching, the Guru Granth Sahib, the Bahai scriptures, the Book of Mormon, the Jain sutras, and the practiced philosophy of Native Peoples all over the world. Christians, what does Jesus say but to be like the servant who works because it is his duty, not even expecting thanks. Only we who fool ourselves think we own anything to give! Muslims and Mormons, your Quran and the Book of Mormon especially stress this fact. ("Moneyless World")

Suelo's principle is universal: to share and give is a natural act. Hoarding resources, possessions, or money, are all counterproductive to the spiritual underpinnings of all religious systems. In giving up material possessions, Suelo suggests we can finally be free of the hold systems of domination have over us: "Actually, when we finally realize we own no possessions, we have nothing to steal, and nobody to trespass against us, and nobody can have power over us" ("Moneyless World").

The spiritual dimensions of Suelo's rhetoric provide for an interesting contrast with other interpretations of various religious systems. For example, it has long been argued that Christianity contained within it the seeds of environmental devastation. One of the most widely circulated accounts of this argument was advanced by Lynn White, Jr. in a 1967 *Science* article. For White, "Human ecology is deeply conditioned by beliefs about our nature and destiny—that is, by religion" (1205). For one view of Christianity, the Earth was given to humans to use and the end of days doctrine will make any environmental issues moot, so why not deplete resources? Why not live out of balance? Suelo explicitly rejects this understanding by emphasizing an alternative morality: "You can keep procrastinating and wait for zillions of years for Messiah to come to zap everything right. Or, you can realize what your own scriptures teach you, that Messiah is in you, your Hope of Glory. You are the Hands and Feet and Eyes and Mouth and Breath of Messiah. Wake up and realize that Messiah will never, ever, ever come, except through you. Take Responsibility" ("Moneyless World").

Although the spiritual elements of Suelo's discourse are important factors to consider, many observers might worry about where they would get their next meal if they did not have the money to buy it. The answer

Suelo offers is a simple one: "Have faith that everything comes as you need it in the moment" (Suelo, "Moneyless World").

Present Opportunity and Everyday Materiality

It is in living in the moment that the material aspects of Suelo's performances come into sharp focus. According to one observer,

> Suelo lives an abundant albeit frugal life, thriving on the waste of a small town. Every week, he inspects Moab's trash, finding more than he needs. Supermarket throwaways keep him well-fed. He eats healthily, often eschewing the abundant supply of day-old doughnuts or expired sweets – although, he says, chocolate is "my gold." The wild onions, watercress, prickly pear fruit, serviceberries, globe mallow and pine nuts that grow near his home add fresh-grown flair to the trash-bin-derived dishes he cooks over fire-branded coffee cans molded into stoves. He occasionally cooks roadkill gathered around Moab, and says he has never fallen ill from spoiled food. (Blevins)

Suelo's life decisions, including where and what he eats, allow others to see an alternative way of living, one where identity is not tied to an economic position. How much one pays for his or her meal, and how and where one eats that meal, does not determine one's worth. This observation is also noted by Horton: "People literally eat their way into identity positions. Like food shopping, the eating of some foods and the refusal of others powerfully communicates lifestyle" (71). The lifestyle Suelo wishes to live is one that is consistent with his spiritual understanding of how humans should exist in balance with nature.

The idea of using what is readily available does not mean Suelo is a Luddite. In fact, Suelo is technologically savvy, making use of public resources such as computers available at the public library to disseminate his ideas via his blog. Suelo gives his blog readers another example of how living day to day, free of capitalistic concerns, was liberating and a blessing. He tells of an encounter he had while "dumpster-diving at the thrift-store to find warmer clothes for winter," how he was thinking about how nice it would be to learn how to play the guitar:

> The dumpster was so full of junk it was overflowing—stuff piled around it. I dug around a bit and found a booklet on how to play the guitar. "What a coincidence." I thought, "But I don't have a guitar," my

other voice reminded me, again. As I was getting ready to leave the dumpster, I took a last glance back and noticed I hadn't checked the stuff piled against it. I lifted up a box and noticed a guitar case underneath. "Nice case. I have friends who might need it," I thought. I lifted it, and it wasn't empty! I opened it up, and, voila, a guitar! "Surely there must be something wrong with it for it to be here," I thought. I brought it back to the farm, checked it out the next morning, and found it was virtually new and flawless! There were also some instructional DVDs included in the case and two extra strings. If ever I got a clear message to do something, this time it was, "Learn to play the guitar." ("Moneyless World")

Suelo's real life experiences inform the narratives found on his blog and in his interviews. Living in the moment saturates all that he does. When filling out a common online list of "get to know you" questions often circulated in spam emails, a conscious awareness of the here and now is ubiquitous. His favorite movie: "The movie I am watching now." His favorite music: ". . . the sounds around me right now." His favorite book: "I'm living my favorite book and you are too." Not a moment is unappreciated.

Of course, Suelo understands that not all of his narratives make his lifestyle sound rosy to his readers or those who speak with him in person. But struggle is natural and not something to shy away from: "That it's hard is exactly the point, he says. 'Hardship is a good thing. We need the challenge. Our bodies need it. Our immune systems need it. My hardships are simple, right at hand—they're manageable.'" (qtd. in Ketchum 66). Whether dumpster-diving or living in the moment as he experiences the joyous sounds of nature, Suelo is also aware that his life is a performance for others to see, an act(ion) to which they can respond.

Natural Living as Performance and Perspective

Suelo is indeed keenly aware that others are watching him. His life is so different from the mainstream lives of those working within capitalism that it is not unusual for Suelo to draw the gaze of others. His response to the attention is simply to make his beliefs transparent for all to see: "I've been saying for the past few months that I decided to make my life an open book, including the good, the bad, and the ugly" ("Moneyless World"). There is a brutal honesty to Suelo's everyday performances, a kind of perspective that forces observers to see something about their daily lives that they had not observed before. After all, he was once like his observers. However, he noticed things in a slightly different manner. Take, for example, what Suelo has to say about his life within capitalism before he stopped using money: "Every time I made a resume for a job, signed my name to a document, opened a bank account, or even bought a banana at the supermarket, I felt a tinge of dishonesty, like I was not letting my yes be yes and my no be no" ("Moneyless World"). Suelo provides us with an alternative form of being in the world, a way of engaging nature not available to all within capitalism. By making his life an "open book," he allows audience members to see how he started as someone just like them, but became someone else, someone who arguably lives in harmony with nature.

Although Suelo does not explicitly say he is out to persuade others that his way of living is the right one, there is a hint of this intent in his writings. Suelo's creations of a transparent life could simply be a way of inviting others to see what it is he sees. But there is more to his life choices. Indeed, there is a clear persuasive element to what it is Suelo is doing. Take the following excerpt as an example of Suelo's clear sense of advocacy in favor of a different form of being in the world: "Live communally right here, right now, where we are, in this very society. Infect society with it, until people wake up and realize money and possessions are simply illusions, realizing that there can be no balance until everybody freely gives & freely takes" ("Moneyless World"). Suelo asks his readers and all who see his life to not only change the way they live their everyday lives, but he asks them to also become advocates on their own. Of course, when an alternative to systems of power exists, systems of power and those influenced and/or controlled by it will often attempt to maintain and defend what they believe seems "normal."

Audience Reactions

Assessing Suelo's effect on those who have read his writings or heard him speak in person is difficult. There seem to be two major reactions to Suelo's everyday life as a form of performative critique. Predictably, some audiences accuse Suelo of being a hypocrite; a parasitic bum who lives off the generosity of others. According to Mills, Suelo has, "also ignited an angry backlash from others who complain that he is only too happy to make free use of the costly internet facilities that others are paying for through their taxes. 'Who do you think pays for the internet at the library where you write this blog?' complained one reader. 'You have the qualifications to get a job but, instead, you choose to leech off society'" (35). For another writer, "It seems fair to suggest that Suelo couldn't have the lifestyle he has now if everybody else did the same. For a start he doesn't seem to be producing his own food or clothes" (Osborne). But how do we make sense of these reactions? According to one of Suelo's college friends, Damian Nash, "'I think he makes people angry because they have this belief that if only they had a little more money, they'd be happy,' Nash says. 'His lifestyle is a challenge to their Holy Grail, the American consumer capitalist dream'" (Blevins). But we can further ex-plain this negative reaction in Burkean terms: those who accurately per-ceive Suelo's critique against modern capitalism as one requiring a sig-nificant change in lifestyle see his life as an impious one; they remain devoted to the piety of free market economics. There is a breakdown of what Burke would call the "identification" process (*Rhetoric* 19-28). In other words, the perspective by incongruity has functioned to draw the fire of those living a mainstream lifestyle. Unable to identify with the impious position advocated by Suelo, their only recourse is to attack Seulo in order to remain pious to their own beliefs and values.

But how does Suelo answer the charges made by his critics? Is he really a "leech"? For Suelo, using the free Internet access at the local library is not a hypocritical act. He often offers an analogy to explain his position: If a bird were to build a nest using human-made materials, or build that nest in a human-made structure, would humans be angry at the bird for living as naturally as it could? If not, why be angry with Suelo? Suelo sees nothing wrong with using materials that are freely given and freely taken. In fact, according to one observer, living naturally means one is more connected with things and people rather than less:

> Self-sufficiency isn't a goal in his moneyless life, he says. So, he will sometimes house-sit, but it makes him antsy and he pines for his cave. If someone presses him to take something, he doesn't argue. He recent-ly began taking yoga classes offered by a friend. If they insist on giving him money, he gives it away immediately. 'We are all completely de-pendent on everyone else. The point is to live freely, in the present, freely giving and freely taking, which is the way of nature,' he says. 'The idea is to give up control of credit and debt, and just trust the cy-cle of nature . . . .'" (Blevins)

Despite the critics, Suelo seems to be undeterred. He continues with his unorthodox preaching and everyday performances. In fact, Suelo's response to his critics may be read as a commentary on *their* performances. The scripts his critics follow in defense of "normal" lifestyle choices illustrate the incongruity between their respective positions: each side defends what Burke would call a piety, while appearing impious to the other.

Although Suelo has received his fair share of criticism, others have looked at Suelo's life and have seen much to admire. They are confronted with a different perspective, a perspective that appears to be giving Suelo benefits few others find. Nash observes, "He is truly the happiest person I have ever met. He is so deeply peaceful, it's contagious." Nash continues, "He is living proof that money can't buy happiness" (Blevins). While many may feel sorry for Suelo, that he most likely will die somewhere in the wild, for Suelo the thought is not a depressing one: "'I'll do what creatures have been doing for millions of years for retirement,' he says. 'Why is it sad that I die in the canyon and not in the geriatric ward well-insured? I have great faith in the power of natural selection. And one day, I will be selected out'" (Ketchum 66). Suelo's life—his everyday performances—bring the larger questions of what it means to be a part of nature to our attention. What is Suelo doing? How are we to live our lives? Is there another way? For Suelo, the answer to the latter question is a definitive "yes."

Conclusion

In this chapter, I have examined Daniel Suelo's everyday life as a form of embodied performance and environment-related critique. This case study underscores the way that persuasion can not only function *as* a tactic to be used in a performer's everyday life, but, more importantly, how a performer's everyday life *is* a tactic against the strategies employed by dominant systems of power. This analysis has implications for understanding the strengths and limitations of Burke's perspective by incongruity as it is used to advance environmentally friendly actions and Certeau-inspired conceptions of everyday performance.

To the extent that Suelo's everyday performances provide a point of comparison for observers who live their lives within the confines and discourses of capitalistic and environmentally damaging systems of power, audiences of Suelo's self-performance are forced to see the world in a new and alternative fashion. In this sense, audiences are exposed to an embodied perspective by incongruity where they are invited to alter their notions of "how things were, how they are, and how they may be" (Burke, *Permanence,* 14). But what are we to make of this invitation in light of the mixed audience response? How do we make sense of the visceral and vilifying reactions when placed next to the reactions of worship and praise? On the one hand, it is possible to argue that Suelo's performance is partially successful in the way that the incongruity jars audience members out of their comfort zones. Suelo has successfully used perspective by incongruity as an "opening wedge" for a number of observers to rethink their pious positions in relation to economics and the environment (Whedbee 48). However, an equally strong reading is one that argues Suelo has taken the incongruity too far. The idea that Suelo's incongruity gives that appearance of not having enough in common with his audiences is not lost on Suelo:

> But I do think there's a certain kind of person who is willing to go to eat at something like Free Meal or Food Not Bombs. It's a person willing to forget class and ideology and sit humble on the grass with everybody else and just be sincerely human. I'm realizing that that's what's the only real common [thing] among us all: simple human-ness. When we try to find people with things "in common" with us, trying to find people who "think" like us, that's not the common I'm talking about here. Our common-ness isn't in what we think. Our common-ness is when we *give up thinking.* It's not about *belief,* it's about *Being,* which is the *True Faith.* (Suelo, "Moneyless World")

With such a strong reaction against the norms of everyday life—as it is experienced by the majority of observers who still use money, live in houses, and concern themselves with what they have "in common" with others—Suelo has alienated many of his onlookers. Even Suelo's understanding of what "common" means is different from how members of his audiences may understand it. In other words, Suelo's performance is so incongruous it has created a problem for the identification process Burke so highly prized in persuasive appeals (*Rhetoric* 19-28). Suelo's performance is, in essence, divisive. It is in this division where we encounter the paradoxical strength and limitation of using perspective by incongruity in environmental performances.

As activists of all stripes begin and continue to use perspective by incongruity as a powerful tool to advance their agendas, they should do so with caution. Audience members should ideally think, "If he can do it, so can I," not "He can do it because he's not like me." In addition, scholars who further investigate the use of perspective by incongruity as it is used with environmental performance critiques, such as in the recent film *No Impact Man*, should make it a priority to investigate cases where incongruity does not lead to audience alienation. At what point does the identification process breakdown? How far can activists push the envelope? These are questions that have yet to be sufficiently addressed. Although Suelo's performance does not allow us to answer these questions here, and, in fact, gives us more questions than answers, it does provide us with an important point of comparison for future studies.

In addition to allowing observations about the strengths and limitations of perspective by incongruity as it is used in environmental performance critiques, this case study also allows us to address Certeau's tactic/strategy dichotomy. While Anna Schober has criticized Certeau's work by noting strategies and tactics, "never appear in a 'pure' way," this chapter articulates another concern with the dichotomy (qtd. in Bell and Jones 230). While it is easy to conceptualize the powers Suelo is fighting against as the same systems of power that Certeau would say employ strategies to maintain their positions of privilege, it is not so clear that Suelo's acts of resistance in his everyday life are reduced to being categorized as tactics. Unlike the example of "the wig," Suelo's life is openly observable. Of course, this is not to say that all tactics must be hidden from the surveillance of those in power, nor should scholars oversimplify Certeau. It is to say that the dichotomy of strategy and tactic must be amended and expanded upon. Suelo's embodied performance and environmental critique clearly illustrate additional possibilities for understanding resistance in/and everyday life. One does not resist *during* one's everyday life; one's everyday life *is* the act of resistance.

In their now canonical article on performance studies as a paradigm of intellectual scholarship, Ronald J. Pelias and James VanOosting have observed that the case has been made "for viewing performance as fundamental to everyday life" (223). Indeed, Bell and Jones have gone so far as to call the "stage of everyday life" one of three major strands in performance studies perspectives. Turning to Suelo's self-performance has allowed us to further extend the stage by complicating the dichotomy found in Certeau. As we better understand how postmodern theories have "shifted the emphasis from 'grand narratives' of oppressive power to the *local, the subaltern, and everyday practices as resistance* in micropolitics of contemporary life," we are reminded of the importance of what it is we do to "make do" on our stages (Bell and Jones 200). Every act is reactive, every stage is a restaging of everyday power relations.

On October 27, 2010, Suelo participated in an online meeting with other "lifestyle gift economists" (Suelo, "Moneyless World"). Using public libraries and free Internet connections, the "economists" could chat and network with other like-minded individuals doing the best they could to change the world. Garcia notes:

> Though Suelo's story is a particularly riveting one, less radical communities of "freegans" are cropping up in places like San Francisco and New York. These groups have risen out of a desire to boycott what is seen as an unethical corporate system and to minimize the waste of resources. To varying degrees, freegans salvage edible food from dumpsters, squat in abandoned buildings, and encourage a reconsideration of the benefits of leisure and play as opposed to excessive work.

That there are others like Suelo living their lives in ways that differ with the "mainstream" and "normal" only highlights the importance of studying the connections between environmental performance and environmental critique. Even if one does not become a dumpster diver or a building squatter, the lesson to be learned is a valuable one: we should all harness the power of self-performance—what many may see as the only real form of agency we have left—to act favorably on nature's behalf. Let us hope that freely giving and freely receiving is one day part of the everyday for everyone.

Works Cited

Bell, Elizabeth, and Stacy Holman Jones. "Performing Resistance." *Theories of Performance: Selves, Scenes, Screens.* By Elizabeth Bell. Thousand Oaks, CA: Sage, 2008. 199-231. Print.

Besel, Richard, and Reneé Besel. "Polysemous Myth: Incongruity in *Planet of the Apes.*" *Millennial Mythmaking: Essays on the Power of Science Fiction and Fantasy Literature, Films and Games.* Eds. John Perlich and David Whitt. Jefferson, NC: McFarland, 2010. 51-66. Print.

Blevins, Jason. "Moab Man Embraces Simple Life in Cave." <DenverPost.com>. 22 November, 2009. Web. 22 November, 2010.

Bolton, John H. "Writing in a Polluted Semiosphere: Everyday Life in Lotman, Foucault, and Certeau." *Lotman and Cultural Studies: Encounters and Extensions.* Ed. Andreas Schönle. Madison, WI: U of Wisconsin P, 2006. 320-344. Print.

Burke, Kenneth. *Permanence and Change.* Berkeley: U of California P, 1984. Print.

————. *A Rhetoric of Motives.* Berkeley: U of California P, 1969. Print.

Certeau, Michel de. *The Practice of Everyday Life.* Berkeley, CA: U of California P, 1984. Print.

Clark, Nigel. "Feral Ecologies: Performing Life on the Colonial Periphery." *Nature Performed: Environment, Culture, and Performance.* Eds. Bronislaw Szerszynski, Wallace Heim, and Claire Waterton. Oxford: Blackwell, 2003. 163-82. Print.

Cooks, Leda. "You Are What You (Don't) Eat? Food, Identity, and Resistance." *Text and Performance Quarterly* 29.1 (2009): 94-110. Print.

Eckert, Andreas, and Adam Jones. "Historical Writing about Everyday Life." *Journal of African Cultural Studies* 15.1 (2002): 5-16. Print.

Foucault, Michel. (1979). *Discipline and Punish: The Birth of the Prison.* Trans. Alan Sheridan. New York: Vintage, 1979. Print.

Garcia, Gabriela. "Man Had Lived 9 Years Without Money—Social Rebel or Simply a Mooch?" <Matadornetwork.com>. 18 September, 2009. Web. 18 August, 2011.

HopKins, Mary Frances. "The Performance Turn—and Toss." *Quarterly Journal of Speech* 81 (1995): 228-36. Print.

Horton, Dave. "Green Distinctions: The Performance of Identity among Environmental Activists." *Nature Performed: Environment, Culture, and Performance.* Eds. Bronislaw Szerszynski, Wallace Heim, and Claire Waterton. Oxford: Blackwell, 2003. 63-77. Print.

Ketchum, Christopher. "Life On Zero Dollars." *Details* August 2009: 66. Print.

Lefebvre, Henri. *Everyday Life in the Modern World.* Trans. Sacha Rabinovitch. New York: Continuum, 2002. Print.

————. "The Everyday and Everydayness." *Yale French Studies* 73 (1987):7-11. Print.

Mills, Tony-Allen. "Struggling US Envies its Cashless Caveman." *The Sunday Times* 30 August, 2009: 35. Print.

Osborne, Hilary. "Daniel Suelo: Free Spirit or Free Loader?" *The Guardian.* 23 July, 2009. Web. 26 October, 2010.

Pelias, Ronald J., and James VanOosting. "A Paradigm for Performance Studies." *Quarterly Journal of Speech* 73 (1987): 219-31. Print.

Rockler, Namoi R. "Overcoming 'It's Just Entertainment': Perspective by Incongruity as Strategy for Media Literacy." *Journal of Popular Film and Television* 30 (2002): 16-22. Print.

Suelo, Daniel. "Living Without Money." n.d. Web.11 November, 2010.

————. "Moneyless World—Free World—Priceless World." n.d. Web. 11 November, 2010.

Wander, Philip. Introduction to the Transaction Edition. *Everyday Life in the Modern World.* By Henri Lefebvre. Trans. Sacha Rabinovitch. New York: Continuum, 2002. vii-xxiii. Print.

Whedbee, Karen. "Perspective by Incongruity in Norman Thomas's 'Some wrong Roads to Peace.'" *Western Journal of Communication* 65 (2001): 45-64. Print.

White, Lynn, Jr. "The Historical Roots of Our Ecologic Crisis." *Science* 155 (1967): 1203-7. Print.

Part II

PLACES AND SPACES

Chapter Six

Reinhabiting the Land:
From Vacant Lot to Garden Plot

Barbara Willard

Introduction: Gardening as Performance

It's July, 2010, and I'm exploring the streets of the Fuller Park neighborhood on the south side of Chicago, looking for signs of "nature"[1] in a dense urban environment that is dominated by concrete, industry, and freeways. I drive by trash-strewn vacant lots, abandoned homes with plywood covered windows, dilapidated structures, and failed businesses. But upon closer inspection, here and there I see a few modest, well cared for homes. I see children playing a game of pickup basketball. I see a barbecue on the sidewalk, a local church inviting the community for burgers and prayer. And periodically, next to the vacant lots, abandoned homes, and dilapidated structures, I find a community garden where neighbors are making earnest efforts to convert the spoiled and polluted spaces of the inner city into spaces of hope and community transformation. These gardens represent the best of the intersection of nature and culture.

Community gardens are public and physical expressions of the community's relationship with the land. Because of their visibility, these spaces communicate the gardeners' values, tastes, and needs to all those who observe the garden. In this fashion, the practice of gardening is a "kind of performance. Gardeners use gardens, consciously or unconsciously, to shape and maintain a self-image, as well as a public image" (Dunford 1). I see the act of gardening, in this respect, as a performance of reinhabitation, as a way of reclaiming land cast aside as useless and separate from the productive life of the city. Reinhabitation of land occurs when people collectively organize to reclaim their neighborhoods "as watershed, as community, as the sum total of the relations which sustain us–where human culture is formed" (Andruss, et al. 3). These gardening practices, whether those gardens are for the creation of food or beauty, function as an embodied and performative rhetoric that signals a reconnection with and transformation of a landscape from one marked as a spoiled and polluted space to one that is welcoming to the community and its visitors.

In this chapter I explore the performative process of reinhabiting blighted urban spaces through the creation of gardens. I examine this reinhabitation based upon data gathered from four focus groups conducted over the summer and fall of 2010 with residents of neighborhoods from the south side of Chicago. Each focus group was conducted at a different site. Three of those sites were garden sites: Eden Place Nature Center (with four participants–two women and two men), the Artists' Garden (with seven participants–three women and four men), and Gary Comer Youth Center (with six participants–four women and two men). The fourth focus group was held at a coffee shop in a south side neighborhood and was made up of six female gardeners from various sites around the community. The following questions were asked of all focus group participants:

1. What motivated you to become involved in gardening at the community garden (e.g., a friend, a community center)?
2. For what purpose(s) do you garden there (e.g., food, relaxation, meeting with friends)?
3. What does the garden represent to you (e.g., community space, source of food, peace, tranquility, hard work)?
4. What, in your observations, is the meaning of the garden to the surrounding community?
5. If it weren't for this garden, what would be missing from this community (e.g., place to gather, source of fresh fruits and vegetables)?

The analysis of the focus group transcripts and the physical space of the garden draws upon a combination of ethnographic, participant-observation and rhetorical/critical approaches. I farmed at the Eden Place Urban Farm from August, 2012, through November, 2012, with twenty-seven of my students in my Urban Agriculture class taught at DePaul University. Our primary task was to work with Eden Place staff and other community members to start a four-season farming program in their hoop house. My embodied practice of urban farming also allowed me to experience the performative nature of community-building that often accompanies this practice. During this time, I took field notes regarding my observations in terms of the meaning of the landscape to the surrounding community and the way in which community members have been impacted by the creation of the urban farm.

The chapter combines my own analysis based on these observations along with the analysis of the focus group transcripts. I first offer a theoretical grounding for the analysis. I follow this with a description of two of the gardens that are representative of many of the urban agriculture sites in

Chicago. I then go on to identify the various themes that arose from the focus groups. Finally, I conclude the essay by describing how the performance of reinhabitation is a tactic and means of resistance.

Performing Reinhabitation

The neighborhoods where the community gardeners who participated in the focus groups live can be considered what Camilo José Vergara has defined as a "green ghetto." These urban sites are characterized by depopulation, vacant land overgrown by nature, and empty lots covered with debris, trash, and toxic waste. They are viewed as an urban wasteland "subtracted from the life of the city. Contradicting a long-held vision of our country as a place of endless progress, ruins, once unforeseen, are now ignored" (Vergera 716). But in the case of the community gardens that I visited, the neighbors regard these green ghettos as opportunities for reinhabitation. While many individuals can and do see these vacant lots as community deficits, some neighbors see them as assets because of the possibilities of their transformation. Because of their asset-oriented vision, some residents have been reclaiming the abandoned homes and vacant lots that constitute their neighborhood and replacing them with vegetable and flower gardens. The neighbors engaging in this reclamation often have little power to change the physical conditions (let alone the socioeconomic conditions) of their neighborhood; but, the transformation of vacant lots allows them to enact civic agency and actively participate in rewriting the future of their community. Thus, reinhabitation serves many purposes and functions, addressing important practical and immediate concerns even as it responds to wider civic, social, cultural, and even political matters.

In the past decade cities across the United States have witnessed a growth in these unconventional sites of nature—community gardens where nature and culture blend together in a harmonious space testifying to the strong bond between humans and the land. In this way we inscribe cultural meaning into the landscape. But these gardens are more than just an opportunity for gardening. These sites function as transformative spaces that offer a visual and embodied rhetorical experience for those working in, living by, and visiting them. They act as spaces of possibility, where the natural world can coexist with culture, in an environment that is heavily populated, blighted, and most definitely urban. The visual contrast that these idealistic community gardens provide to the surrounding urban setting illustrates the ways in which alternative spaces and practices interrogate the urban excess and human hubris around them. These landscapes, that many would call "nature," have thus taken on cultural meaning and act as communicative artifacts. As texts these landscapes function to shape a particular understanding of the natural world and its relationship to human culture. These gardens, along with human interpretation, have the capacity to influence human thought about "nature" and its relationship to culture—and in the process inspire action.

Clearly then, these gardens are more than just an opportunity to exercise one's green thumb and consume healthy, local produce. Because these residents often live in highly polluted inner cities, they often have a sense of disconnection from their surrounding landscape and the natural environment. This "'non-functional' relationship with nature that results from living in an impoverished, polluted environment may produce a disabling alienation that breeds hopelessness in local communities" (Di Chiro 312). Often, the only knowledge these city residents have of their surrounding landscape is of the "destruction of nature and natural systems in their local communities" (314). But it is this "[e]xperiential knowledge of environmental degradation and toxic poisoning" that ultimately mobilizes their community activism (314). The cathartic act of removing toxic debris, putting in raised beds filled with healthy compost and soil, planting seeds, watching them grow, and consuming the vegetables, functions as a material and embodied rhetoric of spatial transformation. As one urban farmer, Lorraine Johnson, states, "[c]ommunity gardens are, essentially, participatory landscapes, places where people shape the shared resource of public land" (135). Sociologist Thomas Lyson maintains that the act of making improvements to the land and engaging in "soil citizenship" through small-scale agricultural acts such as community gardening fosters a stake and a role in a commonly held public good, the land, and builds the problem-solving capacity of citizens within their local spaces (105).

Hope in a Garden—Eden Place Nature Center

So that's what I went off to find in July 2010: hope in a garden. I traveled from my home on the north side of Chicago to neighborhoods in the south side of Chicago to discover how gardeners have reshaped their communities through transformation of the land. I went off to discover the possibilities that the beautification of vacant lots and polluted public spaces can offer to the surrounding neighborhood. I found it at Eden Place Nature Center in the Chicago community of Fuller Park. Fuller Park is just south of Comiskey Park (now known as U.S. Cellular Field) with a predominantly African-American population (95 percent) with 40 percent living below the poverty line. While this is not the sort of neighborhood where you would expect to find a nature center, through the vision of Michael Howard, a longtime resident and community activist, a nature center is exactly what you will find among the boarded-up homes, cracked sidewalks, and shuttered factories.

Eden Place sits on a three-and-a-half-acre site sandwiched between an alley and a raised railroad track heavily traveled by trains hauling freight to the inner city. It was a former illegal dumping ground that was used by a variety of businesses and Chicago residents, producing mountains of industrial and household waste (Smith). In 1997 Howard had a vision about how to improve the conditions of his community by transforming the dump into an urban oasis. With the help of his wife and five children, he organized the neighbors, requested whatever resources he could get from the city and, over a three-year period, moved 200 tons of debris from the site, covered the tainted lot with compost and fresh topsoil, and began to plant a garden (About Us). Today it is a breathtaking scene of beauty designed to replicate the Midwestern prairie and woodland ecosystems that once were abundant throughout the region. The site tells a "story of environmental redemption" where residents can "feed farm animals, grow vegetables, and nurture a habitat for monarch butterflies" (Smith).

Eden Place is a scene that one would expect to see about 100 miles west of Chicago. There is a small prairie with goldenrod, purple coneflower, butterfly weed, and black-eyed Susan sprinkled throughout the native grasses where monarch butterflies spend their summers as they migrate between Canada and Mexico. There is a wooded area that looks much like the Native American communities that used to populate this region before European inhabitation. It boasts a small pond and a wigwam, made out of tree branches, where children gather inside to hear tales of how Native Americans used to live off the land. The crow of roosters can be heard throughout the grounds, an aural signifier of the chickens that live in the small red barn, providing fresh eggs for the community residents. There is a wetland area with a pond where a flock of good-natured white Pekin ducks make their home year-round, gliding over the waterways and through the clumps of cattails, delighting young and old alike as they quack and waddle their way around Eden Place.

Food Desert to Food Oasis

More recently, staff and volunteers installed vegetable gardens to provide fresh produce to the surrounding community. Fuller Park is considered a food desert, a neighborhood where large grocery chains are faraway or nonexistent. Food deserts are

> large geographic areas with no or distant grocery stores–[where residents] face nutritional challenges evident in diet-related community health outcomes. Those outcomes worsen when the food desert has high concentrations of nearby fast food alternatives. We call this the Food Balance Effect. (Mary Gallagher Research & Consulting Group 6)

Residents, in other words, cannot easily access fresh meat and produce; however, they have plenty of convenience stores and fast food restaurants that sell inexpensive, low-nutrition, highly processed, and high-calorie packaged food. There are a number of areas in the south side of Chicago that have been classified as *food deserts* (Mary Gallagher Research & Consulting Group 8).

In the face of these conditions, which exacerbate the problem of obesity and inadequate nutrition among those living in urban poverty, gardens like those found in Eden Place offer a fresh supply of high-quality nutritional food at a low cost. With the expansion of their small vegetable gardens into larger greenhouses, 2009 marked the inauguration of the Eden Place Farmers Market–held every Saturday from June through September. It has been a struggle, during its first two years, but the staff at Eden Place Nature Center is still trying to expand the urban agriculture program. It turns out that it is not easy to change the diet of a community that has grown up on fast food and packaged foods for most of their lives. Michael Howard states that,

> For years the Fuller Park residents have been surrounded by fast food restaurants and gas stations that sell junk food. This is what they are used to. That is the only diet they know. Many of them are not aware of how to cook the fresh vegetables that we grow so we offer cooking classes from Chicago chefs so they can see how easy and delicious it can be to consume fresh produce.

A hoop house has been erected on an empty lot adjacent to Eden Place so that they can now grow vegetables year-round. Needless to say, the four-season hoop house is a highly unusual yet welcome use of space here on the south side of Chicago. By growing their own food in community gardens and, in some cases, selling it to their neighbors through small farmers' markets, they are overcoming the nutritional and economic challenges created by food desert conditions. These types of small-scale local food systems, so common to urban agriculture, operate as a type of political, economic, and social resistance to large-scale industrial farming practices.[2] They function to build small local markets where farmers sell directly to consumers. Often, these small-scale farms and local farmers' markets can redefine "profitability and success in terms of care, responsibility to the public and connection to the farm" (Trauger, et al. 53). In this fashion, the consumers can get to know their farmers, the source of their food, and the conditions of production. The gardens/farms help to build community capacity and empower local economies.

These gardens not only offer a fresh supply of high-quality nutritional food but also can result in a source of income and a way of reconnecting with a landscape that had previously been a source of neighborhood scorn. The reclamation of this spoiled space allows gardeners to communicate to themselves and others that they can rescript their physical surroundings and "make a place" that is vibrant, safe, beautiful, and welcoming to all who live in and visit the neighborhood. Gwen Beatty, a community gardener at Eden Place Nature Center, states that as she has watched Eden Place change "so has the neighborhood. We never had a community space like Eden Place where neighbors, especially teens, could feel they have a space safe to enjoy nature. There is a lot of gang activity around here and this is an alternative for the kids so they don't have to hang out with the gang members." Community activist and master gardener Greg Bratton (a.k.a. Mr. Green Jeans) states, "The gardens help to establish pride in residents of all ages, and 'greens up' the neighborhood at the same time. If given a choice of an empty lot versus a food producing community garden plot, I think it's a safe bet that folks would opt for that lot to be a help to the community, rather than an eyesore." In this sense the act of gardening has both a material and a rhetorical function. Through their performance of making place, the gardens become landscapes of reinhabitation, human-made landscapes created and interpreted via processes of cultural (re)signification. Indeed, the gardens challenge the existing arrangement of the urban blight–redefining material and social community. The meaning of the garden is thus established through its relationship of difference/contrast to other spaces that surround it (the abandoned buildings, the liquor store on the corner, the weedy lot where gang members gather).

The transformation of vacant lots into community gardens that produce food allows the neighbors to enact what Lyson calls "civic agriculture" (1). This form of food production stands in contrast to our conventional industrial agricultural system where citizens, especially the poor and disenfranchised, have little choice in their food selection. Lyson states that "Through active engagement in the food system, civic agriculture has the potential to transform individuals from passive consumers into active food citizens . . . someone who has not only a stake but also a voice in how and where his or her food is produced, processed and sold" (63-64). Civic agriculture is a challenge, even for communities with land, knowledge of gardening, and economic resources. But for these neighborhoods with contaminated soil, little knowledge of gardening practices (especially in cold winter climates), and virtually no economic resources, it is a miraculous undertaking. However, the embodied and material benefits of civic agriculture are numerous and well worth overcoming the challenges, especially for urban residents in impoverished neighborhoods. These benefits include "bodily health, safe spaces and empowerment . . . In many cases, the farm itself became an integral part of the product or service to be consumed, and as such, the farm became a public space for civic work" (Trauger et al. 53). Urban farms add value to the community beyond aesthetic improvement. They function as community-building sites that encourage civic participation in the creation of safe, healthy, and connected communities.

Food Safety

Many of the gardeners I spoke with stated that the gardens offered a place to get fresh, local, affordable organic produce. This type of produce, free of pesticides and other chemicals, is very important to them, especially the Mexican and Asian immigrant communities that are not used to industrial agricultural food systems. Many of the gardeners at the Artists' Garden, described below, are immigrants and indicated they have a distrust of our agricultural system due to its reliance on fertilizers and pesticides. However, because of the high cost, they cannot afford organic produce sold in grocery stores. In their respective homelands they often grew their own food, which ensured that "it was all natural, grown with no chemicals." A number of focus group participants stated they are suspicious of produce purchased at the grocery store because, as one woman stated, "You just don't know what the people put in it when you buy it in the store"; but when you grow it yourself, you know "there's nothing in there and it's very fresh." One Eden Place participant complained that the "produce at the excuse we have for a grocery store is disgusting. I wouldn't make my dog eat it. It is often rotten or if it looks okay, it has no taste. And heaven knows what they put in it for that tomato to last for a month or two sitting on the store shelf." Participation in civic agriculture, then, allows residents to operate outside the industrial agricultural food system, a system that forces them to consume food tainted with the residue of fertilizers and pesticides, and meat from livestock fed with antibiotics. In addition to the healthy, organic quality of the produce, one focus group participant from Eden Place commented on the importance of knowing who grows the food, and how much care they put into their practice. She stated the importance of consuming food from community gardens comes in ". . . the quality of not just the produce, but the love that comes from the vegetables. Because I think that you can grow anything for the most part, but all the love that goes into growing; it just tastes so good!"

Building Community Capacity

Community sites such as Eden Place offer more to the surrounding neighborhood than just urban agriculture. They also have a strong capacity to build community, creating a "more beautiful, peaceful and safe place to live" (Dunford 4). Eden Place hosts hundreds of visitors each year: school groups bringing inner-city children who rarely experience nature, community groups interested in learning about the possibilities that open space can provide for urban regions, and volunteers who hope to get their hands dirty by tending to the perennial garden, feeding the chickens, or helping weed in the prairie (Smith). Anyone who visits will no doubt hear a talk on the importance of environmental stewardship and the human need to connect with nature and community. Eden Place, then, is a site that brings together nature, culture, and human community in the most unlikely of places.

A number of the gardeners and young students who participate in a youth development program at Eden Place called *Leaders In Training*[3] stated that it is a site of community and hope. It even has a monument on its site dedicated to hope called, appropriately, The Hope Mound. One Leader in Training, John, stated that "The Hope Mound was the first thing planted here" after transforming the three-and-a-half-acre lot from an illegal dump. It is "the first area where we put fresh dirt down and we planted. So every year we maintain the actual mound, but it will stay there no matter how far Eden Place goes. It is a reminder of where we came from." Troy Howard, Michael Howard's son, states,

> I believe that every community usually has a central area where everybody comes; usually it's like a gym or a hall that everybody can claim as the community. And this is Fuller Park's central area. I think this is the meeting ground for everyone in the community where everyone can come and sort of relax and talk. And just have a peaceful place to come. It's a great place to have in the city. So it's pretty much like our oasis. It's often called the "Oasis in the City."

This oasis is more than a chance to commune with nature. It is an oasis from the crime and blight continuously faced by its residents.

Vacant lots often attract crime and are the site of illegal dumping. Consequently, the illegitimate power structure of gangs and other criminal activity is challenged when vacant lots are transformed into community gardens. Recognizing the transformative power of creating community gardens, the city of Chicago has instituted an "Open Space Plan" that includes a means for vacant lot acquisition. The city plan states, "Vacant lots become magnets for illegal dumpers and other destructive behavior . . . Transforming a vacant lot into a park or garden allows the neighborhood to build a sense of pride and community spirit and sends a clear signal to others that the residents care about their neighborhood and will not tolerate destructive or criminal behavior" (7). Glenda Daniels of Openlands, another nonprofit organization that helps neighbors acquire vacant lots for community gardening, states that "[p]eople are eyes and ears on the street. If people are out there taking care of their garden, the gangs and drug dealers are going to go somewhere else" (Christoph). Gangs can be resistant to the creation of community gardens. In 1997, when Michael Howard was cleaning up the vacant lot in Fuller Park, he found a bomb with a lighted fuse in his mailbox, which fortunately did not go off. This was followed by someone throwing a Molotov cocktail through his window that caused a small fire, which Howard put out with an extinguisher.

He assumed the perpetrators were gang members fighting back due to their anger at "his efforts to clean up land they used to stash drugs and burn cars to collect the insurance money" (Smith). The transformation of vacant lots into community gardens allows for residents to deny the ways in which gangs define the use of open space in their neighborhoods. Gang members often use vacant lots as sites for the drug trade that provides income for their operation. By taking back these vacant lots from gang members, the neighbors resist the tyranny of their power.

Community gardener and Toronto resident Lorraine Johnson maintains that,

> Community gardens may be centered on the activity of growing food, but many of the most powerful and lasting effects of these gardens have less to do with vegetable production and much more to do with social interaction and growth. I'm convinced that community gardens, while functioning in the public realm, are also very intimate spaces. Where else, in public, do we carve out such declaratively personal territories of individual expression and creativity? (135)

Indeed, because urban agriculture sites are often created by the residents themselves, they see it as an extension of themselves and their community. It represents their material presence in the neighborhood and their enactment of agency.

A number of gardeners in the focus groups talked about how the landscapes became, for them, sites not just to grow produce and flowers but also to "grow community." That is certainly the case at The Gary Comer Youth Center, located on Chicago's south side. It is in the Greater Grand Crossing neighborhood with 98 percent African American residents, 20 percent of whom live below the poverty line. The Greater Grand Crossing neighborhood is also in a food desert (Mary Gallagher Research & Consulting 8). Gary Comer is an organization that provides "positive extracurricular alternatives in a welcoming and safe environment" (About GCYC). Their mission is to give inner-city youth from low-income neighborhoods on the south side of Chicago a chance at success by preparing them to graduate from high school, go on to college and/or pursue a career. One of Gary Comer's youth initiatives is the Green Teens, a program that prepares students for careers in the green-collar industry and urban agriculture. It has a rooftop garden and a large community garden. The 8,600-square-foot rooftop garden sits atop the three-story building where students and community members grow annuals, perennials, and vegetables that are used by the center's cafeteria in food preparation and sold to Chicago restaurants. Across the street from Gary Comer Youth Center is the one-and-a-half acre community garden that was erected on a former Brownfield[4] and has a raised-bed garden, a hoop house for four-season farming, and an orchard (Reinwald). Students and community members work together to learn the art of successful urban gardening, food preparation, and food sales. One gardener from Gary Comer stated that "the community really gets involved in developing and forming relationships with the kids and among themselves." Another Gary Comer Youth Center gardener teaches at-risk youth in his neighborhood how to grow produce in community gardens. He described the community-building importance of these sites as follows:

> I have children that come to the garden and sit and do their homework. So they find it as a place of peace and sanctuary. I have seniors that come just to gather, some can't pick up a shovel, but like I tell them, they don't have to be a gardener to be a member of the community garden. If you can conversate, you can pass water out or if you can flip a burger, there's [sic] a lot of hungry volunteers in the garden. And that makes you a member.

The way in which these gardeners describe the community-building capacity of the gardens resonates with Victor Turner's notion of *communitas* (45). Of the three types of communitas identified by Turner, it is normative communitas that most resembles the community-building that takes place through the act of community gardening. Turner describes normative communitas as an enduring social system, "a subculture or group which attempts to foster and maintain relationships of spontaneous communitas on a more or less permanent basis" (47). These relationships are not beholden to the structure of the institutionalized social system from which the community seeks autonomy. Normative communitas is characterized by "something of 'freedom,' 'liberation,' or 'love'" (47). This does not mean that normative communitas is a revolutionary or rebellious acting out against the power structure. Turner states, "*communitas* does not represent the erasure of structural norms from the consciousness of those participating in it; rather its own style, in a given community, might be said to depend upon the way in which it symbolizes the abrogation, negation, or inversion of the normative structure in which its participants are quotidianly involved" (45). The community symbolizes its "abrogation" and "negation" of structural norms by transforming the degraded sites typical of low-income, inner-city neighborhoods. The societal norm in response to these degraded sites is to either further pollute them or to ignore them altogether. The gardening communities come together of their own volition, challenging the institutional and criminal use of the landscape in an effort to develop relations outside these realms. The communitas created among the members is all the more strengthened by its autonomous creation outside of the existing social order. It is an organic community that grew out of the shared desire to improve the neighborhood by fostering relations among the people and their environment. Through normative communitas residents locate their collective sense of identity in place and thereby claim that place as their own.

Bridging Communities–The Artists' Garden

I also found clear evidence of the community-building possibilities created by the intersection of nature and culture farther down the expressway in the neighborhood of South Chicago. This neighborhood was once home to the mighty U.S. Steel South Works, the largest steelmaking operation in Chicago and, at one point, in the United States. After years of layoffs during the downfall of the steel industry, U.S. Steel finally shut its doors in 1992, leaving behind 576 abandoned acres, a host of unemployed workers, and an economically depressed community. Today, it remains one of the poorest areas of Chicago. A few blocks away from the old U.S. Steel site, among empty lots, boarded-up houses, and other common signs of urban poverty, one can find the Artists' Garden, a community garden that sits on four vacant lots. According to Sarah Ward, the Director of the South Chicago Art Center and founder of the garden, it "promotes friendship, cultural pride, and civic engagement" in the neighborhood. And, I would add, an impressive strawberry patch in June and fanciful sunflowers in August. This string of former vacant lots was transformed into a thriving produce garden that functions as a community space for surrounding residents. Ward felt that this garden was needed not only to provide fresh fruits and vegetables in this food desert, but also to offer an open space for neighborhood gathering in an area suffering from gang violence, racial strife, and severe poverty. The garden bridges two distinct ethnic housing areas, a predominantly African American Section 8 housing complex on one side and a row of modest homes with primarily Mexican immigrants on the other. Ward describes these four lots as "a place for community members to come together for the common purpose of growing and doing something positive. In a racially divided and gang infested area, [the garden] is a neutral area." The Artists' Garden as a space of neutrality allows for community residents to gather in a place where, from a material perspective, they have common goals—to produce food. However, the material space becomes a communal space through the performance of a community centered on urban agriculture. Here racial and ethnic differences can be temporarily, even permanently, overlooked in an effort to work toward their common interests.

Throughout the garden one can find a variety of fruits, vegetables, and herbs including tomatoes, cucumbers, raspberries, basil, dill, collard greens, kale, Swiss chard, radishes, and broccoli. The produce that isn't used by the gardeners is taken to the nearby Ada S. McKinley food pantry, a community organization that among its many services also provides food to those with disabilities and other limiting conditions. The garden is also used as a place for community education. Children who attend classes at the South Chicago Art Center come to the garden to be inspired and practice their watercolor painting and sculpture. It offers garden classes for children where they learn to farm the land. Farming is a skill that one wouldn't expect urban kids to acquire and yet, in a green economy that is increasingly turning to urban agriculture as a legitimate source of food, it could provide future jobs. The Art Center also offers cooking classes where kids can learn how to prepare nutritious meals from the garden's produce. The children take these recipes and garden produce home to their families, thus sharing in the garden's great bounty and illustrating how a local site can provide a healthy alternative to the packaged foods found in the convenience store down the street. Also, in recognition of the garden's aesthetic contribution to the neighborhood, it won Second Place in Chicago Mayor Richard Daley's 2009 Landscaping Award for community landscapes. But the garden offers far more than produce and natural beauty; according to Ward, it is the "interactions and relationships forged between neighbors" that attest to the truly transformative capacity of this site.

In addition to the food produced by the garden, I find artistic displays and structures, colorful signage, rocks decorated with beautiful tile mosaics, and a gazebo with seating for weary gardeners to gather after a day of harvest. During my visit to this site, I find a group of men resting in the gazebo. I get a personal tour from one of them, Miguel, a Mexican immigrant who lives just behind the garden in a house off the alley with his immediate and extended family. He takes pride in showing me the variety of produce grown here and the lush flower beds. As we walk the paths that lie between each of the twenty-five community garden plots I hear the crow of roosters in the distance. I ask him where the chickens are and he tells me they are in "Crazy Hat's" (a fellow gardener) backyard just across the alleyway from the Artists' Garden. He takes me through the back gate of Crazy Hat's house, where I find a beehive, an outdoor adobe oven, and a flock of chickens wandering the yard. For a moment, I feel as if I am transported to a bucolic scene, but no, I am indeed in the middle of the third-largest city in the United States witnessing elements of rural living. Miguel notices that there is a beehive that is out of place, too high in the tree where they will "become confused" and unable to thrive. He excuses himself to fetch a ladder so he can move the beehive lower to the ground. I am astonished at the seemingly rural practices that are taking place in the urban environment.

The Artists' Garden is a site that allows the citizens of the neighborhood, many of them immigrants from Mexico, to perform familiar farming practices and "follow tradition." Miguel stated that he was from a small town in Mexico where they "all lived off farming." "We farmed beans, peppers, corn . . .," he shared; "Whatever we didn't need, we'd sell it to another town." He said they had fond memories of their farming days: "It was fun watching my father doing it . . . . We had horses, donkeys, chicken, sheep, all those kind of good things . . . . This is kind of like memory lane." A number of the Artists' Garden gardeners also see this site as a place of escape from the stressors created by urban living. The relaxation and tranquility that the community space affords provides a safe haven for the neighbors. One gardener reflected upon the healing quality of the space, "I live close [to] here, so I come and look at the garden, look at the flowers, talk to the people, pass time in the garden, [it is a] beautiful time to heal and enjoy the plants . . . ." Another gardener reflected more specifically on the relaxation that he finds by being in the garden, "It's something to do that's relaxing and something nobody tells you to do. You do it for the fun, to enjoy what you're doing. It's not like work or nothing; it's just a way to relax, almost as good as fishing." Relaxation and communal gathering are important aspects of the gardens, turning them into social spaces as well as gardening sites. One focus group participant stated that the primary characteristic that drew her to the garden was the social element, stating that, "the gathering and being able to associate with friends and someone else that has the same passion for something you love" was what caused her to spend so much time at her community garden. The Artists' Garden, as it is performed and embodied by the gardeners, has a number of functions. It helps to foster community among diverse groups. It offers immigrants the opportunity to maintain their traditional foodways and agricultural practices. It allows for artistic expression and the opportunity to inscribe meaning into the landscape through creative outlets. And it provides an escape; like Eden Place, it is an oasis from the stress of living in an urban environment.

Garden Tours: Performing Reinhabitation

The community gardeners' performance of reinhabitation of place is not just limited to their own neighborhood. Many of these gardens offer regular tours for visitors from around the Chicago region.[5] Tour guides and gardeners proudly describe the history of the garden itself, its transformation, what is currently grown, the farming methods, and the plans for the future. They name their gardens to reflect the tale behind the transformation, with names like the "Hot Wheels Senior Growing Plot," created for senior citizens in motorized wheelchairs, and the "Heal Thyself Garden," an herbal garden created and cared for by at-risk youth. One of the women I spoke with who works in the "Victory Garden" stated that she wasn't sure why the garden was named the "Victory Garden" but she had her own meaning, because, as she said "[e]ver since I started working there, good things have happened for me. It is my own victory. I have had some hard times lately but that garden has brought me some victories. I don't know why."

Much like "toxic tours,"[6] these garden tours have a highly rhetorical function; but unlike toxic tours, they do not raise awareness about the toxic burden the neighbors bear but the transformation of the landscape the neighbors have enacted in their own communities. The tours illustrate how these sites act as spaces of opportunity set among a human environment that is heavily populated, blighted, and urban. Pezzullo identifies the possibility for material rhetoric to influence embodied practice because the "materiality of place promises the opportunity to shape perceptions, bodies, and lives" (9). The gardeners in these urban farms construct a site that is both a space of symbolic transformation as well as a material rhetoric through which stakeholders, city residents, community gardeners, and farm employees witness and engage in civic agriculture and embodied alternative agricultural practices. It demonstrates the potential of a community to influence their surrounding cultural and natural environment. This performance displays the capacity of individuals to gather together to enact change and to perform possibilities for what the community can become and is becoming.

Conclusion

In the *Production of Space*, Henri Lefebvre writes of the communicative function of "social space" as it creates symbolic associations through the metaphorical and cultural dimensions of the social. He states: "[i]tself the outcome of past actions, social space is what permits fresh actions to occur, while suggesting others and prohibiting yet others" (73). Here he implies that spaces—like these urban gardens—have the capacity to impact behavior. In addition to the symbolic elements of space, Lefebvre identifies the communicative capacity of the material aspects of space. When we move through space and confront structures such as buildings, roadways, paths, and gardens, we are placed in a relationship with that space that suggests our position in society and, I would add, in the natural environment.

The community gardeners obtain the land on which they farm and garden in a number of different ways. Chicago has approximately 70,000 vacant lots that can be acquired through the city or through the help of private organizations. The lots are either private or public property and by contacting the city or NeighborSpace (a nonprofit organization in Chicago) they are able to either use the publicly owned land or they can pay the property taxes on a privately owned lot that is in arrears and take possession. These transformed spaces thus become ways in which community members take public spaces and express civic agency, civic agriculture, creativity, and autonomous connection with the land. They are given land-use guidelines that they must follow in order to remain on and use the public land, such as allowing public access and following safety codes like not creating ponds or placing other bodies of water on the land. Otherwise, within the legal limits, they are able to do what they desire with the land. Consequently, this public space becomes a private expression of their relationship with the land, each other, the urban experience, and the socioeconomic conditions imposed on them. Michel de Certeau might argue that this is an example of how the disempowered give expression to power through the use of tactics in their everyday practice. He describes tactics as

> a calculated action, determined by the absence of a proper locus. No delimitation of an exteriority then provides it with the condition necessary for autonomy. The space of a tactic is the space of the other. Thus it must play on and with a terrain imposed on it and organized by the law of a foreign power . . . . (36-7)

The law of the foreign power in this case is the city of Chicago, but it is through the public expression of their land use that residents gain power over their local space. They perform their civic agency and civic agriculture in this public space so that they can express to themselves and others that this land is their own and the actions they perform on it "gain validity in relation to the pertinence they lend to time—to the circumstances which the precise instant of an intervention transforms into a favorable situation . . ." (Certeau 38).

Gardens like Eden Place Nature Center and the Artists' Garden operate outside the typical conditions of many urban landscapes and interrogate the existing community practices: crime, disregard for human and nonhuman life, pollution, disconnection from neighbors. They create a visual and spatial oasis that invites residents to think of other ways of being in their community. They challenge the existing spatial order in which they are situated, acting as counter-sites that suggest—in and through material and embodied choices—an alternative way of experiencing the cultural use of space where residents can enact and embody their relationship to "nature." They challenge the agricultural-industrial complex that surrounds the Chicago region. They challenge an American diet that contributes to high rates of obesity and Type 2 diabetes. They challenge the idea of urban space as necessarily void of greenery and natural beauty. They challenge the lack of community participation in food production.

Gardening for residents becomes, at least potentially, a dialogue between nature and humans ("we can work together and grow food, beauty, hope . . ."), between community members ("we can create a space of sanctuary and peace, we can take back our community . . ."), and between urban residents and visitors to the neighborhood ("we have taken back our neighborhood and transformed it from a vacant lot to a site of beauty"). These gardens ask people to peacefully and harmoniously coexist with other life-forms (and by implication, other people). The "author" of these gardens, a community of activists like Michael Howard and Sarah Ward and the many gardeners that work along with them, constructs a site that is both a symbolic space as well as a material rhetoric through which stakeholders, city residents, and visitors both witness and engage in embodied alternative urban practice–experiencing "nature" in the city. These author-gardeners are thus not only planting fruit and vegetable seeds but also the seeds of community and connection to all lifeforms. They are doing nothing less than planting hope.

Notes

1. "Nature" is a term that Raymond Williams called "perhaps the most complex word in the language" due to its multiple meanings (1980, 67). In an urban environment, the idea of nature is particularly complicated by the prevalence of human culture and a built environment that alters most elements of the natural world. In this chapter, I refer to nature as any flora or fauna that exists outside brick-and-mortar structures. In urban environments this is often referred to as "greenspace" or "openspace."

2. See, for example, Hinrichs 295, Feenstra 99, Allen, et al. 61, Lyson, 63, and Trauger, et al. 43.

3. The Leaders in Training program is a summer youth program sponsored by the U.S. Forest Service where inner-city at-risk youth have the opportunity to learn entrepreneurial skills in organic farming and through selling produce at the farmer's market. Additionally, they participate in nature conservation and community service at Eden Place and throughout the neighborhood.

4. The site had a gas station and a distribution center for chemicals and petroleum but was remediated by the Environmental Protection Agency.

5. I have attended two of these tours. The 10th Green Summit Bus Tour has been an annual event since 2007. The 10th Ward residents charter a bus and take visitors to various community gardens in their neighborhoods. The bus stops at each garden where the tourists get out and hear the garden's story and purpose. Typically, tourists are gardeners from around the Chicago region (many from the north side of Chicago and a different demographic group, i.e., white, middle-class) who wish to see the beautification efforts of residents of the south side residents of the 10th Ward.

6. Communication scholar Phaedra Pezzulo describes toxic tours as a rhetorical tactic employed by environmental justice activists seeking to raise awareness and share personal stories of environmental injustice and inequality with "tourists" who are willing to expose themselves to toxic sites and the residents of these sites who would normally be unseen and unheard (3).

Works Cited

"About GCYC." Gary Comer Youth Center. 2006. Web. 24 February 2012.

"About Us: History." Eden Place Nature Center. Web. 10 August 2010.

Allen, Patricia and Margaret Fitzsimmons, Michael Goodman, Keith Warner. "Shifting Plates in the Agrifood Landscape: The Tectonics of Alternative Agrifood Initiatives in California." *Journal of Rural Studies* 19.1 (2003): 61-71. Print.

Andruss, Van, Christopher Plant, Judith Plant, and Eleanor Wright, eds. *Home!: A Bioregional Reader*. Philadelphia: New Society Publishers, 1990. Print.

Certeau, Michel de. *The Practice of Everyday Life*. Trans. Steven F. Rendail. Berkeley: U of California P, 1984. Print.

Christoph, Ella. "The Garden Party: The Dirt on Chicago's Resurgent 'Urbs in Horto' Movement," *New City.* 7 July 2010. Web. 15 August 2011.

"CitySpace Plan: An Open Space Plan for Chicago." City of Chicago. 1998. Web. 25 August 2011.

Di Chiro, Giovanni. Nature as Community: The Convergence of Environment and Social Justice. In Cronon, W. (Ed.), *Uncommon Ground: Toward Reinventing Nature* (pp. 298–320). New York: W.W. Norton & Company, 1995. Print.

Dunford, Christine. "What Does a Garden Show? Vacant Lot Gardens in North Lawndale." *Perspectives on Civic Activism and City Life* 1.2 (2000): 1–12. Print.

Feenstra, Gail. "Creating Space for Sustainable Food Systems: Lessons from the Field." *Agriculture and Human Values* 19.1 (2002): 99-106. Print.

Hinrichs, C. Clare. "The Embeddedness of Local Food Systems: Notes on Two Types of Direct Agricultural Markets." *Journal of Rural Studies* 16.2 (2000): 295-303. Print.

———. "The Practice and Politics of Food Systems Localization." *Journal of Rural Studies* 19.1 (2003): 33-45. Print.

Johnson, Lorraine. *City Farmer: Adventures in Urban Food Growing*. Vancouver: Greystone, 2011. Print.

Lefebvre, Henri. *The Production of Space*. Malden, MA: Blackwell, 1984. Print.

Lyson, Thomas. *Civic Agriculture: Reconnecting Farm, Food, and Community*. Lebanon, NH: UP of New England, 2004. Print.

Mary Gallagher Research & Consulting Group. *Examining the Impact of Food Deserts on Public Health in Chicago*. Chicago, IL, 2006. Print.

Pezzullo, Phaedra. *Toxic Tourism: Rhetorics of Pollution, Travel and Environmental Justice*. Tuscaloosa, AL: The U of Alabama P, 2007. Print.

Reinwalk, Peter. "Comer Youth Center Project is a Garden in the Desert." *Chicago Tribune* 11 August 2010. Web. 10 February 2012.

Smith, Gerry. "Eden Place Nature Center Serves as Model for What Urban Communities Can Do With Vacant Land." *Chicago Tribune* 25 April 2011. Web. 15 October 2011.

Trauger, Amy, Carolyn Sachs, Mary Barbercheck, Kathy Brasier, and Nancy Ellen Kiernan. "'Our Market is Our Community': Women Farmers and Civic Agriculture in Pennsylvania, USA." *Agriculture and Human Values* 27.1 (2010): 43-55. Print.

Turner, Victor. *Process, Performance and Pilgrimage: A Study in Comparative Symbology.* New Delhi, India: Concept, 1979. Print.

Vergara, Camillo Jose. "The Ghetto Cityscape." *The New American Ghetto.* Ed. Vergara, Camillo Jose. New Brunswick, NJ: Rutgers UP, 1995. 714-9. Print.

Williams, Raymond. *Problems in Materialism and Culture: Selected Essays.* London: Verso, 1980. Print.

Chapter Seven

"Progress Fell Upon Us": Ecotourism, Culture, and Performance in the Peruvian Amazon

Jnan A. Blau

Our early history is lost in mist. It seems all we ever did was break rocks and beat each other with clubs. But one might well ask: Weren't we able to survive, when survival was all but impossible, because we learned to share our food and band together for defense? Would today's me-first, do-your-own-thing civilization have lasted more than a moment?

—Eduardo Galeano, Latin American historian from Uruguay (4)

Our world has never before cried out so need fully for understanding among us all. Never has a sense of the other seemed more crucial for our own humanity.

—Wallace Bacon, oral interpretation of literature scholar from the United States (97)

Considering Performance(s) and Ecotourism . . .

The Amazon Basin looms large in discussions of the environment. It is a physical place, a site possessing immeasurably rich biodiversity and serving a vital function as Earth's single largest carbon sink—as, almost literally, our planet's lungs. It is an experience, providing both its inhabitants and its visitors with a powerful setting for interaction with and appreciation for nature as phenomenal performative display—an experience that is rife with relationality and citationality: humans and animals and plants interconnected, interaffected, depending on each other, counting on each other, hailing each other. It is also a site of contestation, a locus for the complex sociopolitics of the human-nature-culture interaction, where the fate of human and nonhuman life on Earth is being worked out. Put differently, the Amazon is a place, a space, and a case: a place where much happens and is at stake; a space of and for the unfolding of interrelated phenomena; and a case study, a site for deriving scholarship and insight.

There is much to understand about Amazonia—and about our selves, our world(s), our interconnectedness. In what follows, I search for understanding(s). I weave, on the page, an (auto)ethnographic and performative tapestry. I use for this weaving threads from my own thoughts, feelings, and observations, together with strands of thinking and the keen, insightful voices of a range of scholars and scholarly disciplines. I draw primarily from my experiences during two visits—as a tourist, teacher, and scholar—to the Tambopata National Reserve in the Peruvian Amazon during the summers of 2010 and 2011.

What I posit here is a collection of vignettes and arguments and quotes.

And interruptions.

This work is tentative and contingent, purposefully furled, and necessarily incomplete, as I both describe and unpack the multiple levels of critical, theoretical, and performative insights that inhere in the jungle. At the heart of my work is the strong hunch that, in dealing with and talking about the Other outside our own subject position (be that Other nature or environment, or a human or nonhuman living Other), there is a fundamentally important shift from a discourse and self-performance of *relationship to* to a *relationship with*. In other words, the necessity for proceeding in terms of a more active and reflexive self-implicature is explored and laid bare. Our relationships, then, are cast into relief. We find ourselves, it seems to me, ineluctably entwined in a dynamic of co-performance: with living people, of course, but also, perhaps most importantly, with the environment itself, which I believe we must now understand qua co-participant.

At Posada Amazonas, where I stayed, an interesting model of eco-tourism and resource conservation is in evidence, one seeking to balance a series of more or less productive dialectical tensions. Here, conservation of both nature and the culture and rights of the native Ese'Eja people meet up with the demands of running a successful, for-profit lodge. On the surface, ecotourists enjoy the spectacular natural performances in/of the Amazon. Behind the scenes and below the surfaces, a host of cultural, social, political, and economic performativities are at work—and at stake. Places like the Amazon, indeed, "are not only destinations on an itinerary: they are also nodes in a network of attractions that form the recreational geography of a region and, increasingly, the globe. [Such destinations], by whatever name, are also an integral part of natural, historical, and cultural sites" (Kirshenblatt-Gimblett 132). Posada Amazonas's partnership with the Ese'Eja thus functions as a rich site, with important implications: for the sustainable future of the environment; for profit-motivated enterprise in the area (and beyond); for tourism; for sociocultural well-being; and for a geopolitics in/of global(ized) times and spaces.

. . . in the Peruvian Amazon

Lago Tres Chimbadas, also known as Oxbow Lake, is located inside the Infierno Ese'Eja preserve. It is an elbow-shaped body of water that, while once a part of the Tambopata River, is now a tucked-away natural sanctuary. It is a key destination—a must-see—for all visitors to Posada Amazonas. It is where Mother Nature readily offers up some of her most spectacular displays of plant and animal splendor.

* * *

Before we continue, I wish to cite two guiding dictums from Richard Schechner:

> [. . . .] the performance is the whole event, including audience and performers (technicians, too, anyone who is there). It is hard to define "performance" because the boundaries separating it on the one side from the theater and on the other side from everyday life are arbitrary. (85)

And, also:

> Performance is the widest possible circle of events condensing around the theater. The audience is the dominant element of any performance. Drama, script, theater, and performance need not all exist for any given event. But when they do, they enclose one another, overlap, interpenetrate, simultaneously and redundantly arousing and using every channel of communication. (91)

I have always been drawn to, and found useful, Schechner's conceptualization of the concentric circles of drama, script, theater, and performance. They tune us in(to) the many levels of performativity and iterativity that inhere, and are present, in any given moment of human communication. They blur the lines between performer and audience and environment. They focus us in(to) the micro-level minutiae even as they widen our perceptual and analytical lens by drawing our attention to ineluctable macro-level contextualities.

* * *

We wake up before dawn, and have a quick breakfast. After hiking through the jungle to get from the lodge to the riverside dock, my students and I find ourselves on two long river boats, twenty or so of us evenly distributed on both sides of the two boats' long benches, for balance purposes. Our guides are with us: Willian and Robin in my boat, Ivo and Paula in the other. We're all silent, partly because of how early it is, but mostly because of the nature of what we are doing at this very moment. We're going about thirty minutes farther up the Tambopata and, already, this is awe-inspiring.

The horizon is just beginning to inject light into the retreating night's sky. The air temperature is about perfect: a little humid, of course; neither hot nor cold. My body feels at home, perfectly content and at ease with(in) the environment. The boats slowly glide upriver, skimming its surface like floating arrows. On either side of us, the jungle is darkly silhouetted against the just-brightening sky. A company of parrots flies silently in the distance, probably headed to one of the salt and mineral licks that jut out along the river's banks. I take it in with fullest intent. This is special, a real privilege. My personal history imbues this experience with deep meaningfulness. Indeed, this is meaning-full. For me, and, in each of their own ways, for my students.

Our boats eventually pull up to our riverside destination. Our guides prop long planks of wood down from the front of the boat to the semifirm mud banks. A set of basic wood stairs with one rickety railing takes us up onto terra firma. We hike, now, for another twenty minutes, reinterning ourselves into the jungle. The guides point out key features along the way. A walking palm tree. A particularly splendid epiphyte. The distinct sounds of a distant pack of howler monkeys. The call of a nearby parakeet.

My senses are on alert. I am a willing and most earnest spectator.

Finally, we reach Lago Tres Chimabadas, a.k.a. Oxbow Lake. After a quick briefing from the guides, we are ushered onto two catamaran-like boats, each with three rows of rough benches. The guides take turns steering and propelling us with a giant oar-like contraption attached to the back of the boat.

We as a group had been chatting during the hike. But now, we fall silent again. If we are lucky, we are told, we will get to see some of the many beautiful, interesting, and sometimes rare species of fauna that have turned this lake into a nature preserve and tourist attraction.

* * *

My experience in, and understanding of, my time in the Amazon is absolutely wrapped up in my being a performance studies scholar.

The foundation of performance studies—as academic discipline, as theoretically informed praxis, with the distinction between the two hopelessly, wonderfully blurred—is the aesthetic component of communication. To elaborate, performance theory-practice is a heightened act, set apart and oriented toward with special attention (Bauman 41). Performance is also something that takes place with and in a social context, and is thus always already a social contract (Langellier 122). Performance occurs on/as a continuum of sociohistorical (f)acts, its own special thing, yet inextricably linked to wider contexts and concerns. Given this, as Elizabeth Bell points out, performance studies' work "quickly slides into ethical and moral issues," and maps "a geography of accountabilities and responsibilities" (369). I, like Bell, understand that performance's "hue and cry" is particularly strong at "times of change and crisis," that a performance studies sensibility is valuable inasmuch as it asks us—calls us—to account for our place in the world as actor-agents (369). My every moment—which is always already a moment-*in*, not a moment-*with*—is laden, is charged with significance, with effects, with affect, with relationality, with process(es).

One of the thematic threads of my work—both explicit and implied—is that the environment (and more specifically, nature) be considered qua performer. I cannot understand what I did, and what I experienced, in the jungle without casting nature into a definite role. Truly, I was not so much *in* nature as I was *with* it. Time spent in the jungle as an ecotourist is, really, a heightened time: time spent in a particular place, which I regard with special intensity, and which I feel and think about deeply. I am hyper-aware as an ecotourist. I am tuned in, open. I am explicitly interested in "nature" as a beautifully complex system of which I am only a small part, a walk-on actor. Or, put differently, I am paying close attention to the "environment" as an aggregate of physical, biochemical, ecological, and sociocultural systems. The Amazon *is* both a place and space. It is: soil and air; flora and fauna; nonhuman and human performance/performing.

* * *

For three nights and four days, we are guests at Posada Amazonas, within the Infierno community, inside the Tambopata Reserve, in southeastern Peru. It's a wonderful experience. A real treat. My students will cite this time—time spent in the Peruvian Amazon—as a definite highlight of their six weeks studying and traveling in Peru. The Posada (which translates as "lodge") was built in the mid-nineties, as part of a relatively novel enterprise. Rainforest Expeditions ("Rainforest," as the Ese'Eja say) is a for-profit ecotourism company based in Lima, Peru. They have partnered with the Ese'Eja, an indigenous Amazonian tribe, in a venture that is interesting and that is in need of praise and support as well as of close scrutiny for what it may or may not portend.

The model under which Rainforest and the Ese'Eja work is fairly unique. In a nutshell, it is a partnership between two cultures, between two groups of people that are geographically, culturally, and economically very different from each other. Proceeds from the enterprise are shared, with 40 percent of the profits going to Rainforest and 60 percent to the Ese'Eja.[1] Rainforest have provided the venture capital needed to build and maintain the enterprise, the tourism business know-how and connectivity, and the staff training. The Ese'Eja, on the other hand, have provided the land, the people, and the bulk of the labor force needed to build, maintain, and run the whole enterprise.

Rainforest operates three lodges within the Tambopata reserve: Posada Amazonas, Refugio Amazonas, and the Tambopata Research Center. The following is what Rainforest claims to provide, as found on their website:

> Each Amazon lodge provides access to a unique set of ecotourism experiences in the jungle of southeastern Peru. We offer a true ecotourism experience by working closely with the *Ese' eja Native Community* to generate sustainable local development while caring for the environment. Visitors to our lodges are completely surrounded by nature due to our location in the *Tambopata-Candamo National Reserve*. Rooms constructed from bamboo and adobe give visitors a unique experience in the jungle without sacrificing comfort and quality. All of these factors combined have earned us numerous awards including the *Ecotour-*

ism Excellence Award and certification by the *Rainforest Alliance.* ("Rainforest Expeditions Lodges")

It is indeed a wonderful place to spend time in, and with, the jungle. A series of thatched-roofed structures, interlinked by long walkways, the lodge is a mix of rustic and stylish. It's a wide-open feeling space. The rooms, to illustrate, have no windows, and only a sparsely slatted, waist-high wooden railing and grate separates my room space from the jungle space. The jungle is right there, ten feet away. The jungle, really, is the wall, its lush intensity rising out of the ground just past the cleared buffer around the lodge's perimeter.

The whole thing is clearly about jungle as spectacle.

You can lie on your bed, or sit in your hammock, and all the sights and sounds of the jungle are cued up. Birds and other creatures swing by at all times. All manner of critter communication and activity, of rustling leaves and jumped-upon branches, offer up a near-constant aural tapestry. Howler monkeys make noise in the distance, sounding strangely like a roaring jet engine. A pack of smaller brown capuchin monkeys saunters by.

The whole thing is clearly about jungle as spectacle.

Later that night, dinner in the big open hall is excitedly interrupted by the appearance, out behind the staff quarters, of a huge rainbow python. Someone had spotted it and sent the word. We scramble down the steps to find an older man from the kitchen staff holding it up on the end of a long, thick stick, for all of us to get a good look. Appreciative oohs and aahs mix in with the obligatory squeals of the reptile-adverse young women in our group.

As a snake lover, as someone who has determined that the snake is my "power aninal," I had silently asked the jungle—formulated the thought in my being, and put it out there to whatever forces I imagined to have a say in these things—that I might be able to see a good snake.

After most of the crowd has gone back to the lounge for after-dinner drinks and conversation, I linger a bit more. I ask to touch the snake, but the man handling it urges me not to. It's a bit riled up. "No le vaya a hacer algo, profesor!" We wouldn't want anything to happen to our esteemed professor visiting us from the United States, now, would we?!

The whole thing is clearly about jungle as spectacle.

* * *

"But what kind of participation, we might ask, is being modeled here?" (Fancy 64). Indeed. I, like David Fancy, am very interested in deepening my/an understanding of "the role of the encounter between the audience and the actor" (63). I could feel and adumbrate the implications, the theoretical possibilities, then and there, and am attempting to grasp them more fully now and here.

The overwhelming, nagging insight is that there is/was a problem of interaction—a crisis of inter-action—at work in the jungle. While I hesitate to posit this as an absolute, clear fact, I could not shake the feeling that my relationship with what and who I was encountering in the jungle was quite different—was of a different nature—than that of my students. Fancy's work with geoperformativity and immanence, drawing from the work of Deleuze and Guattari, provides an invaluable assist here. In his important essay, Fancy helps me understand that traditional conceptions of actor and audience, left unquestioned and unchallenged, work from/as an ontological understanding that is (appears to be) dangerously stable, at best, and harmfully enacted, at worst. A more desirable state of affairs, in theory and in practice, is one in which we resist "a movement that precedes representation;" in which we complicate "a becoming that precipitates or territorializes into certain machinic configurations of gesture, sound, light, colour, voice, and so forth" (Fancy 69). Again, while I want to be careful to not assume a facile and self-serving distinction between me and my students, my impression and concern was often that, for most of us there in the jungle, "the human is seen as the active force engaging in a passive background substance of 'nature,'" and that, given this, "then nature is separated from its own force or power and is at the whim of active human interference" (Fancy 65). My observation of my students' experiences with/in nature was that they marveled at what they saw, but didn't *really* take it in. They were experience-spectating more in terms of a *relation to*, and less in terms of a *relationality in* or a *relationality with*, nature. I know this claim about my students—this judgment about their comportment—runs the risk of being both unwarranted and unkind. And I don't know how to properly address this problem. I don't want to point to—to call out—specific behaviors. And I certainly don't want to speak for my students, or to lump them and all their varied and complex experiences, together into one undifferentiated whole. At work here is a problem of measurement. How do I measure *awe* and *reverence* of nature? How do I account for the quantity and kind of *respect* and *understanding* of what's there, what's at stake, what it all means?

* * *

Rainforest Expeditions' own website proclaims that a trip to Tambopata is "for those looking for a short stay in the rainforest with the promise of an authentic eco-tourist experience." My research turned up this statement early in the writing process. Interestingly, when I return to it at a later time, wanting to verify the source for citation purposes, my Internet search turns up an array of sites (travel sites, tourism-promotion sites), many of them not at all associated with Rainforest Expeditions, that all have this exact wording in their content. The people at Rainforest have clearly been doing their work, harnessing the power of the Internet and yoking it to the power of the desire, on the part of so many in the developed world, to "look" for and find ecotourism. The statement is rife with language worth unpacking, with just about every word in it chock full of rhetorical appeal.

To be sure, "promise" and "authenticity" are words that do a slick, and very effective, performative dance. They ask us—the privileged, White tourists able to afford such an excursion/intrusion—to come and partake in this most exciting and noble form of tourism, this "ecotourism experience." The words are designed to lure our dollars and our bodies away from the civilized world in which they are normally, happily ensconced. The force pulling us out and away from our everyday lives— lives lived out as a *habitus* entailing a large carbon footprint, one that has constituted and perpetuated the very environmental crisis that tunes us into the jungle in the first place, bringing us to this space with this reverent and thankful attitude—is Nature, ostensibly.[2] But, really, it is Nature cast in a particular role, thrown onstage, put under a spotlight, and asked—expected—to perform for us.

I am thus not unaware, as I have my "authentic ecotourist experience," of the fact that this is both enjoyable and critique-able. A double consciousness is at work here for me—in me. I am most definitely "aware that I [am] being 'guided' by an economically driven tourism industry"; and that this (f)act is undeniable, inescapable (Shaffer 143). My critical cultural sensibility, my (auto)ethnographic I/eye, is, if not ruining my experience, at least tainting it, rendering a certain distance. My time in the jungle is indeed centered around notions of "authenticity," which is nothing if not a socially derived understanding structuring my self-in-the-jungle. My aspirations and expectations as an ecotourist almost require me to act and feel certain ways. Moreover, even as this performative requirement lays out for me what "specific acts" I am supposed to execute in order to have my "authentic ecotourism experience," these very acts, this purposive, basically scripted approach serves to render my ecotourism experience in/authentic, im/possible (Shaffer 154). It is the ineluctable dialectic of tourism. It is, following Eric Peterson and Kristen Langellier, the eternal double bind which "surpasses the performing/audiencing boundary by *creating* performance" (Peterson and Langellier 250, emphasis added). The mind reels at the implications. How can my experience qua ecotourist ever really be authentic? How can I not be complicit? How can my interaction with the flora and the fauna and the people not occur without my being ever-aware of the oceans of distance separating us—even as we touch, as we interact? How can I condemn or negatively judge my students for somehow being less tuned in, less good at being ecotourists?

But, it must be said, I am all too happy to be cast into my role. And to play it to the hilt.

I *am* happy to be here, happy to make the most of the opportunity before me. Happy to be, as Jamaica Kincaid puts it, an "ugly" tourist (17). I am happy to be *that* kind of person-in-the-world at this moment, in this place; a person who is all too ready, willing, and able to leave the banality and boredom of my own native space, my "back home." And I am happy—to a large extent—to not think too much about what all this really means. My students and I are indeed happy to not think too much about the deeper implications and effects of our having come here. We don't dwell on the fact that we took numerous airplanes, buses, and boats to get here, thus leaving behind a significant energy-and-pollution wake, an undeniable carbon footprint. We don't spend much time thinking about the fact that, even as we enjoy our interactions with the Ese'Eja, we are basically encouraging and expediting their modernizing, their industrializing, their joining—finally—the ranks of Western (i.e., White) culture, socioeconomics, and politics. In order to maximize our joy, and perform our awe, and play out the already-laid-out script, we are all too glad to *not* focus on what brought us here, and how our being here affects the environment. We do not want to spend time dwelling on the everyday details—and much less on the wider geopolitical and sociohistorical conditions—of the lives of the Ese'Eja. We don't want to let our consciousness linger long (if at all) on the fact that

They are too poor to escape the reality of their lives; and [that] they are
too poor to live properly in the place where they live, which is the place
[I], the tourist, want to go—so [that] when the natives see [me], the
tourist, they envy [me], they envy [my] ability to leave [my] own banality and boredom, they envy [my] ability to turn their own banality
and boredom into a source of pleasure for [myself]. (Kincaid 19)

Yes. It must be said (admitted?). I am all too happy to be cast into my
role. And to play it to the hilt.

* * *

To look closely at the history and ongoing events of the region is to come
face-to-face with a very complex, very fraught narrative. Much of it, as
one commentator puts it, "pits self-determination against the fiction of
progress" (Garabano 351). It is interesting to note, however, that indigenous peoples across South America—who have long been forced to play
the role of the subjugated, the ignored, and/or the oppressed—have been
re-casting their role in current affairs. This is most certainly the case in
the Amazon basin.[3] Indigenous tribes in Peru, Ecuador, and Brazil, with
"widespread support from both [national] and foreign social movements,
trade unions, NGOs, and political leaders," are attempting to take control
of the narrative of their lives and their lands (Hughes 89). As usual, it
boils down to resources and the needs, and ravenous appetites, of those
who live far afield from the jungle.

The broad plot lines and the archetypal protagonists of these stories,
I expect, are more or less familiar to my reader: the explorations, extrac-
tions, and exploitations of oil, forestry, agroindustry and energy companies leave a wake of social and environmental degradation. Highly valued resources are taken out of the jungle, and animals, plants, and people
are left behind in an impoverished, worse-off state. All in the name of
modernity, all for the sake of progress.

In conversation with our guide, Robin, I learn, for example, that one
of the (many) problems facing the Ese'Eja is the mining of gold in the
Tambopata River. Though the fact that the Infierno area has been de-
clared an ecological preserve means that dredging for gold is officially
outlawed, clandestine operations persist. In addition to the social and
economic consequences of the predictably lopsided distribution of the
profits from such operations, this activity has the effect of causing severe
damage to the river ecosystem itself. Mining for gold in the Tambopata

leaves behind harmful amounts of arsenic and mercury, byproducts of the process, killing fish and other river and river-dependent life.[4]

The problem, as critical cultural studies scholars Jennifer D. Slack and J. Macgregor Wise note, is that all this "progress" is mostly only measured in terms of *material betterment*, and not in terms of *moral betterment* (12). In other words, progress is measured in facile, quantifiable ways. Progress is measured and discussed as: profits, tons of material extracted and exported, Gross Domestic Product, market growth, etc. Betterment is not measured, instead, in terms of that which matters most but which is not easily quantifiable, as: happiness, quality of life, cultural preservation, social functioning, a sense of peace and harmony among all living and nonliving things, etc. Indeed, so far there has not been enough of an attempt to strike a balance "between material prosperity as the mark of progress, and moral and spiritual growth as a mark of progress" (Slack and Wise 14). Moreover, even the material betterment upon which the prevailing, received view of progress focuses has tended overwhelmingly to favor both the few and the far away.

* * *

Robin is one of the four guides assigned to our group while we are in the Amazon. Over the four days that we're there, we establish and enjoy a nice interpersonal connection; we enjoy talking to each other, and do so repeatedly. A native Ese'Eja born and raised in Infierno, Robin had plenty of valuable and interesting things to share with me—and he seemed quite happy and eager to do so. The phrase that titles this essay comes from him. I was inquiring about how the Ese'Eja had come to play the role that they were playing in modern-day Amazonia, especially interested in how the Rainforest-Ese'Eja partnership had come to be.

Up until the early 1990s, this corner of the Amazon Basin was fairly quiet and unnoticed—undeveloped, to put it in Euro-American terms. Brazil had long been synonymous with the Amazon, anyway, and most of the development of the Peruvian Amazon, whether in terms of the extraction of resources or the tourism industry, mostly took place farther north. Iquitos, several hundred miles to north, is considered the capital of Peruvian Amazon. By contrast, Puerto Maldonado, the city nearest to Infierno, was a sleepy little town well into the 1990s. What got things going was an influx, starting in the early 1990s, of European and American researchers drawn to the area's striking biodiversity (this part of the Amazon is richer in biodiversity than most any other part of the jungle).[5]

After a while, as word spread about this Edenic corner of the world, the more adventurous and hardy tourists followed. Things, of course, kept going and building from there. "Progress fell upon us," Robin told me—with a very mixed-feelings tone of voice and look on his face.

* * *

Our third night at the lodge. Our final one. We find out that we're going to be party to a special treat. About once a month or so, Ese'Eja school-children come upriver to the lodge and dance for those present (the Infierno Ese'Eja live scattered on mixed-use land not too far from, and now also in, Puerto Maldonado). It's cultural pride meets cultural display. Not all lodge guests get to see this performance (I saw it during my second visit, but was completely unaware of it on my first), but, since we happen to be there at the right time, we, the lucky ones, are going to experience this event.

The lodge's biggest structure is the dining/lounge area. Guests are served buffet style, all of us (from our big, thirty-plus group to other smaller groups to an Irish couple on their honeymoon) seated at four very long shared tables. The dining area takes up about half of the structure's space. The other half is comprised of a lounge area and a bar (specializing in selling jungle-specific cocktails, with liqueurs and/or fruit drawn from the area) where guests can relax and converse, play games, read books, check email and/or charge devices (a wireless Internet connection is available only here, and only for limited windows of time, when the gas-powered electricity generators are run twice daily).

The announcement comes toward the end of dinner, as we're shifting into lounge mode. The music at the bar is stopped, and those present are told what's about to happen. Excitedly, couches and coffee tables are cleared, to open up a space for the performance event about to occur. As this is happening, we see that the group of Ese'Eja have arrived. They line up and wait in the separate adjoining reception structure. It looks to be about twelve children, around ten to fourteen years of age. There's an older male, who appears to be a chief or leader. Also, we can see four or five other adult males carrying instruments. They are all dressed in "authentic" garb, as they proudly tell us.

An interruption: "Authenticity is not found in objects or places, it is found in the body and its interactions and contexts" (Shaffer 141).

Once we're all in place, and after an introduction and explanation from Posada's manager (himself Ese'Eja), the performance begins. In orderly fashion, the children, musicians, and chief walk across the breezeway connecting the reception and lounge structures. The musicians take their place at one corner of the assembled crowd, and the children file into the circle, dutifully taking their place in front of the musicians, the girls kneeling in front of the boys. The chief then steps in and previews for us what we're about to see. He explains that, in an attempt to preserve the culture of the Ese'Eja, the children are taught the music and movements of their ancestors, as part of their school's curriculum. They live and attend Peruvian public schools in "regular" clothes, but they are proud to wear their authentic Ese'Eja garb and give us guests a taste of their age-old music and dancing.

An interruption.

I am not sure I need—or want—to issue a full description of what then took place. We know, I suspect, how this goes. I am presuming that many of my readers are culture- and diversity-sensitive. You, my reader, have probably come across some version of this in your own lives. Perhaps a Native American music-and-dance performance on a university campus—in all likelihood, as part of, billed and framed as, a "cultural" or "multicultural" event. Maybe something at a county or state fair. Maybe a performance in some sort of performing arts center.

Or some of you might remember the opening ceremony of the Vancouver Winter Olympics in 2010, in which a decent amount of show time was turned over to the Aboriginal Peoples of Canada as they welcomed the world to the event with a carefully chosen and enacted display of their own culturally authentic performances.

You've seen this show before.

It clearly is all about spectacle.

* * *

Indeed, if you, my reader, were expecting in the above (interrupted) vignette, a description of this micro-performance on the part of the Ese'Eja children in the jungle—the ones we were so "lucky" to have been able to audience—then I'm sorry to disappoint. I am interrupting and resisting that expectation here, deliberately. For I am less interested in describing the specifics of what the performers did and said, and more interested in writing through—and in expressing, getting out—*my* experience and observations, and some of the insight and implications inherent in this moment (and so many like it).

The problem for me—then and there, and here and now as I write—is that I am all too aware of these sorts of "authentic" cultural performance events as a display-medium in which there is a gaping distance between that which is (ostensibly) on display and those who are "enjoying" it.

Indeed, I want to listen to "the voices that are telling me to be uncomfortable with being comfortable" (Warren 165). For that is what happens to me when I audience these sorts of performances. It happened to me when I watched the opening and closing ceremonies of the Vancouver Winter Olympics, and it happened to me at Posada Amazonas as I watched the Ese'Eja children dance.

An interruption. An interruption *is* called for here.

I've tried explaining this to family members and to my students. What it boils down to, as far as I'm concerned, is that there is an element of consumption that, if acknowledged, is quite troubling. When audiencing these sorts of "special," "authentic," and "genuine" performances, I cannot shake the feeling that this is just not right.

An interruption. An interruption is at work here.

I'll try to get at this with the example of the Vancouver Olympics ceremony, which I very much did experience in this way. As I watched the ceremony, hard questions arose, and deepened thinking and critical insights ensued for me. As soon as the Canadian Aboriginals were announced and came onstage (onto the ice, in this case), my mind reeled. I thought of the history of these people, one heavily pervaded by domination and violence at the hands of White colonizers. I thought of what was irretrievably lost as (that) history ran its course. I thought of the innumerable silenced experiences; of very real, very material, very painful loss. I thought about how disingenuous, and how woefully facile, this "wonderful" such act of "inclusion and celebration" really was. This was somehow supposed to make up for that history? This was evidence that things have been worked out, that we're "all good" now, that we've learned to "get along," that we are gleefully "post-racial"? Did anyone watching—or, for that matter, participating in—this performative moment think about the length, weight, and nature of the history preceding it, framing it, leading up to it? Did anyone stop to consider that these dances, these performance rituals, were not really "entertainment"; that they are—or once were—deeply woven into the fabric of a culture and a cosmology about which they may know little to nothing?

An interruption. An interruption is missing here.

I want to interrupt the ease with which these sorts of performances occur. I want—I need—critical intervention. I want to interrupt and complicate the ability of the audience member to engage in what I think of as a sort of performative consumption.

I know (I think) that the vast majority of those audiencing such performances are enjoying it on two levels—which brings us back to the Ese'Eja and their Amazon dance. We are enjoying it on an aesthetic level, delighting in the artful flair that is undeniably a constitutive feature of these on-display rituals. And we are enjoying it on a cultural level; that is, we are enjoying being "exposed" to a different people, an alternate worldview, a new set of embodied behaviors. This is a coming-to-know the ineffable Other, the exotic foreigner. And we feel good about this. We delight in being able to now be able to say that we have sat through and enjoyed this performance. We like what this means. We are going to like how it sounds when we tell friends and family members and colleagues back home about this experience. It neatly and efficiently affirms our self-image, our ability and desire to say that we are kind and open-minded people.

An interruption. Yes, an interruption. Given the stakes, an interruption.

What hits me, every time, is an unshakeable feeling that, in taking in and "enjoying" these sorts of performances, I am—we are—participating in a process of performative erasure. I am in a very real way consenting to the elision(s) inherent in the very (f)acts of the display taking place in front of me/us—i.e., in front of a White audience that may or may not be engaged in careful (self)reflexive understanding/audiencing. This was the case for me and my students in the Amazon, watching the Ese'Eja children dance for us; watching them put themselves on display for us, we who felt so privileged to be there on that night, for that performance.

The matter, of course, is not a zero-sum game. I do not mean to discount or underappreciate the fact that these performances *are* meaningful, for both the performers and the audience members. But, my understanding and acceptance of this double bind does not make it easy for me. Which, of course, is the point; is the critical insight called for and being put forth here.

In *Destination Culture: Tourism, Museums, and Heritage*, Barbara Kirshenblatt-Gimblett notes that "Immersion in a world other than one's own is a form of transport [. . . .]. What is most ordinary in the context of the destination becomes a source of fascination for the visitor [. . . .]" (132). It was certainly the case that the guests at Posada Amazonas on that special night were fascinated—even thrilled—by the fact that they had been there on that night. I overheard plenty of "Cool!," "That was so special," "I can't believe we just saw that," "They're so cute, those kids, especially in those outfits," and "What interesting dancing and music" comments in the moments bookending the performance.

Kirshenblatt-Gimblett, again: "Once it is a sight to be seen, the life world becomes a museum of itself" (132). I am, in other words, too aware of the fact that "whiteness and racial power are [being] constituted through the repeated and mundane communicative acts" taking place in moments like this; and that are, really, working to "sediment and reify our understanding of race and difference" (Warren 160). The Ese'Eja are there, in front of us, in flesh and blood. But, they are also not there. Because we, as spectators, are not, really, *with* them. The Ese'Eja are, for us, more of a fantasy, a simulacrum: a hyperreal representation, charming and ephemeral, of *our* ideations.

* * *

We are expectant, wanting a good show.

The occasion is tinged with rare-opportunity excitement. We are mostly quiet, and definitely reverent, as we make our way out onto the waters of Tres Chimbadas. A surreal mist hangs over the lake, as the horizon begins to brighten in earnest.

Let the show begin.

It's just us, on our two catamarans, and whatever the Amazonian rainforest sees fit to put in front of us. Anticipation is high.

We are expectant, wanting a good show.

Reeds and fog are first up. Already, a splendid spectacle, here in the Amazon, as dawn blooms before us. We marvel at the quiet majesty of the unfolding scene, one we enter as benign intruders. The lake is rimmed by jungle, and the dead-still air renders the lake's surface a mirror.

A cobweb laced with dew, constructed between two high reeds and with the early morning light behind it, draws the attention of several of our cameras.

We were expectant, wanting a good show.

Ivo and Paula are both using binoculars to scan the area. Their job is to facilitate for us ecotourists the best possible experience; and now, on this lake, it is all about spectacle.

We are a primed and ready audience, eager to play our role: awed and reverent appreciators of Mother Nature. If only she'll cooperate. After all, she's a fickle performer. We've been told you never know what to expect. She may deliver the goods (hers to offer or withhold, after all), or she may not.

And then, a key actor enters the stage. Paula quietly but excitedly motions for us to look about thirty yards in front of us. There's a black caiman in the reeds. It's backed into them, but well visible to us. This, Paula reminds us, is a fairly rare species. Once hunted to the brink of extinction, it is "estimated to have been reduced in numbers by 99% in the space of the last century," mostly so that its skin, which can be transformed into shiny black leather, could become yet another commodity for White/Western consumption (Britton). It is now listed by the International Union for Conservation of Nature (IUCN) as being "conservation dependent" ("Melanosochus niger").[6]

In other words, this is special.

We quiet down as we slowly approach and glide by the caiman. It's a striking creature. Around six feet long, it's a big animal. From its vantage, backed into the reeds halfway, it doesn't move. But it sees us. It is surely keeping a keen eye on us. And it is those eyes that I connect with most. Somehow, they convey tremendous power and beauty to me. I can still picture them in my mind's eye, many miles and months away from them.

I know this animal is not to be messed with.

It's a truly sublime experience. My absolute awe is mixed in with gratitude for the opportunity—along with a healthy tinge, an awareness, of fear.

* * *

Visiting the Amazon, for my students as well as for me, *positions* me/us. Our being there *places* us. It *locates* us within interlocking, complexly interrelated realities—or, if we want to cite Beaudrillard's notion of *hyperreality* once more, within realities in which the distance that separates the simulation from the "reality" is hard to bridge or apprehend. Most immediately, the jungle is taken in in vivid, fascinating detail. But what underlies this moment is a complex mix of experiences and implications. And our experience of it is not more than that: an internal experience that is far removed from the actualities and interiorities of what is *really there*.

Indeed, the jungle offers up its manifestations. I know that each one of these, though unique and discrete and wonderful, always and already has a relation to "the world in which it is generated and consumed" (Cook 2). The caiman and I: here and now in the jungle, but also then and there in the large(r) world. Schechner's concentric circles—drama, script, theater, performance—are operant here, to be sure.

* * *

We have been on the lake for a few hours now. We have fished for piranhas. We have seen beautiful birds fly over us, or perch on lakeside branches. We have taken gobs of photographic shots, hunting, attempting to somehow capture that which we see and feel. Of course, paraphrasing the opening sentence of Eugenio Barba's "Four Spectators," the theatre of nature is ephemeral (96). But, we persist, we insist. We are ineluctably cast into this play, and cannot not carry out our roles.

The climax to our collective narrative comes around mid-morning, as we near the end of our time on the lake. We are close to the edge of where we're allowed to go. The apex of the lake's oxbow shape functions as a boundary, an imagined and artifical, but very much real, line that effectively splits the lake. One half of the lake is open to tourists, to those who would tread its surface on the two catamarans (the only means of enjoying this guarded lake preserve). The other half is off limits. This is so primarily because a family of giant river otters lives at Tres Chimbadas.

Even more so than the black caiman, their numbers are perilously low, and their very existence on this planet is imperiled. They are, undeniably, endangered. Indeed, "threatened by multiple anthropogenic influences," they have: been hunted mercilessly for their pelts; suffered mercury poisoning as a side effect of gold mining; become exposed to "canine diseases such as parvovirus and distemper transferred through the domestic stock [that] are[,] as yet, an incalculable threat"; and generally had their habitat encroached upon, in a host of ways and with a bevy of interrelated effects, by deforestation and the supposed needs and advances of the civilized world ("Pteronura Brasiliensis"). There are just not many giant otters around, and these are to be protected. Only a few thousand remain in the world (estimates vary, but no more than 5,000 or so); and these over an area of land roughly the size of the continental United States.

Yes, the other half of the lake is *their* half. So that their skittish nature (and who can blame them for such an attitude?) can be given proper consideration.

Ivo had noted, as we set out onto Tres Chimbadas, that the far half of the lake is off-limits because not only are these creatures worthy of space and respect, but also because their numbers necessitate a high degree of care and concern. Nursing mothers, when subjected to the stress and strain of contact with humans—even well-meaning ecotourists, like us— can stop lactating.

There is no shortage of ways, it seems, to inflict damage in the jungle.

Paula, always scanning the lake with her binoculars, quietly but excitedly calls for our attention. She has spotted some otters. They are off a distance from us, two hundred yards or so from our catamaran (the other catamaran, with my colleague and the other half of our students, is even farther away). Chatter and movement quickly settle down, and we begin to watch them.

Paula's excitement has a particular cast to it. I remember that, as we set out, our guides had told us (not quite in these words) that one just never knows what will come onstage for audiencing tourists. Just seeing the otters at all, already, is a treat. It seems a mother and three pups have ventured from the safe haven of their side of the lake. We watch them swim along. They're far enough that we cannot see them in much detail, but close enough so that we are in their orbit, very much cast into our spectating spell.

As we continue to watch, one of the pups breaks away from the romp (one of a few terms, and the most wonderful, I daresay, for a group of otters). The young, regardless of species, seem ever pulled by their curiosity.

Slowly but surely, the pup keeps coming closer. It's swimming straight for our catamaran. If we weren't still and quiet enough before, we are now. The proverbial pin drop would not go unnoticed. Not a whisper among us.

It keeps coming toward us, head poking out of the water. Leading with its nose, it snorts and sniffs rather loudly. It keeps coming, somehow drawn to us.

The awe and excitement on the catamaran are palpable. I catch Paula's eye, and we share a glance that says so much. A moment of recognition: of the special moment unfolding before us; of the coeval nature of this magic-of-nature spectacle; of our individual(ized) yet somehow intermingled experience(s).

The otter pup ends up coming within about forty feet of our catamaran, before turning around and rejoining its family. I am able to see the whites of its eyes. I take a picture of it with my camera, knowing full well that this is an exercise in futility, as far as capturing the moment goes. I snap just at the moment when it gets ready to turn back.

* * *

The image I end up with is grainy from the need to zoom in.

* * *

Barba states: "The performance dances not only on the level of energy but also on the semantic level. It is its *meaning* which dances [. . . .]" (97). Moments like the otter encounter on Tres Chimbadas will be with me forever. And I mean that quite literally: the moment will be *with* me. It will live inside me. But the question of how and why such moments can come to become *part of* us is an interesting one. Is this a matter of memory? Is it a matter of psychology, of emotion? Is it a matter of a connection felt—between me and the otter, between human and nature, between possibility and actuality—that will, in one way or another, show up in my being-in-the-world? Surely, the fact that I experience(d), and have here "written up," this moment as deeply meaningful is a testament to the power of performance, of co-present bodies in space, inter-affecting each other, somehow and on some level. I think, here, of Strine, Long, and HopKins's seminal essay, and want to play with the key thesis they lay out (and challenge): "The common presupposition here [is] that [performances] are repositories of enduring insight and value, and that latent meanings and values embedded within [performances] become manifest and most fully accessible when experienced holistically through [and as] performance" (182).

Perhaps most interestingly, performance's meaning(s), performance's meaning-fullness, is a matter of degrees. It is one thing to claim, poetic though it may be, that all of us on that lake on that day had our lives touched by that magical encounter (the word "magical," though much overused, *was* in the air that day). It is quite another to understand that claim in more "real" terms. While I know I cannot position myself as having had a better, more efficacious experience than my students because of/as part of that encounter, it is nonetheless true that the experience is radiating—forward, outward, from then and there—differently in and from *me*. This writing, this book chapter, is an undeniable, material consequence of that encounter.

* * *

The image I end up with is grainy from the need to zoom in.

* * *

During one of our hikes, not far from the lodge, we come across *Pseudomyrmex Triplarinus* and *Triplaris Americana*. We witness, in other words, how a particular ant and a particular tree are so intricately (inter)connected that they are practically a microcosmos unto themselves. The ant intensely fights off any and every thing that even comes near the tree. The ant performs its duties as a zealous gardener (vigorously attacking foreign species and pruning); which of course allows the tree to thrive, to perform well qua tree—and qua host (Weir, et al.).

Symbiosis. A relationship of mutual benefit. A beneficent mutuality.

* * *

Of course, the complex reality of Amazonia's flora and fauna entwine with the reality and well-being of the Ese'Eja and other indigenous tribes who have been living in relatively perfect symbiosis with the jungle since, seemingly, time immemorial. And we can ride the concentric circles out from there . . . the lungs of the planet; the policies enacted by local, national, and transnational governmental agencies; the decisions and priorities of resource-extraction (mega)companies, all or most of which are based far, far away from the places and people on which they inflict so much damage, even as—as a necessary condition for—the reaping of (outlandish profits).

* * *

Speaking and thinking and theorizing in/from the jungle, for me, means coming face-to-face with connections, with binaries, with relations. There are dialectics in place that, even as I acknowledge them, I want to transform. The *separating lines*—between human and nature, between

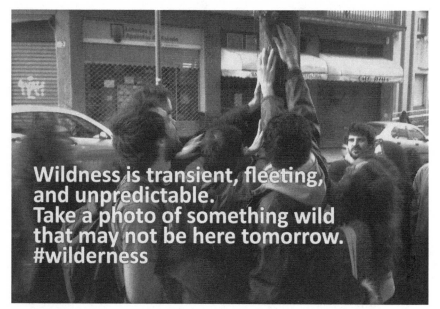

Figure 9.1. Wilderness is unpredictable. Photo provided by EcoArtTech.

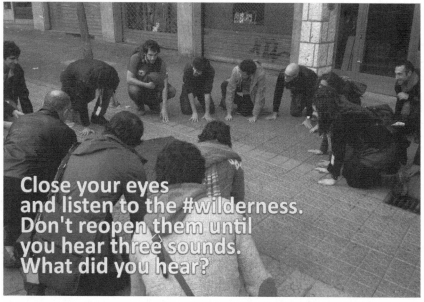

Figure 9.2. Listen to the wilderness. Photo provided by EcoArtTech.

Figure 9.3.   Symbolism in wilderness. Photo provided by EcoArtTech.

Figure 11.1.   Fashion Trashion. Photo taken by author.

Figure 11.2.   Eco-invention. Photo taken by author.

Figure 11.3.   Eco-collage and assemblage. Photo taken by author.

local and tourist, between other and self, between spectator and spectacle, between affected and affecting, and between so many other uncriti-
cally accepted conceptions and performative enactions—are both trou-
bled and troubling. I want to dance with them, open them up. I want to
call them into question, complicate them, confuse them. Indeed, "this
confusion is manifested in the careful patrol of performance: the negotiation and redistribution of power among performer, text, and audience are
in constant tension" (Bell 370). At least as I understand and value it, performance studies' relationship to, and its insistence on drawing upon, a
wonderful array of academic disciplines—too many to list here—has
very much helped to shed light on stable categories, unchecked episte-
mologies, and taken-for-granted ontologies very much in need of being
shaken up, resisted, subverted, re-visioned.

At the heart of the matter, and of the critical-cultural-performative
lens being deployed here, lies the ineluctable need to point to and deal
with power. "Locating the *power* of the performance in the performer,"
Bell posits, "is an historically, culturally, and aesthetically frightening
strategy." Of course, we must now add to this list the phrase *environmentally frightening*. Given what is at stake in all of this—given the all-too-
real vicissitudes of global climate change as part and parcel of glob-
al(ized) socioeconomic change—the power of the performance does indeed lie in the performer. In us. In each and every one of us. Indeed: "the
world itself is imbued with creative forces that continuously generate its
untold number of assemblages and their infinite relationship" (Fancy 69).

The whole experience, upon close reflection, feels like something
that occurs in a huge, performative bowl. At least I experience(d) it in
this way. A double consciousness pervaded my time in the Amazon. I
loved every moment of it, truly. I was immersed in tremendous, awe-
inspiring beauty, face-to-face with a web of natural expression and
Earthly manifestation that was just sublime in its scope; a scope which is
both physical and meta-physical.

As I look to draw this writing to a close, I am unsure about how to do
so. This seems telling, and worth noting/sharing.

Voices and strands of thought seem to be all I can turn to, all I have
left.

I turn, once more, to Elizabeth Bell's work, in which she discusses
performance and communication as a tripartite phenomenon involving
sight, site, and citation. Indeed, the Amazon is something to behold; and
is a place to be in and a part of; and readily calls forth—hails—more than
that which is being seen and moved through. My time in the Amazon

reminds me that "the relationship between performer and audience is a skirmish on the borders of display" (Bell 363).

My time in the Amazon was fleeting, a brief moment or two in the span of my life thus far. Hard not to speak in tired clichés, but: its grandeur lingers, its vastness still suffuses me with awe, the thoughts and feeling—especially, the feelings—persist. Barba's words, again, speak to me particularly well, have much to say at this point:

> "Ephemeral" means "that which lasts but one day." But also means "that which changes from day to day." The first meaning evokes the image of death; the second, on the other hand, evokes the ever-changing flow which characterizes being-in-life.
>
> It is the performance, not the theatre, which lasts only a short time. The theatre is made up of traditions, of conventions, of institutions, of habits which endure throughout our time. The weight of this endurance is so heavy that if often prevents life from emerging and replaces it with routine. Routine is another of theatre's natural boundaries. (96)

I realize, with Barba's eloquent help, that what I'm after with this essay, and what coursed through my thinking and experiencing whilst in the jungle, is a particular sense of performance. This is performance-with-eyes-wide-open; performance that is self-aware even as it is (necessarily) self-leery. Performance that is nature-aware even as it is, by nature, hardly aware of all that is going on, all that is involved, all that is at stake. Performance in which the environment—in complex, ineffable ways that we *need* to pay attention to, to understand, to think though, and to learn from—is co-participant, co-present. Barba, once more:

> There are spectators for whom the theatre is essential precisely because it presents them not with solutions but with knots. The performance is the beginning of a longer experience. It is the scorpion's bite which makes one dance. The dance does not stop when one leaves the theatre. The aesthetic value and the cultural originality of the performance are what make the sting sharp. But its precious poison comes from somewhere else. (98)

* * *

Of course, the voice(s) heard—then, and now, as I write—include the people(s) in/of the jungle. I hear/listen to the Ese'Eja, with whom I interacted while in Infierno. I hear/listen to the Guarani, from the film *The*

Mission that my students and I watched together in Cuzco, who were so brutally entangled in the Spain-Portugal and Catholic-Jesuit sociopolitics of Eighteenth Century Colonial Latin America. I hear/listen to the Awajun and Wami people who got caught up in what is now known as the Bagua Massacre in northern Peru.[7] Indeed, I think of the important work of Scott Wallace who, in his important book *The Unconquered: In Search of the Amazon's Last Uncontacted Tribes*, states the Amazon is "where indigenous people [are] manning the front lines against the advance of bulldozers and drill rigs that [signal] the global economy's final offensive on the planet's shrinking pockets of primordial wilderness" (3).

My students and I read Peruvian writer Mario Vargas Llosa's novel *The Storyteller* together (and, in an instance of beautiful fortuity, he was awarded the Nobel Prize for Literature a few months after our return in 2010). I hear, in and through Vargas Llosa's words, the voices of the junglepeople crying out—a powerful, deeply metaphorical and ineluctably allegorical cry:

> How many times have I had to leave where I was because they were coming? Since before I was born, it seems. And that's how it will be as I go and come, if my soul doesn't stay in the world beyond, that is. We've always been leaving because someone was coming. How many places have I lived in? Who knows, but there have been any number of them. Saying: "We're going to look for a place so hard to reach, amid such a tangle, that they'll never come. And if they do, they'll never want to to stay there. But they've always come and they've always wanted to stay. That's just how it is. No mistake about it. (138)

So, so true. So poignantly true. And I was/am part of that coming and going. I was there, with the Ese'Eja. Hesitantly, very hesitantly forging an empathic connection with their existence in Infierno, even as my being there to connect and to care meant that I was being complicit in driving them further away from the way of being-in-the-world that they once knew.

* * *

I have sought, here, to give proper weight to the (inter)influences that pervade our everyday lives. And to (re)assess our role(s) in/as performers. We simply must begin to take seriously the notion that that which we do—as human behavior—*matters*; that our exercise/ing of agency is an ongoing process in which at least two iterations are put forth simultaneously: 1) a unique, of-the-moment and of-the-person creative flourish, an assertion and coming-to-be of a human existential fingerprint, and 2) a repetition of a past, but ongoing, trajectory of history, culture, and politics.

I feel that what I have done here is both an exploration and an invitation. I have explored my own experiences. And, to much lesser extent, and perhaps only by implication, or extrapolation, I have explored the experiences of the Other (now understood in productively broader terms?). I have explored my explorations in and of Nature, with and in the Environment. I have explored the (f)act that there *is* a role that the physical environment plays in our performed lives. Moreover, I have explored the concept/theory that it's *all* roles, all the way down: roles in the play of Life, on this world a stage.

If my work in this chapter is successful (and it is mightily helped by the work of my fellow contributors in this volume), this exploration functions, I hope, as an invitation: an invitation to look and to listen closely, to give a participative voice—a role—to the each and every performing agent in our Life, so that, as we nuance our understanding of performance, we also come to understand the performers, and the performances, anew.

* * *

Still struggling to provide closure to this writing. My mind's eye—as if on its own, as if on cue—goes back to the Amazon. Part of me is still there. I close my eyes, casting out/back . . . .

The image that comes, the feeling that bubbles up, the experience that presents itself, is of me and a group of my students atop a canopy tower. One hundred and twenty feet and a few hundred steps up into the jungle air. Above the trees. So that, from our small viewing platform, all we see, all around us, is jungle. The only interruption of the jungle is the lazy flow of the river, the Tambopata, as it rounds a bend on its gradual wending toward the mighty Amazon.

It's a vast, vast expanse. All one can do, quite literally, is stare out in wonder.

We're there, as the fates would have it, right at sunset time. And we're the last group up, so we don't have to hurry back down so that others may have their turn. So, we're there in peace. In acceptance. In reverence.

There's more silence than talk. And when we do talk, it's with a hushed, respectful tone. The glory of it is humble-making, I suppose. Gratitude, too, seems to tinge the air between us.

We take pictures with our cameras, of course. Though we know, we surely know, that no digital facsimile could ever hope to encapsulate this 360-degree vista.

Patches of clouds in the looming distance add texture to the view, make the horizons of our visual experiences that much richer. Especially as the setting sun goes down, hiding behind them and then reappearing. The play of light and dark and color and hue at this hour—this hour upon which the sun has decided to cast a new, different, more vivid, yet more peaceful, light.

The whole thing is clearly about jungle as spectacle.

The image I end up with is grainy, from the need to zoom in.

Notes

1. At Posada Amazonas, we heard this information repeated a few times. We were told that this about the arrangement between Rainforest Expeditions and the Ese'Eja by the tour guides with us on the bus ride from the airport in Puerto Maldonado. And, a few days later at the lodge, have this information reiterated and further explained during an evening presentation on these matters.

2. My use of the word "habitus" here is based on the work of Pierre Bourdieu. The conception, as I understand it, posits an understanding of power in which agency (the ability and propensity of individuals to exercise their free will) and structure (the workings and interests of social, cultural, and political institutions) are engaged in a constant, be it destructive or productive, back-and-forth.

3. Of course, as I endeavored to make clear to my students in Peru, these unfolding matters extend well beyond the jungle. The Quechua in the Andean highlands of Peru, the Aymara on the Peruvian and Bolivian altiplano, and the Mapuche in south central Chile, to name a but a few, present instances of rising socio-political tension between indigenous populations and the White/Western context(s) in which they live. I am heartened, and particularly intrigued, by what I see as a very positive trend in the region. Starting in particular in the 1990s, there has been increased visibility for, concrete actions by and for, and, most important, actual policy-making centered upon indigenous rights. From the rise to power of Evo Morales in Bolivia (setting aside the presidency of Mexico's Benito Juarez in the mid-1800s, as an Aymara, Morales is Latin America's first "indian" president) to the creation, and ratification by many countries' governments, of the United Nations Declaration on the Rights of Indigenous

Peoples, the scales of justice seem to be tipping, slowly but surely, in the right direction.

4. This is a serious, complex, and ongoing problem in the Amazon basin (and beyond). See, e.g., Barbieri, Cournil, and Gardon; Clark; Fialka; and Telmer et al.

5. Our guides repeatedly stated that the Peruvian part of the Amazon Basin, in general, and the southeastern part of it, in particular (where the Tambopata Reserve is located), has a higher biodiversity than the Brazilian Amazon (which is what most people think of when they think of the Amazon). While this claim is a bit tricky to substantiate, it appears that, particularly when it comes to bird and butterfly taxa, it is largely accurate. For a useful document touching on this topic (and containing an extensive and useful Works Cited section) see the Natural Resources Information Clearinghouse's "Conserving Biodiversity in the Amazon Basin: Context and Opportunities for USAID."

6. For additional information, consult http://www.iucn.org/ and http://www.iucnredlist.org/. The IUCN is "the world's oldest and largest global environmental organization," supporting species status awareness, knowledge, and research ("About IUCN"). The IUCN Red List of Threatened Species includes entries for the black caiman and all other threatened, endangered, and/or extinct species, such as the giant river otter, mentioned below (*The IUCN Red List of Threatened Species*).

7. In June of 2009, long-simmering tensions between Amazonian indigenous peoples and the (empowered, privileged) forces of Peruvian institutional power and neoliberal capitalism erupted in a bloody massacre of more than thirty natives, who then retaliated by killing and kidnapping police officers. The Awajun and Wami had been protesting, for a while and with little sign of respect or progress, their treatment and the conditions of imposed and unjust development in the area (see, e.g., Jaña and Romero).

Works Cited

"About IUCN." *IUCN, International Union for Conservation of Nature.* International Union for Conservation of Nature, 27 February 2102. Web. 4 July 2012.

Bacon, Wallace. "The Interpretation of Oral and Ethnic Materials: The Ethical Dimension." *Literature in Performance* 4 (1984): 94-97. Print.

Barba, Eugenio. "Four Spectators." *The Drama Review* 34.1 (1990): 96-101. Print.

Barbieri, Flavia Laura, Amandine Cournil, and Jacques Gardon. "Mercury Exposure in a High Fish Eating Bolivian Amazonian Population with Intense Small-Scale Gold-Mining Activities." *International Journal of Environmental Health Research* 19.4 (2009): 267-77. Print.

Bauman, Richard. "Performance." *Folklore, Cultural Performances, and Popu-*

lar *Entertainment: A Communication-Centered Handbook.* Ed. Richard Bauman. New York: Oxford UP, 1992. 41-49. Print.

Beaudrillard, Jean. "The Precession of Simulacra." *Cultural Theory and Popular Culture: A Reader.* 4th Ed. Ed. John Storey. 2009. Harlow: Longman, 409-15. Print.

Bell, Elizabeth. "Performance Studies as Women's Work: Historical Sights/Sites/Citations from the Margin." *Text and Performance Quarterly* 13 (1993): 350-74. Print.

Bourdieu, Pierre. *Distinction: A Social Critique of the Judgment of Taste.* London, Routledge: 1984.

Britton, Adam. "Melanosuchus Niger (SPIX 1825)." *Crocodilian Species List.* Web. 22 Dec 2011.

Clark, Matthew. "Environment: In Peru's Amazon, Finding Gold but Leaving Mercury." *The Christian Science Monitor* 5 Jan 2010: 10. Print.

Conquergood, Dwight. "Rethinking Ethnography: Towards a Critical Cultural Politics." *Communication Monographs* 58 (1991): 179-94. Print.

Cook, Nicholas. "Between Process and Product: Music and/as Performance." *Music Theory Online: The Online Journal of the Society for Music Theory* 7.2 (2001): 1-24. Web.

Fancy, David. "Geoperformativity: Immanence, Performance and the Earth." *Performance Research* 16.4 (2011): 62-72. Print.

Fialka, John J. "Backfire: How Mercury Rules Designed for Safety End Up Polluting." *Wall Street Journal* 20 Apr 2006: A1. Print.

Galeano, Eduardo. *Mirrors: Stories of Almost Anyone.* Trans. Mark Fried. New York: Nation, 2009. Print.

Garabano, Sandra. "The Brilliance of Progress: People, Nature and Nation." Trans. Sander Berg. *Journal of Latin American Cultural Studies* 25.4 (2011): 343-54. Print.

Gorenflo, L. J., Suzanne Romaine, Russell A. Mittermeier, and Kristen Walker-Painemilla. "Co-occurrence of Linguistic and Biological Diversity in Biodiversity Hotspots and High Biodiversity Wilderness Areas." *Proceedings of the National Academy of Sciences of the United States of America.* Ed. B. L. Turner. 7 May (2012): 1-6. Web. 18 May 2012.

Hughes, Neil. "Indigenous Protest in Peru: The 'Orchard Dog' Bites Back." *Social Movement Studies* 9.1 (2010): 85-90. Print.

The IUCN Red List of Threatened Species. International Union for Conservation of Nature and Natural Resources, n.d. 2012.1. Web. 4 July 2012.

Jaña, Elsa Chanduvi. "Report Blames Amazon Indians for Violence." *NotiSur Peru* 29 Jan. 2010. *Latin American Database: News and Educational Services.* University of New Mexico. Web. 15 Oct. 2011.

Kincaid, Jamaica. *A Small Place.* New York: Penguin, 1988. Print.

Kirshenblatt-Gimblett, Barbara. *Destination Culture: Tourism, Museums, and Heritage.* Berkeley: U of California P, 1998. Print.

Langellier, Kristin. "Forum: Cross-Gender Performance." *Literature in Performance* 8.1 (1988): 120-122. Print.

"Melanosuchus Niger." *The IUCN Red List of Threatened Species.* International Union for Conservation of Nature and Natural Resources, n.d. 2012.1. Web. 4 July 2012.

Michalski, Fernanda, Paula C. Conceiçao, Joyce A. Amador, Juliana Laufer, and Darren Norris. "Local Perceptions and Implications for Giant Otter (Pteronura Brasiliensis) Conservation around Protected Areas in the Eastern Brazilian Amazon." *ICUN Special Otter Group Bulletin* 29.1 (2012): 34-45. Print.

Natural Resources Information Clearinghouse. "Conserving Biodiversity in the Amazon Basin: Context and Opportunities for USAID." *United States International Agency for International Development.* May 2005. Web.

Ohl-Schacherer, Elke Mannigel, Chris Kirkby, Glenn H. Shepard Jr., and Douglas W. Yu. "Indigenous Ecotourism in the Amazon: A Case Study of 'Casa Matsiguenka' in Manu National Park, Peru." *Environmental Conservation* 35.1 (2008): 14-25. Print.

Olcese, Cristiana. "Review Essay: Latin American Movements and Neoliberalism." *Social Movement Studies* 10.3 (2011): 299-303. Print.

Peterson, Eric E., and Kristin M. Langellier. "Creative Double Bind in Oral Interpretation." *The Western Journal of Speech Communication* 46 (1982): 242-52. Print.

"Ptenonura Brasiliensis." *The IUCN Red List of Threatened Species.* International Union for Conservation of Nature and Natural Resources, n.d. 2012.1. Web. 4 July 2012.

"Rainforest Expeditions Lodges in Tambopata." *Rainforest Expeditions*, n.d. Web. 21 December 2011.

Recharte, Maribel, Mark Bowler, and Richard Bodmer. "Potential Conflict between Fisherman and Giant Otter (Pteronura Brasiliensis) Populations by Fishermen in Response to Declining Stocks of Arowana Fish (Osteoglossum Bicirrhosum) in Northeastern Peru." *ICUN Special Otter Group Bulletin* 25.2 (2008): 89-93. Print.

Romero, Simon. "9 Hostage Officers Killed at Peruvian Oil Facility." *New York Times* 7 June 2009 late ed.: A8. Print.

Schechner, Richard. "Drama, Script, Theater, and Performance." *Performance Theory.* New York: Routledge, 1998. 68-105. Print.

Shaffer, Tracy Stephenson. "Performing Backpacking: Constructing 'Authenticity' Every Step of the Way." *Text and Performance Quarterly* 24.2 (2004): 139-60. Print.

Slack, Jennifer Daryl, and J. Mcgregor Wise. *Culture and Technology: A Primer.* New York: Peter Lang, 2005.

Strine, Mary S., Beverly Whitaker Long, and Mary Frances HopKins. "Research in Interpretation and Performance Studies: Trends, Issues, Priorities." *Speech Communication: Essays to Commemorate the 75th Anniversary of the Speech Communication Association.* Ed. Gerald M. Phillips and Julia T. Wood. Carbondale: Southern Illinois UP. 1990. 181-204.

Telmer, Kevin, Maycira Costa, Romulo Angelica Simoes, Eric S. Araujo, and Yvon Maurice. "The Source and Fate of Sediment and Mercury in the Tapajós River, Pará, BrazilianAmazon: Ground- and Space-Based Evidence." *Journal of Environmental Management* 81.2 (2006): 101-13. Print.

Vargas Llosa, Mario. *The Storyteller.* New York: Picador, 1989. Print.

Wallace, Scott. *The Unconquered: In Search of the Amazon's Last Uncontacted Tribes.* New York: Crown, 2011. Print.

Warren, John T. *Performing Purity: Whiteness, Pedagogy, and the Reconstitution of Power.* New York: Peter Lang, 2003. Print.

Weir, Tiffany L., Scott Newbold, Jorge M. Vivanco, Megan van Haren, Christopher Fritchman, Aaron T. Dossey, Stefan Bartram, Wilhelm Boland, Eric G. Cosio, and Waltraud Kofer. "Plant-Inhabiting Ant Utilizes Chemical Cues for Host Discrimination." *Biotropica: The Journal of Tropical Biology and Conservation* 44.2 (2011): 246-53. Print.

Chapter Eight

"On Finding Ways of Being":
Kinesthetic Empathy in Dance and Ecology

Julia Handschuh

October 1st, 2010—It is 8 a.m. and a fine, cool mist is gathering into cold drops that saturate Brooklyn and Manhattan. The clouds are low, condensing the sky close to the earth, and I am walking along 58th Street West toward the Hudson River, mentally preparing myself to be wet for the next three hours. The Hudson River Greenway just north of the sanitation building at 59th Street is a sculpted terrain of concrete, gravel, grass, trees and Astroturf that divides NY Highway 9A from the waters of the Hudson. It is here, at a concrete ramp ending in rotting wood and water looking out to the skeletal remains of a historic pier and beyond to New Jersey, that the process begins.

This may be the first time I've stopped to take in the land of Manhattan.

Jennifer introduces herself, Maggie, Chris and Kate to the small group of us who have come for this interactive presentation of SIP (Sustained Immersive Process)/Watershed. In a low whisper while holding solid eye contact she explains that they have been working together for a number of weeks and have developed some ways of investigating and engaging with the environment. She pauses between thoughts, sinking in . . . that they are going to share their process with us . . . and that we are welcome to participate to whatever extent we feel comfortable. If we become too wet or cold there are some dry places below the highway where we can gather.

The following are six scores, or sets of instructions, which were given throughout the morning to engage us in their Sustained Immersive Process:

1. A grounding of the feet, a centering of the breath, a circular motion of the arms, movement inspired by Qigong; arriving here in this body, in this space, connecting breath to body to *There is a familiarity, a sense of willingness in my body and desire for physical release. I am circulating my arms toward my core as we stand witness to the movement of the gray waters in*

ground to landscape.

front of us and the expanse of silvery gray sky stretching out from side to side.

2. Forming partners and taking turns leading and following. Holding hands, the leader chooses a place of interest and goes there, the follower takes the opportunity to explore how one might orient themselves along the journey to this chosen place, to their own body, to their partner, to sight, sound, smell, touch, to imagination, to scale, to temperature, shifting perceptual focus as a way to find new orientations in space. Upon arriving at the chosen location the partners switch roles and repeat; follower becomes leader and chooses the next destination.

Chris is lightly grasping my hand as we move at a slow pace through the gray landscape. I feel a different sense of time, something slower or wider, and a willingness to release to curiosity. Water shoots down gray green drainpipes as big around as my head, a series of multiples stretching out in great lines to my front and back, circulating water off the highway above our heads.

3. Gather and watch the water. Seven minutes. Find a partner. One person begins moving in response to watching the Hudson River. The other witnesses and then responds to the response to water. Continue repeating responding to response three times.

Jennifer's hands cut playful and erratic movements along and through the negative space of the shrubs lining the walk, inspiring me to take off at a quick gait down the hill and around the willow tree, wet branches whipping me in the face. I come to a halt that lands me on the ground. Laying on my back, hands upward to the gray sky, arched upper back and neck head reaching for the earth, fingers and arms stretched overhead, fingers pointing downward to distinct blades of grass framed within blue (gray?) sky and willow tree.

4. Find a place on the horizon as far away as you can see. Trace a line from this point on the horizon to where you now stand, as if your gaze is a pencil or record needle. Do this three times with three different points.

There is a difficulty of holding imaginary lines in actual space and an attention to intricacy that creates distance and space and scale between me and one thing and the next. A meditation; we're creating a container for fine-tuned attention that allows us to hold the action of drawing an imaginary line while witnessing the mind wandering, rambling away and back again to the presence of what the eyes can see. I am left with thoughts of scale and perspective; a centering of self in relationship to a vast intangible whole.

5. Find a partner. Person one watches the water. Person two repeats the line-tracing exercise while physically tracing the bones of their partner's body with their hands. Switch roles and repeat.

Feeling the juxtaposition between projected line and solid bone, the exacting massage of fingertips through muscle. Working my eyes along the particularities of cityscape and then moving water that is so hard to hold with a focused and constant gaze.

6. Walk through the environment. As you are walking, listen. Find a sound that is far away, live with this sound, become accustomed to it. Find a sound that is closest to you, live with this sound, become accustomed to it. Find a sound that is in the middle, live with this sound, become accustomed to it. If a louder sound comes along and covers the sound you chose let it

It's difficult to hear anything over the rush of highway to the right. Suddenly, I realize the rush of wind shaking the plastic poncho against my cheeks and the splatter of rain close to my ears and eyes.

cover it and try to listen to it
through the louder sound.

***

The first time I spoke with Jennifer Monson, dancer/choreographer and
founder of iLAND (Interdisciplinary Laboratory for Art, Nature and
Dance), about her creative process, we were ascending a steep hill in
New York City, away from the Hudson River inland toward 12th
Avenue. It was raining and we had just spent the morning together with
five or six others along the banks of the Hudson, immersed in an
interdisciplinary investigation she and her collaborators are calling SIP
(Sustained Immersive Process)/Watershed. I asked Jennifer about how
she experiences her work in relationship to ecological issues. Amidst the
rain soaking our clothes, punctuated by pauses for thought, she used the
word "empathy." It was this word and its sentiments that have stayed
with me as I've grown to know Jennifer. That day she spoke of a desire to
have an empathetic exchange with her environment, that her embodied
practice leads her to question notions of power in how we approach each
other and our surroundings. These are important issues to consider in the
face of climate change and the pressing need for ecological
sustainability. To think in terms of a relationship *with* the environment as
opposed to *to* the environment begs us to listen more and be in touch
with our surroundings.

iLAND is a dance research organization that fosters cross-
disciplinary investigation of the ecology of New York City. The
organization's ethos is grounded in Monson's many years of
improvisational dancing outdoors and a firm belief in the power of
kinesthetic awareness to influence other fields of research. Focusing on
kinesthetic awareness and impact demands a reorganization of the
senses, which calls into question how we as humans tend to navigate,
understand, and inhabit an environment. I have become involved with
iLAND over the course of 2010 and the work cultivated through this
organization has inspired me to think of my own process of
improvisational dance and environmental action in terms of ecological
empathy. In my practice-based research I've begun to track the
experience of my body in relationship to my surroundings and to unpack
what trainings and practices I've acquired and developed that encourage
me to lean toward an empathetic exchange with my environment. This

has led me to question the role of embodied experience in our understanding of and response to environmental issues, particularly in light of cultures of capitalism and consumerism that often disregard impacts on bodies and land due to profit-driven initiatives. The work of iLAND counters this tendency by cultivating embodied experience that grows out of and into the interconnected systems of which we are a part.

What follows here are documents and ruminations on the kinesthetic relations between body and place. The writing moves between theoretical analysis and poetic documentation, culled from my engagement with iLAND and the public presentation of SIP/Watershed, as well as by my own solo movement investigations that are inspired by my recent move from rural Massachusetts to New York City. My research is an investigation of the built environment through a rural- and dance-trained body. It is a project of proximity, a performative and analytical process to invest in the possibility of forming an empathetic exchange between body and place, an exchange that could subsequently lead to a reorganization of how we value each other and the environment. I am writing as a practitioner and observer, balancing the task of filtering conversations, research, and experience through movement and words.

***

It's so different here. New York City. A place of endless connections, networking, socializing, career building, dream making.
And disconnection.
At home in the hill towns of Western Massachusetts I am reminded of the quiet. And what six miles into town feels like on a bike. The gradual receding of the countryside to clustered homes, college campus, city hall. Six miles to school here in New York City is a stream of one concrete ecosystem interrupted by the water under the Williamsburg Bridge. I privilege the "natural" ecosystem of home and its green spaces. "Natural" in quotation marks because there too we have reconstructed land from forest turned farmland turned strip mall intercepted by conservation lands and old growth trees. But I privilege this reconstruction of land; it feels smaller and more expansive in its simplicity. I feel more distant from the urban landscape than a part of it and yet the intellectual-cultural-technological huuuummmmm of urban space stirs me.
Something expansive in its own right; but closed, too—and other.

In *Choreographing Empathy: Kinesthesia in Performance*, dance writer and anthropologist Susan Foster engages in a close tracking of the evolving cultural meanings of the terms kinesthesia and empathy. She explains empathy as the sensory experience felt in the body invoked by encountering another, be that "other" inert, active, human, or otherwise; and kinesthesia as the awareness of bodily orientation in space. Kinesthetic empathy thus implies an awareness of how our bodies sense and respond in overt and minute ways to the world around us. Vernon Lee suggests that the capacity for an empathetic experience originates "in one's own awareness of the kinesthetic responsiveness to the object"; that we must feel the world with our bodies before we can empathize with it (Qtd in Foster 155). Kinesthetic empathy, then, can be thought of as a dialogue between that which is within and without; as an attunement to the body's capacity to register sensory shifts in relation to the multiplicities that constitute an environment.

Recent research in neurobiology suggests that empathy is integral to how we construct meaning; in other words, it is linked to knowledge production, and is a form of orienting self to world (Foster 178; Gallese 771). Susan Foster's work illustrates how dance practice, in particular, cultivates kinesthetic empathy by making one aware of bodily interactions in time and space. This work, held in tandem with Jennifer Monson's dance research and those practices proposed and supported by iLAND, leads me to consider how kinesthetic empathy might produce new ways of knowing the spaces and bodies that we inhabit. This process of meeting the world and self through kinesthesia is one of proximity rather than distanced, objective observation and is subject to the particular body through which the information is channeled. How, then, does dance, and more specifically dancing outdoors, train a body or audience to approach the world with empathy? Does the cycling of data through a kinesthetically attuned body invoke alternative ways of being in the world? Perhaps the cycling of the environment through the body heightens our awareness of the reciprocity inherent in our relationships with other people and our surroundings.

***

ABANDONED LOT:
Movements at the corner of Kent and 6th
Brooklyn N.Y.
October 31st 2010

I don't trust this dirt; I trust these weeds.

Riding my bike over the Williamsburg Bridge each day I pass by a vacant lot far below with deep rivets cut in the earth and gravel piled high covered in scraggly green. Large steel beams frame half the lot overhead, just begging for a swing to be hung surreptitiously in the night. I can imagine swinging out high over the weedy rubble and dream of building a little off-the-grid shack nestled into the hollow of the bygone building.

Yesterday I went in search of this lot and found it cordoned off by plywood strewn with graffiti, prohibiting entrance to this dreamy space of possibility. I pressed onward to other streets in hopes of a weedy encounter. A little later I found it through a gap in razor and barbed wire tangle on 6th Street. Slipping through with a couple of snags through blue wool and green canvas I stepped into a sunny open space left in the wake of some previous structure. Lined by buildings on two sides and streets on the other, I am protected from ground-floor view by a metal wall that rises high overhead.

Abandoned lots. Lots of abandon. Move with abandon; reckless abandon. Abandon self. Let go. Of what would I let go? A practice of holding. A delineation of holding the things worth holding. Nestling into an unsettled place.

Take stock: to take in the land. Do wild spaces dictate wild movements? Becoming wild. Becoming animal (Deleuze and Guattari 335). Becoming human. To make this space resonate through experience and attention to micro perceptions. Becoming place. If anywhere in New York City is wild this is close to it. Unplanted and unplanned.

After burning there is re-growth. After upheaval there is re-growth. After building and demolition there is gravel and toxins and re-growth. The weeds are the land pushing through.

I do not trust this dirt. I trust these weeds.

A tree stands in the corner of the lot growing around metal I-beams of an industrial gate disfiguring both itself and the beam, twisting it mercilessly and gorging a deep scar in itself as it envelops the rusting metal. Climbing through the brambles and trash I perch myself on the gate and find contact with the tree. Shoulder to branch, cheek to bark, hand to twig, spine to trunk, wedging myself into the tangle of metal and alive wood. Round yellowing seedpods hang like fruit around my head, some sprung open and passed (dead) like tiny mouths still clinging. I feel protected here, in and among the arrow-shaped leaves, looking out across the open weedy expanse, beyond to tagged walls and cityscape, holding leaves and metal and seeds and gravel and bark and buildings.

Two tasks/scores. Task one: Delineating a thing to hold: a perception score. A dance of the eyes. Holding a stick and remaining focused on a metal beam five feet away. The stick becomes transparent and I can see the beam through the stick. The stick splits. Becomes two. Holding each in perfect focus without joining the two. Soft brown, speckled with dark spots, slightly raised, which I can feel where the bark meets my skin. Holding two sticks and one rusted yellow beam. Switch. Blend the sticks and the beam becomes two. The softened focus is a doubling of the world. An overlap. Holding focus sharp and soft in the same moment. Holding two kinds of focus in two different spaces. *Experiencing the tentative line of holding multiple realities in a singular observation.*

Task two: finding this tentative line in movement. Running through space. Body in motion switches between two modes of focus: one of play and observation, and one of thinking and audience. Self watching and imaginary other watching, creating an articulation that is bound to a preoccupation with ideas of successful communication, impact and impression. *A split between concept and movement*, between self as mover and witness. Holding both simultaneously. Playful investigation moves toward trying toward thinking toward performance. Toward dance? The awareness of moving and the choice making, the desire to let go of preconception and exterior watching, to move the body as the body wants to move, as the land wants the body to move. Charting a trajectory from perception to movement to placement, to awareness to thinking, to choice making, to communication. When does this sense-perception-turned-movement turn into dance?

***

In "Movement's Contagion: The Kinesthetic Impact of Performance," Susan Foster draws a lineage of the study of kinesthetic perception. In the late nineteenth century kinesthesia was identified as a kind of "sixth sense" connected to the awareness of one's existence to space and time. This definition was refined and articulated as researchers learned more about how this "sixth sense" is connected to the musculature and proprioceptors of the body that process the intake of sensory experience and articulate the expression of movement, from something as unconscious as breathing to the self-aware gestures of dance (47). "Kinesthetic empathy," "inner mimicry" or "metakinesis" became known as terms that refer to the imaginary sense of movement felt when observing someone (or something) in motion. Kinesthesia is now understood as the sensorial awareness of movements and their orientation.

In the 1930's American dance critic John Martin wrote about kinesthetic empathy in relation to the emotional transmission of modern dance as exemplified by the work of Mary Wigman and Martha Graham. To quote John Martin at length:

> Since we respond muscularly to the strains in architectural masses and the attitudes of rocks, it is plain to be seen that we will respond even more vigorously to the action of a body exactly like our own. We shall cease to be mere spectators and become participants in the movement that is presented to us, and though to all outward appearances we shall be sitting quietly in our chairs, we shall nevertheless be dancing synthetically with all our musculature. (53)

Recently, neuroscientists have connected this sense of "dancing synthetically" to the presence of mirror neurons, which "resonate" in similar ways regardless of whether we see an action or perform it ourselves (Rizzolatti 253). We feel the movement that we see around us as if we ourselves were moving. Regardless of whether we are aware of this process it is always happening, the movement of the world is replayed through our muscles and brains in minute ways. In other words, when we witness an action we are effectively rehearsing the possibility of fully embodying it as a way to connect with and understand our surroundings. Gallese speaks about this process as creating a shared body-state in which observer and observed are linked in an inter-subjective relationship (771). Our orientation to the world, indeed our very sense of self and reality, are deeply informed by a constant neural and physical response to our surroundings whereby our body/minds actually repeat, or mirror, the world around us. *We perform the world in minute neural-muscular gestures.*

In the context of this project I am particularly interested in our kinesthetic response to the environment. If our neurons fire appropriately upon seeing a turn or leap or fall, what is firing upon living in a city, forest or field? Might we find ourselves in an intersubjective state with our environment? Some would argue, as is evident in many of the experiments recorded in *The Secret Life of Plants*, by Peter Tompkins and Chris Bird, that the transference of feeling or sense from one object or being to another is not a purely human experience.[1] These experiments suggest that we are part of a network of kinesthetic response in which all things are informed by each other. Animate or otherwise, in motion or stillness; we are in a constant state of re-orientation, sensing and feeling our environment as if it were ourselves.

What are we sensing in our bodies as we witness shots in the chest, or scars in the land? How are these experiences being tracked, traced and archived by our bodies?

Mirror neuron theory gives scientific credibility to experiences that I think are very familiar to improvisational dancers. There are many improvisational techniques that teach you to pay close attention to your surroundings, its form and movements, how it impacts your body and what choices to make from within a constantly shifting landscape and (subject) position. An example of this is the practice of Authentic Movement, a contemplative improvisational dance technique which engages people in two different roles, that of mover and that of witness. The mover closes his or her eyes and moves in whatever way he or she wishes. The witness remains still and monitors the sensations that arise while witnessing the other. The witness is often described as creating a container for the practice; his or her act of attention holds space for the movement of someone else while taking note of his or her own body's response. Each role in Authentic Movement requires an attention to what is arising from within, the mover witnessing self, the witness regarding mover, each in a state of nonjudgment, seeing what is and letting things arise and pass. They are bound in a reciprocal engagement in which their movements define each other. I grew up dancing this witness from within and witness from without.

What is it to witness this earth?
This space?

This place?
This city?
What container are we creating in order to witness and respond to our actions?

Practices such as Authentic Movement have informed Monson's work and this is evident when I spend time with SIP/Watershed. I see it in the ways in which they give spaciousness to their investigations, listen to each other, dig deep into internal kinesthetic response, and reflect on findings as a catalyst for continued exploration. They are consistently observing their own experience within the container of a shared practice. These practices build relationships between self, site and other that resonate for me beyond the explicit space of dance. They infuse the way I inhabit my body, my environment, and my relationships with a kinesthetic awareness and attentiveness.

I am not of this place. I come from a rural place.

Through the displacement of my body—which is trained in techniques of contact improvisation, climbing trees, yoga, catching bugs, tuning scores, hitchhiking, body-mind centering, buying local, laying in grass, conceptual performance art, riding bicycles and authentic movement[2]—I become aware of the tension and juxtaposition between built and natural space. I become aware of the strangeness of land reclamation, box stores, parking lots, and parks. I also become aware of a general sense of displacement. The displacement of people by colonialism, capitalism, and environmental force, the displacement of land from under our feet by corporations and agribusiness resulting in a place-less-ness that is pervasive and deep.[3] With this displacement also comes a lack of orientation, and so it seems to invoke a shoring up of those things I think I know so that I can relocate my body-self-sense in this foreign land. Dance practice, and in particular improvisational and site-specific practice, provides a framework with which I can be present to the passing sensation and constant re-orientation to body to thought to place to land. Dance has intention, a survey of possibilities, and a contextual reorientation that *leans toward the possibility of an empathetic exchange.* Through training and attention I grow aware of my body pressing into this possibility. As I find meaning in movement and space for consideration I also encounter the demand to reckon with the implications of my actions and the recognition that I have the capacity to shift perspective and direction.

SIP/Watershed:
164th St. on the Hudson River
Manhattan, N.Y.
October 8th, 2010

You cannot take 164th Street all the way to the Hudson. You must access the river farther south or north and travel a path between railroad tracks and the water. Near where 164th would intersect with the Hudson, the land is a long wide green expanse along the steep rocky edge of Manhattan.

Was it always like this, or carved away for rail and recreation?

Here the river is wide and even, flowing toward the city to the left and upstream, lined with rocky outcroppings aglow with autumn colors. These kinds of landscapes, with their northeast waters, wood, and rock, are familiar to me. We meet in the shadow of the George Washington Bridge at a discharge site for combined sewage overflow during rainy weather. There is a sign cautioning to beware of toxins released in the advent of a storm. Following a similar pattern of warm-up to the first day we ground our feet and find our breath.

It's gray but not raining.

Standing here and taking in the landscape there is always more than appears or is perceived. What embodied and environmental cues are edited out in the process of understanding? Is this how we understand the terrain; through mapping and flattening it out to make way for transportation?

We hold hands and lead each other to points of interest.

Editing to create order, not the natural order of growth and decay cycling back onto itself, but the clean precise order of grass mown, leaves raked, pavement mended, and shrubs clipped.

I fit my hipbone into the hollow of the shore and think about how water edits stone.

Departments of recreation, sanitation, environmental protection.

We rearranged objects and bodies in relationship to each other and sound.

An ordered body.

We played the landscape.

An ordered landscape.

We made sounds and drawings, diagrams that mapped the

soundscape.
> What order are we to follow with our bodies in this
> place?
Drawing sound, drawing out sound, sounding drawing, diagrams of
sound and space.
> Does SIP embody and engender a new order?
We spoke in whispers, treading the line of intelligibility between
sound and speech.

***

The embodied research practice proposed by my experience with iLAND engages a cross-disciplinary approach to dialogue with the environment. The tools brought forth in sound, architecture, and dance infuse and inform the process, creating a relational network of sound, space, and movement. This form of research imagines a way to approach a conversation between humans and built and natural environments by turning toward the environment through the body. iLAND proposes a space where boundaries are blurred between disciplines. Dichotomies such as performer/audience and expert/novice are diffused into a shared space of exploration, expression, and meaning-making. Rather than define each collaborator or audience member within specific roles, everyone becomes involved on multiple and shifting levels. The exploration is not conclusive or didactic but instead proposes a deep attentiveness and interrogation of a kinesthetic response to internal and external composition. The site is equally regarded in this process as it influences the form of research and data collection used by the various disciplines represented. This exchange between environment and dancer, and dancer and audience, completes a kind of kinesthetic empathetic feedback loop from the environment to the body to another body and back to the environment. SIP may not completely break down socially prescribed ways of being, but it does practice it by following a more fluid engagement of inquiry and reciprocity. This challenges presumptions of defining the world based on notions of truth or fact by calling attention to the nuanced textures of lived experience.

In *The Lie of the Land,* Paul Carter proposes that Western relationships to physical and theoretical landscapes have been predicated on colonialist practices of erasing physical and cultural details which allow for the construction of an artificially flat ground on which to lay claim to territory and authorship. Carter beautifully uses the metaphor of poetry, whose meandering trajectory folds along the details of the terrain, as a contrast the the linear and cutting marks of colonial navigation. For Carter, poetry allows for a sympathetic tresspass and expression of experience, which I feel is akin to my nuanced time passed within this Sustained Immerisve Process. After my first day participating in SIP/Watershed at the Hudson, memories and experiences became linked to the minute details witnessed in the space opened by sustained kinesthetic engagement. What was once only a park between highway and waterway becomes a container for a multiplicity of happenings and investigations. I begin to know the space in another way. Carter argues that forming a detailed relationship to people and place counters the totalizing narrative of the State.[4] I believe that kinesthetic investigations are one way to form narratives counter to mainstream capitalist and colonial ideologies. By aligning oneself *with* the environment and others, we perform a reorientation toward a more ecological way of being.

How are our understandings of power and subjectivities changed if, instead of being defined by a single call-and-response of one human to another, we instead turn toward the soil, a river, or a storm?[5] Understanding our identities as constituted by both human *and* environmental relations thus requires that we give credence to the landscapes we inhabit. The ways in which we manipulate, use, and respond to our habitats affect the kinesthetic relay that defines our experience and understanding of ourselves. It would seem, then, that an increasingly resource-deleted, paved, privatized, and war-stricken world would reproduce a particular kind of subject; and in the face of this, it becomes important to interrogate our notions of self and other and the response mechanisms that these positions reproduce.

In *Relationscapes* Erin Manning speaks about proprioceptive awareness in terms of feeling ecologically, stating that "we feel the world ecologically before we know exactly what it is" (73). In other words, our ability to recognize or name the world is pre-empted by sensory perception, which raises questions for me about our ability to listen, or feel, without jumping to hard and fast conclusions about ourselves or the world around us. She also notes that "proprioception provides us with clues that precede our cognitive understanding of where we are going," which suggests that our body begins to process, respond, and perhaps understand before our mind can conceptualize a socially constituted meaning, or a politically correct response (14). Our bodies, we now understand, are hardwired to the world, inextricably linked to our intake of and impact on our surroundings. This, then, is a prelinguistic impulse, which relates to the questions of subjectivity above in that it proposes the possibility of articulating (through movement) an ecological state of being that functions within cycles of reciprocity and constantly evolving patterns of exchange. Dance has the potential to cultivate this state of being by teaching one to hone in on the details of kinesthetic response. It proposes a context for the articulation of movement and composition (read: subject position) that allows for, indeed neccessitates, awareness of mutually responsive and constitutive flows of action not only between bodies but also within the context of a given space.

Felix Guattari addresses similar notions of ecological states of being in *The Three Ecologies,* outlining what he calls an "ecosophy": an articulation of the ethico-political arenas of "environment, social relations and human subjectivity" through the lens of ecology (28). His call to recognize the depth and breadth with which all things are interconnected (not as a singular unity but as a system that consists of a multiplicity of interacting forces) demands a deep interrogation and response to political and environmental issues, both individually and collectively. Guattari argues: "Ecology must stop being associated with the image of a small nature-loving minority or with qualified specialists. Ecology in this sense questions the whole of subjectivity and capitalistic power formations, whose sweeping progress cannot be guaranteed to continue as it has for the past decade" (52). An ecosophical analysis complements the neural and physical aspects of kinesthetic empathy discussed thus far by presenting an ethical imperative bound to the notion of an ecological subject. This suggests that through becoming aware of oneself as an ecological subject one must confront the ways that hierarchical and capitalist systems are incongruous with the relational depth and breadth of human (or nonhuman) experience.

Through my engagement with iLAND I have often spoken with Jennifer about her process, and have been impressed by the sincerity with which she is questioning the notion of "a small nature-loving minority" that is often attributed to environmentalists searching for a practice that is able to grasp, or at least move, in relation to this depth of interaction. The collaborative experience of SIP/Watershed engages with an expanded concept of ecology, one in which the body in implicated within the systems it is investigating. It is important to note that while dance and kinesthetic empathy offer a lens through which to think, feel, and move ecologically, these practices in and of themselves do not inherently lead toward an interrogation of or response to the issues Guattari presents. The collaborative experience of SIP/Watershed thus becomes an ecosophical practice insofar as it is utilizing these practices to inform an expanded concept of ecology and our experience of it.

The concern for how we respond to "capitalistic power formations" and "sweeping progress" is echoed by Foster in *Choreographing Empathy* when she raises the question of how new technologies such as cell phones and the Internet are mediating our kinesthetic capacity; that is, our ability to orient our bodies in space. She notes the disorientation created when speaking on a cell phone in public and the rapidity with which we are fed sensory information (making less time to pause) as two examples of how our kinesthesia is being compromised (or at least changed) in an increasingly technologized world. If attunement to our surroundings is fundamental to our capacity to experience empathy and empathy is a correlate to understanding the self and other, then we may be at risk of a greater sense of disorientation (Gallese 775). In light of these reflections it seems important that we find ways to reorient, read, and respond to our surroundings.

***

I was sitting outside FAO Schwartz next to the glass cube of the Apple Store, on Fifth Avenue, and was approached by a security guard and told I could not sit on the floor. This was striking to me.

Floor.

I was outside and I was welcome to be in the chairs provided, but not on the floor.

I was outside. On a floor.

Silvery concrete and glass stretching out on all sides. Interrupted by fashionistas connected to iPads and iPhones. More like a roof. For below me was the largest Apple Store in the world. On the roof of a subterranean Apple Store; on the floor of the city. Where sidewalk becomes the property of private corporations hidden underground.

My small-town environmental training is made particularly apparent in light of the realities of city life. It's easier to feel as though everyone in the United States has a general sense of environmental awareness and action when living in a town where trash, recycling and compost are proudly carted away by The Pedal People Collective[6] and cloth shopping bags are made by and for the community to substitute for paper or plastic at the local grocery store, not to mention the pervasive "buy local" campaigns,[7] Community Supported Agriculture,[8] and farmers markets. It is these trainings that partially constitute the lens through which I am able to read my body and environment. It is with these predispositions that I find myself in the city.

***

APPLE:
Movements at the Apple Store Plaza, 5th Avenue Manhattan, N.Y. November 13th, 2010

I'm nervous here, I'm afraid to move. I can't move.

I have a deep desire to find a similar release and investigation in this space. What use are these tools (scores, ways of being) if they cannot be used within this system too?
   Be courageous. Move.
   Heart is rapid.
   Gaze is at middle gray and safe. Survey the possibilities.
Learn the rules through breaking them.
   Remember motion. Orientation.
The score of this space is delineated, maintained and enforced.
   I can feel the corporation.
The fountain elegantly redistributes water into frothy white columns that mirror the pillars which frame one side of the plaza. *So many bodies.* Guards appropriately attired in black suits with clear plastic wires protruding from their ears, coiling down their necks and into their collars. Shoppers toting bags, cameras, and children form a line awaiting entry to the subterranean Apple Store. I find purchase in the slightly rounded edge of the stairs that mediate plaza to sidewalk. A slow quiet teeter begins as the concrete splits the length of my foot, folding minute bones and muscles around the architecture to assure balance in a metered walk along this public private edge.

Holding innerscape and outerscape, private space and public space.
My private experience in their privatized public space.
  Am I holding my own private revolution? Is this world-making?
Here is my place: an intimate space between bodies, unbeknownst to the
crowd, unbeknownst to passersby, unbeknownst to the guards, cultivated
through hyper awareness, attention to kinesthetic response and
proximity, existing within and between.
  In a crowd, I am so close. We are so close.
Gray on gray on white on black on gray on silver on clear on white on
gray on silver punctuated by the vibrant Google blue of ties and t-shirts.
Imported melting snow forms dirty slush heaps that frame the curb,
ushering in the shopping season. I hold eye contact with a couple who
sits some distance away.
  Are they conversing about me?
I am moving backwards, attempting to sense a spaciousness around my
back, attempting to feel (see) with my spine. Bodies are in every
direction with a density accumulating at my left as people pause to enter
or snap pictures. My heightened attention makes everything feel hyper
visible: the space between people, the weave of cloth, a conversation, the
temperature. I'm aware of the guard's eyes but do not know who else is
witness to these actions. To my actions. The invisibility of the crowd
mixes with the hyper visibility attained through kinesthesia. Being keyed
in to a shift or gesture or brush or pass or glance.
  I feel invisible and possible.
Who is allowed, forced, denied, privileged, access to their own
disappearance?
  *I'm on my knees now and with arched back, face to sky, bodies and
buildings soar above me.*
Static concrete and frenetic bodies. The scale collapses between bodies
and buildings. Bodies become moving buildings. Buildings become static
bodies. Soaring (towering) up ahead.
  My white rural dance body, clad in blue jeans, slouched on corporate
steps. A playful inching wiggle of torso (ass) leads to the soft thump
down one, two, three, stairs, slick clean gray stairs, landing on the rough
sidewalk, legs spread wide in front of me. In a world where we mask and
bind and build and shave and wax to plug in, strip down, smooth out and
shut up, all categorized, all containment, all the time, where does my
excessive fury-feeling body/self fit in?
  Animal body. Body sense. Animal sense.

Embracing breasts with whiskers; receptors; feeling receptors made for sensory experience.

Sometimes I feel a greater kinship with the tomato plants on my windowsill and their fuzzy stems than with the women on these streets.

***

Ecologically Identified

I am given names. I give myself names. I am naming. *Hippie, anti-capitalist, idealist, unrealistic, tree hugger, witch, childish, fairy, anarchist, artist, weirdo, crunchy, scrub, dirty, hairy, dirt ball, ragamuffin, irresponsible, pacifist, leftist, radical, naive, granola, hipster, privileged, white, mooch, back-to-the-lander, beatnik, bohemian, queer, freak, deviant, dropout, fringe, free, creative, resilient, unconventional, anti-consumerist, environmentalist, ecofeminist, pagan.* I am attempting to build a relational practice predicated on the interstices of biology, perception and cultural identity.
Self-consciously,
    ecologically·
        forming.

Since moving to the city I've needed to reconcile the small local actions that transform one town against the enormity of consumption and waste made apparent in an urban environment. I find myself questioning the value and impact of small-scale actions in the shadow of a nation that propagates environmental disregard and destruction. In Northampton, Massachusetts, our waste may be conscientiously sorted and whisked away without fossil fuels (until it leaves the city limits), but in New York City there is no hiding the plastic to-go containers offered at every turn and mountains of waste on barges and city corners transported to some unknown destination. *In the countryside you can at least pretend that things are sustainable.* Having been groomed in the (mostly white) hippie-land of Western Massachusetts and educated in the tradition of self-conscious leftist activism of rural New England, I am keenly aware that my body is written with innumerable practices that hold innumerable pitfalls and blind spots. However, I also hold that in my body (and in all bodies) there is a kind of truth that we must listen to; that when we hone our attention to that of micro-perceptions and ecosystems, something is revealed with which we must reckon.

Toward what elements of our environment are we trained to pay attention and how can we learn to feel and understand the subtle impulses that our body is constantly receiving and performing?

John Martin assumed the emotional state of the dancer is effectively transmitted to the audience purely through their physicality, thus allowing the audience to experience the same emotional state simply through witnessing the dancers' movements. Susan Foster refutes the universality assumed in Martin's thesis by situating the spectator on a spectrum of capacity for sensory feeling and interpretation that is predicated on a set of social formations and trainings that enable someone to have an approximate read on the experience of the other ("Kinesthetic Empathies" 247). Neuroscientist Vittorio Gallese makes note of this as well when he cites an individual's "idiosyncratic past experiences, capacities and mental attitudes" as having an impact on one's empathetic capability in a given situation (774). These theories of kinesthetic empathy presume that while we may always be sensing the world on a neural or physical level, our capacity to discern and read these impulses as a site for interconnection are reliant on additional factors. These factors are in part based on our familiarity with a given experience, site, or body and our ability, or patience, to hone into the attendant neural, physical and social cues.

Foster, by way of M. le Chavalier de Jaucourt, posits that the experience of kinesthetic empathy is not one of exact representation, but instead is one that produces a "heightened sense of attentiveness" (274). Rather than leading toward an explicit form of understanding or communication, I believe it this heightened sense of attentiveness that can help to reorganize how we value our relationships to each other and our surroundings. I find it difficult, particularly in an urban environment, to remain attentive to my body and environment; yet practices such as SIP suggest ways in which we might give time and space for a closer, more nuanced and sustained examination of how we interact with the world around us. Tapping into kinesthetic empathy, then, can train the body to pay attention to physical response regardless of our ability to immediately name or give meaning to these sensations. Before understanding comes listening, and time spent.

***

The time I have spent with Jennifer, Chris, Maggie, and Kate in their investigation of SIP/Watershed has infused my own process with new considerations: Orientation, Scale, Perception, and Filter. These are entry points into the landscape. Into an experience *with* the landscape. Landscape entry points to ready the mind and body for an exchange with space. With place. With built things and natural things, moving things and static things. An empathetic embodied response: "I move to move with you to move with them to move you moving me" (Manning 25).

SIP. Sustained Immersive Process. To sip; to take in small portions of information. To let things soak in, sip. To mull things over. To give time. To commit to a sustained practice. To a sustainable practice. To pause between. To be open and ready. To let in. To give in . . . to release.

John Martin says an empathetic response is possible when one holds an awareness of self to a degree that allows for holding an other simultaneously. The landscape entry points of this Sustained Immersive Practice were held loosely, reconfigured, and repeated at the Newtown Creek Nature Walk in Greenpoint, Brooklyn.

***

SIP/Watershed at Newton Creek Nature Walk
October 7th, 2010

They tell me we use 1.3 billion gallons a day
They tell me it processes 310 million gallons a day
They tell me they transport 2.24 million gallons a day

When I heard we were going to meet at Newtown Creek Nature Walk I thought I would be going somewhere green near the water, to some winding thing along marshy edges, or to a smooth clear running stream along stones. There would be birds and wooden planked walkways that meander along and dead-end in platforms with benches for pausing and taking things in. "They have this in Queens?" I thought, "How great!"

They do not *have* this in Queens.

The Nature Walk begins on a set of stairs that lead up to a concrete walkway. There is no water in sight. The walk has high walls that grow and arc like the edges of a ship with portholes through which you can catch rounded auditory and visual vignettes of the other side. Gravel pits and cisterns among networks of pale green pipes, yellow trucks, and pink paint on gray concrete. A loudspeaker calls. An office building towers. A truck beeps. The sun is hot and the air is cold.

We repeated score number two of the first day, pairs leading and following through the walkway, taking turns to experiment with orienting our attention to where we have been, where we are, what might be. We stopped to notice the wood grain embedded in the concrete walls, drops of water accumulated on metal and glass, the resonant quality of the metal tubes opening out to another aural realm. Turning at the juncture in the path, the only direction is left; sloping down a long corridor at the end of which we find designed trees, circular benches and . . . water. "Designed to evoke the rich, continually evolving environmental, industrial, and cultural histories surrounding Newtown Creek" (DEP). This feels like an office park.

***

I remember the cranes at Newtown Creek
I remember cranes.
Great green muscle (metal) arms
steady and smooth
swinging out its rusted animal talon

a flick of the wrist

grasping at our waste (like carrion)
what a waste (what a task)

Here a car. A whole purple shining car.
Green arm and rusted hand
clenching maroon car then red car then white car then
beyond disrepair (despair)
beyond demolition derby

Now seeing the pile grow; neatly stacked
Here's a clack
one dropping with a soft sound buried in the other sounds

If a louder sound comes along and covers the sound you chose
let it cover it and try to listen to it through the louder sound.

here
a deep green one

We stood there for a long time. Watching these arms swinging out
and back, we had arrived at the end, or *an* end, looking out from a
concrete platform with benches (to pause and "take things in"), standing
by the rail separating us from the water's edge, out into this deep moving
channel, out to these piles growing bigger from another pile bigger still.
Where are these barges going? What is this churning? Every piece in that
color-coded pile of rust was once new and of use and before that
constructed and before that extracted and before that of the earth. So
much, too much, so what? If we lost sense of our
bodysenseplaceorientationimpact would we just disappear? Disrepair?
Despair? I don't know what to do. So SIP suggests we move.
    Dancing the "I don't know."
    Practices such as SIP orient us to people and place through
kinesthesia. What happens when we encounter a mass of refuse made in
the wake of non-attention? So many things move forward without
consideration for what is left behind. Here we are making room to reflect
on where we have been, where we are, what might be. Paul Carter says,
in all relevance:

> The tracker who tracks his prey also makes tracks, and this sympathetic
> identification, this mark of vulnerability, is also a sign of power. It may
> be that the dionysiac crowd   grows self-destructive precisely because
> it ignores this. Making the mistake of imagining its   tracks   trackless
> wastes, it ends up hunting itself to a sacrificial death. (*Repressed*
> *Spaces*, 188)

It is this sympathetic identification of our own tracks that take witness to
the systems in which we move. To re-encounter what was left in the
wake; recognizing what is ours, what emanates is picked up and cycles
back; or to spend time in the intelligibility of space and scale between
one thing and the next.
    The day at Newtown Creek had its own set of scores to take in and
respond to the phenomena of water:
    We watched the water: *Watch water. We watch water. And all else.*

You find a space to rest on these long wide stairs leading into the water. I trace your body weight as it compresses into the stairs, mapping a shape with my finger of your contact with the land. My body tracing your body tracing the land.

Watch. Watch water. We watch water and all else.

Record needle pencil gaze, tracing distance to nearness to self along buildings and billboards and highways and waterways. Pinpointing self to hear to here to hear to here and now. Tracing bones and muscle tissue and light and difference to approximate distance.

Watch. Watch water. We watch water and all else.

More Scores: endless scores, made to approach and reflect and move, ones that grow out and into ways of being. Drawing and diagramming: now for the watching all else, the taking in of the group of duets and diagramming (drawing) on paper whipped up by cold wind and held down in the heat of the sun. We're making documentation on paper of *what passes what is and what might be.* The im/possibility of catching movement with a pen. *Traces.* What gets left behind. *Outlines.* What we leave in our wake. *What is outside, pushed to the edges.* This orientation through drawing and diagramming is temporal as well as spatial. We're grasping at this residue *(like carrion)* on paper.

***

Tracking (Mapping): Water In Water Out

At 40 degrees 44 minutes 10.3194 seconds North and 73 degrees 56 minutes 48.5952 seconds West, between shrubs on the edge of a concrete walk, below young neatly labeled trees, on a warm day, looking out across a channel of water to the towering eight egg-shaped waste processors, with a concrete wall to my back stretching high over my crouched body, my pee streams into the mulch at my feet. Piss flowing toward my foot, accumulating faster than the earth can absorb. Jamaica Kincaid says that "domestic space is any space in which any one might feel comfortable expelling any bodily fluid" (23). Here I spit. Here I pee. Here I sweat. Here I cry. Here I come. Here I bleed.

40 degrees 42 minutes 41.7132 seconds North 73 degrees 58 minutes 2.8956 seconds West pee mixes with dirt to muddy brown among

pebbles in the abandoned lot. In this (now familiar) weedy lot I find myself contemplating the possibility to be in a space without destruction. To be in a space without destroying. To be aware of what I leave in my wake.
In the wake; to wake up the soil; to wake up the body; to wake.

Wake *noun*

> 1: the track left by a moving body (as a ship) in a fluid (as water); broadly: a track or path left
> 2: aftermath— in the wake of
>> 1: close behind and in the same path of travel <missionaries arrived in the wake of conquistadors and soldiers >
>> 2: as a result of: as a consequence of <power vacuums left in the wake of the second world war >
> 3: a watch or vigil held beside the body of someone who has died, sometimes accompanied by ritual observances including eating and drinking. (Merriam-Webster)

40 degrees 34 minutes 37.6566 seconds North and 73 degrees 53 minutes 42.6042 seconds West the pee disappears into tall grass. Moving away, quickly away. Perched on the eroding shore of Dead Horse Bay. A bit of relocated land that covers (holds) and seeps (reveals) so much past waste now turned treasures. Pissing on past waste and present treasures. Will tomorrow love today's trash?

***

In Closing

What actions and movements create place in a way that is not invasive but invests?
Investigate. Territory. Domestic. Home. Habitat.
    to feel and know
    the spaces and bodies
        we inhabit
Finding a place that is relational.
        A place of reciprocity, which recognizes a connection at some

unknown depth.

A place that we are constantly creating and becoming.

A place where there is room to move.

In the midst of global climate change we cannot rely solely on technological advances and appropriate consumer choices to provide sustainable solutions. I propose that the cultivation of attention to kinesthetic response (and consequently empathy) produces new subjectivities that rely more on a sense of connectedness than on the separation that seems to be perpetuated by present-day neoliberal economics and technology; a separation that has proven destructive to both human and environmental rights and well-being. Practices must be enacted that produce cultural shifts which realign our relationship with the environment. Particularly in the United States, it is time that we own up to our bodies and this Earth, that we shift our weight to the other foot.

This project has been an articulation of a search for an empathetic relationship with my environment, one that is registered by and through the body. I have used kinesthesia as a way to ground myself in a city and perform an empathetic act of place-making. I think of this as a dance, as a kinesthetic exchange between body and place that demands acknowledgment of the inextricable ties between our actions and the world. Neuroscience provides a lens to think of this dance as a honing in on the neural-muscular system with which we are constantly surveying, learning, revising, and rehearsing. Indeed, finding sustainable solutions to ecological issues requires that we implicate our own bodies in the cycle of change. Honing into kinesthetic response necessarily shifts our attention to function *within* ecological cycles. This cannot be fleeting. It must be sustained, translated to state of being. SIP and other forms of improvisational dance enact a sustained process that has the potential to resonate beyond the boundaries of a given collaboration, site, or public presentation, to replay in peoples' bodies and minds, rehearsing and performing a new way of knowing the spaces and bodies that we inhabit.

Notes

1. *The Secret Life of Plants* is a collection of records from science experiments that track the biofeedback of plants in response to various human interactions on and around them using a polygraph machine.

2. Tuning Scores is a practice for ensemble-based improvisation developed by dancer/choreographer Lisa Nelson. Body-Mind Centering is a practice developed by Bonnie Bainbridge Cohen that integrates anatomical, physiological, psychophysical, and developmental principles.

3. See *The Lure of the Local*, by Lucy Lippard, for a conversation about the delocalization of the United States and how this affects our experience of place and identity.

4. For a further investigation of Carter's approach to place-making see Material Thinking: http://www.materialthinking.com.au/

5. In *The Work of Dance*, Mark Franko reads John Martin's analysis of metakinesis alongside Louis Althusser's theory of interpollation to point to the ways in which our sensory experience is implicit in the visceral experience of subject formation (59). As these thories point to how our subjectivities are constructed through interhuman relations I would also like to consider how our identities are formed through relations with our environment.

6. The Pedal People Collective is a worker cooperative based in Northampton, Massachusetts, that provides bicycle-powered waste removal for the city and private residents.

7. Community Involved in Sustaining Agriculture (CISA) launched a highly successful buy local campaign in 1999 that is recognized regionally and nationally and continues to influence the local agricultural movement in the Pioneer Valley of Massachusetts (see http://www.buylocal.org).

8. Community Supported Agriculture (CSA) is a system that mediates the economic risk of small scale farming by selling seasonal farm shares to local members who then receive weekly produce, meat, or dairy.

Works Cited

Carter, Paul. *Repressed Spaces, the Poetics of Agoraphobia.* London: Reaktion, 2002. Print.

———. *The Lie of the Land.* Faber and Faber. 1996. Print.

Deleuze, Gilles and Felix Guattari, trans. Brian Massumi. *A Thousand Plateaus: Capitalism and Schizophrenia.* Minneapolis: U of Minnesota P, 1987. Print.

DEP, *The Newtown Creek Nature Walk.* New York City Department of Environmental Protection. Brochure.

Foster, Susan. "Kinesthetic Empathies and the Politics of Compassion," *Critical Theory and Performance.* Eds. Janelle G. Reinelt and Joseph R. Roach. Ann Arbor: U of Michigan P. 2007.

———. "'Movement's Contagion: The Kinesthetic Impact of Performance.'" In *The Cambridge Companion to Performance Studies.* Eds. Tracy C. Davis, 46-59. Cambridge: Cambridge UP, 2008.

———. *Choreographing Empathy: Kinesthesia in Performance.* Routledge, 2001.

Franko, Mark. *The Work of Dance: Labor, Movement and Identity in the 1930s.* 59-85. Middletown, CT: Wesleyan UP, 2002.

Gallese, Vittorio "Empathy, Embodied Simulation, and the Brain: Commentary on Aragno and Zepf/Hartman," *Journal of the American Psychoanalytic Association* 56, 2008: 769-81.

Guattari, Felix. *The Three Ecologies.* London: The Athlone P, 2000.

Kincaid, Jamaica. *My Garden (Book).* London: Vintage, 2000.

Lippard, Lucy. *Lure of the Local: Senses of Place in a Multicentered Society.* New York: The New P, 1997.

Martin, John. *Introduction to the Dance.* New York: Dance Horizons, 1939.

Manning, Erin. *Relationscapes: Movement, Art, Philosophy.* Cambridge, MA: MIT P. 2009.

"Merriam-Webster." <merriam-webster.com>. Web. 4 March 2012.

Rizzolatti, Giacomo, et al., "From Mirror Neurons to Imitation: Facts and Speculations," *The Imitative Mind: Development, Evolution, and Brain Bases.* Eds. Andrew N. Meltzoff and Wolfgang Prinz, Cambridge, England: Cambridge UP, 2002.

"SIP/Watershed," *iLAND.* Web. 4 March 2010.

Tompkins, Peter and Chris Bird. *The Secret Life of Plants.* New York: Harper, 1989.

Chapter Nine

Indeterminate Hikes+:
Hiking Through the Urban Wilderness

Leila C. Nadir and Cary Peppermint

Indeterminate Hiking

In 2010, the ecoarttech collaborative launched an iPhone/Android mobile app called *Indeterminate Hikes+*, an environmental smartphone performative "happening" that re-imagines ecological awareness. ecoarttech's post-disciplinary work fuses theory with creative practice to deconstruct traditional environmental categories, showing the limits of preoccupations with wilderness, nature, and the rural and exploring the sort of ethics that arise from cities, suburbs, the cultural commons, and even the "virtual" environments created by new media technologies. A significant part of our practice is the effort to rethink the remoteness and inaccessibility so often applied to "nature" or "wilderness" in contemporary critical theory. This separation of the social from the natural has silenced public, democratic discourse about environmental issues, according to Bruno Latour, and for Timothy Morton, modern thinking has turned "Nature" into "a reified thing in the distance, 'over yonder,' under the sidewalk, on the other side where the grass is always greener . . . in the wild," preventing "access to the full scope of [ecological] interconnectedness" ("Ecologocentrism" 75). When we founded ecoarttech six years earlier, our aim was to create eco-art "without nature"—to borrow a phrase from Morton's book, *Ecology without Nature*—and to examine what it means to be an ecological being in the context of convergent networked environments, biological, digital, social, and cultural. *Indeterminate Hikes+* enters into dialogue with theories like those posited by Latour, Morton, and others by bringing nature out from its "reified," faraway realm and into daily life. However, *Indeterminate Hikes+* holds on to the concept of wilderness—not as a synonym for an originary Nature, which is an ethically and intellectually immobilizing concept, as Latour and Morton point out; but rather as otherness, the unimaginable, that is both part of and beyond the self, wilderness can call on us to see un-wild environments in renewed ways (see photo 9.1). In the *Indeterminate Hikes+* smartphone app, the discourse of sublime wilderness is imported into everyday locales, transforming chance encounters on the street into public performances of bio-cultural diversity and wild "happenings." Inspired by the way early- to mid-twentieth-century avant-garde art movements, particularly Fluxus, reinvigorated the way we see mundane life rituals, and drawing from our experience and involvement with the Fluid Frontier art residency program at the University of North Texas, *Indeterminate Hikes+* transforms this ethical impulse into a way to understand contemporary ecological issues and experiences of place.[1]

Fluxus

In 1961, four years after he coined the term, Fluxus artist Allan Kaprow described happenings "as events that, put simply, happen." Unlike theatrical performances, happenings are improvisational, with "no structured beginning, middle, or end." "Open-ended and fluid," they dissolve the artist-audience hierarchy through interactivity, "melting the surroundings, the artist, the work, and everyone who comes to it into an elusive, changeable configuration." Kaprow noted that happenings should take place far away from galleries and museums and instead occupy places such as artists' studios or the "sheer rawness of the out-of-doors or the closeness of dingy city quarters." The more "un-artiness" the context, the better. Adopting a metaphor with ecological and natural history resonances, Kaprow suggests that the most "radical Happenings flourish" in an appropriate "habitat": that is, "the place where anything grows up . . . giv[ing] to it not only a space, a set of relationships to the various things around it, and a range of values, but an overall atmosphere as well, which penetrates it and whoever experiences it." This atmosphere of interconnectedness produces new forms of awareness for all involved—but without any particular, intended goal: "nothing obvious is sought and therefore nothing is won, except the certainty of a number of occurrences to which we are more than normally attentive" ("Happenings in NY" 16-18). The only assured result of such a performance is the possibility of becoming attuned to any number of vague "occurrences."

New media art in general—due to its ephemerality, performativity, interactivity, and use of everyday computing devices—cannot be understood without Kaprow's concept of the happening. In *The New Media Reader*, Noah Wardrip-Fruin writes that Kaprow's essay "'Happenings' in the New York Scene" is "a touchstone for nearly every discussion of new media as it relates to interactivity in art" (83). We would like to show how *Indeterminate Hikes+* performs a particularly ecological, psychogeographical kind of happening, adapting Fluxus guidelines for performances to the democratization and re-imagination of nature and wilderness. *Indeterminate Hikes+* can be performed in two capacities: (1) as an interactive public event led by artists with audience interaction—an open-ended hiking excursion, with no clear beginning or conclusion, conducted by "guides" who facilitate an interactive, un-arty, improvisational tour (see photo 9.2); or (2) as a private event, involving a solo user and her/his smartphone. If we return to Kaprow's 1960s writings, we find that both manifestations qualify as typical happenings: there are "guided tour" performances, but with most happenings, he explains "there should not be (and usually cannot be) an audience" ("Happenings Dead" 64). Providing examples of such solitary happenings, art-as-life activities with no public staging, he includes "the unconscious daily rituals of the supermarket, subway ride at rush hour, and toothbrushing every morning" ("Pinpointing" 87). During an age of ubiquitous computing devices, walking by oneself and using a smartphone for its guiding and mapping tools is surely a new "unconscious ritual" of everyday life.

Here is a technical description of how the app works: Once they have downloaded the app, *Indeterminate Hikes+* participants provide their locations—whether in a mega-metropolis, a remote small town, or a traffic-jammed suburb—and a destination, and in turn, the app suggests a meandering hiking trail. Rather than moving us from point A to point B as quickly as possible, the app reappropriates smartphone technologies, which are generally used as devices for rapid communication and consumerism, as tools of meditation and slowing down. As hikers move along their trails, either alone, or in a group as part of a designated ecoarttech performance, they are notified when they reach a "Scenic Vista," where they are encouraged to pause and contemplate the view, much as they would during a mountain climb or a national park excursion, or at one of those pull-off stops along a scenic highway. At these stops, the app asks participants to engage in a variety activities: stopping, looking around, texting friends, taking pictures, or writing fieldnotes. The directives are designed to transform everyday, mobile spaces into places worthy of the attention accorded to sublime landscapes, such as canyons and gorges. Examples include "Follow the path of falling water," "Listen to the mood of the walking path," "Note the trees bursting from the ground," or "Wander the caverns on the surface of the earth." However, *Indeterminate Hikes+* Scenic Vistas have a decidedly different character than what one might expect on a traditional wilderness excursion. Rather than the stereotypical breathtaking, sublime panorama, where cameras are inevitably pulled from pockets (often among many like-minded tourists) to document one's arrival at a meaningful landmark, *Indeterminate Hikes+* is programmed to choose "Scenic Vistas" entirely at random. Therefore, these directives take on meaning relative to their location. "Falling water" may not be a momentous waterfall but rather a drop of liquid dripping from an air-conditioner unit in an apartment window, which falls to the sidewalk and flows eventually into a street gutter. This water, the app suggests, requires just as much attention, protection, and respect as a historically preserved natural "wonder."

Through backpacking terminology combined with Scenic Vistas' "chance operation"—a term associated with Fluxus performance artist John Cage, with whom Kaprow studied—the performance weds wilderness vocabulary to the most "civilized" spaces. This is not an ironic or sarcastic gesture. A "walking path" may be a nature trail or it may be a well-traveled concrete sidewalk; wandering "caverns" may require spelunking through caves or taking the stairs or elevators, into the vast depths of basements or skyscrapers. No matter the shape of the improvisational moment, both the artist-guides and the audience-hikers are encouraged to give these chance spectacles the attention they would give a sublime natural wonder. As Christine Oravec shows, invoking this sort of response is precisely how U.S. preservationist John Muir generated popular support for the creation of national parks through his natural history writing. Oravec identifies three elements in the "sublime response": "the immediate apprehension of a sublime object; a sense of overwhelming personal insigificance akin to awe; and ultimately a kind of spiritual exaltation" (248). *Indeterminate Hikes+* takes the inspiring "sublime response" and moves it into the space of often-disregarded locations, such as alleyways, highways, or garbage dumps—just as the avant-garde worked to take art out of academia and the privileged art-world and into the ordinary. What if we redirected the sort of sublime response, the awe and respect normally reserved for wilderness parks and nature preserves, toward the rituals and places we experience everyday? What if we call a sidewalk "wild" or toothbrushing "art"? How does this change our imagination of environmental ethics?

For anybody invested in the purity of wilderness or unable to see the ecological "otherness" that exists all around us, *Indeterminate Hikes+* can seem to have made a wrong step, and we have had participants leave our hikes in frustration. One man who found our performance nonsensical exclaimed that there were no "wild animals roaming around" as he stood at a NYC intersection busy with human pedestrians jostling their way into a subway entrance. As with Kaprow's happenings, some hikers "are not sure what has taken place"; however, "when something goes 'wrong,' something far more 'right,' more revelatory, has many times emerged. This sort of sudden near-miracle . . . [is] made more likely by chance procedures" ("Happenings in NY" 20). The growing collection of indeterminate nature photography and texting on our *Indeterminate Hikes+* hike archive demonstrates the de-hierarchization of environments, bringing domesticated, sometimes desecrated landscapes, to the level of consideration usually accorded only to "nature" (see photo 9.3). These anti-spectacles are precisely what one would not expect during a "wilderness" hike, and yet by breaking away from the clichés of traditional nature photography and narration, they create the capacity to imagine the environmental margins. They question why certain facts of modern ecological existence are wiped away from the representation of nature. What parts of nature do we admit into consciousness and what parts do we repress? What are the effects of this selective memory of the details of our lives? Do biological diversity and wildness need to be isolated from human-dominated ecosystems, in fantastical spaces set off from everyday life, such as an elevated train track, a protected nature preserve, or an isolated park? Thinking through these questions about the ecological interconnectedness of all life recalls what Wendell Berry describes as "the forever unfinished lifework of our species": the "possibility that we can live more or less in harmony" with nature (138).

While Kaprow's happenings took high art off its pedestal in part by posing ordinary life, rather than the products of genius-artists, as worthy of aesthetic attention, *Indeterminate Hikes+* uses the "structure" of happenings to bring everyday life into ecological consciousness. Kaprow cast aside the clean white cube of the gallery in favor of artists' messy studios, a place where new creativity thrives, where new ideas are born, where living art actually "happens": "Happenings invite us to cast aside . . . proper manners and partake wholly in the real nature of the art and (one hopes) life. Thus a Happening is rough and sudden and often feels 'dirty.' Dirt, we might begin to realize, is also organic and fertile, and everything, including the visitors, can grow a little in such circumstances" ("Happenings in NY" 18). The app presents improper objects of aesthetic contemplation, including environmental (aesthetic) appreciation. This defamiliarizing gesture, this anti-art anti-spectacle asks us to notice what usually falls out of the official frame, to shake up our modes of perception, and this sometimes requires that we fall away from safe, predictable paths, that we get lost in the uncertainty of the studio of life.

For the French artist-theorist Guy Debord, getting lost had revolutionary implications for the imagination of city landscapes. In his seminal "Introduction to a Critique of Urban Geography," Debord mentions a friend who deliberately got lost by "wander[ing] through the Harz region of Germany while blindly following the directions of a map of London" (7). He used his friend's solitary performance as an example of how one might re-imagine urban spaces, abandoning archaic, "functional" forms, like maps, in order to make way for an experience of a non-utilitarian modern city: what would an urban environment look like without the bias of cartography, without lines, colors, and words demarcating landmarks, highways, and neighborhoods? What if cities need not be organized the way they are, Debord asked. What if they were navigated with an emphasis on "the observation of certain processes of chance and predictability" or transformed according to what he called "psychogeographical possibilities"—that is, attuned to the effect they had on "the emotions and behavior of individuals," on human imagination and well-being—rather than laid out to accommodate "the smooth circulation of a rapidly increasing quantity of motor vehicles" (5)? Debord recommended that pedestrians stop using only "the path of least resistance" to get from place to place (6). Instead, he advocated inefficient, randomized walks, the sort that might be created by mis-mappings—or a "renovated cartography": "more or less arbitrarily transposing maps of two different regions." With *Indeterminate Hikes+*, we seek to ask: How can we hack and reinvent Google maps to navigate space in a non-instrumental way? ecoarttech does not transpose maps of two locations but rather borrows the concepts and vocabulary of natural regions and applies them where they do not belong. Such psychogeographical performances are not undertaken merely as acts of "subordination to randomness," Debord explains, but rather as "wanderings that express . . . complete *insubordination* to habitual influences" (7). By interrupting established, utilitarian patterns—and in the case of traditional environmentalism, sentimental eco-clichés of pleasing birds, flowers, and landscapes—psychogeographical performances, according to Debord, end up "flooding the market . . . with a mass of desires whose realization is not beyond the capacity of man's present means of action on the material world, but only beyond the capacity of the old social organization" (6).[2]

Performing Wilderness at a "Lake" in Denton, Texas

ecoarttech's concept for *Indeterminate Hikes+* was developed while completing a commissioned work for the University of North Texas (UNT) Fluid Frontier art residency program—and is influenced by what we learned from the local ecological and intellectual landscape.[3] As art-residents at UNT, we were asked to collaborate with students and faculty to make a new media work about any aspect of life in the Trinity Water Basin, where water is carefully managed to meet the consumption needs of northeastern Texas, including the town of Denton, where UNT is based, and the entire Dallas/Fort Worth metroplex. Coming from New England and New York State, where water is abundant, we were fascinated by the immense control of the Trinity's watershed. So little H_2O seemed to flow freely: Streams were channeled into concrete structures to prevent flash floods. Rain was routed into reservoirs to ensure that water continued to pour from household faucets. And during a tour of a treatment plant, we learned how efficiently wastewater was filtered, recycled, and returned to streams that fed the Trinity River, for more "natural" filtration, and then channeled again into household faucets. In fact, the Trinity River, over 700 miles flowing through woodlands, forests, and cities to the city, owes its flowing waters to the recycling of water from household drains. However, it became clear to us that, despite these restraints and decidedly unnatural origins, the Trinity River Basin still possessed a wildness, both ecologically and imaginatively; its water seeped beyond its designated boundaries, overflowed its bounds, and produced unexpected occurrences.

The tension between management and wildness intrigued us, and we focused in on a small body of water presented to us by UNT philosophy professor Irene Klaver, called Soil Conservation Services Hickory Creek Basin Retarding Pond #16, also known as SCS#16, or "Little Lake" by some local residents. SCS#16 was built as hydraulic infrastructure yet has come to operate also as a diverse ecological habitat and urban nature retreat. Originally constructed in 1975 as a retention/detention pond to prevent floods like those that devastated downtown Denton in 1957 and 1962, SCS #16 exceeded its function as water-retarding technology, attracting wildlife and becoming host to vibrant, hybrid cultural and ecological diversity in an urban environment. The diversity of flora, fauna, and animals have been documented by Klaver's Philosophy of Water

Project, including great blue herons, yellow-crowned night heron, egrets, ducks, fish, beavers, ballplayers, disc-golfers, kayakers, dog-walkers, picnickers, and fishermen. Through Klaver's description of this water body during one of our research trips, we were inspired by how SCS#16 became a space where social, cultural, mental, and biological ecologies converged, making way for wild events that overflowed official plans.

Although SCS#16 developed into a meaningful place of bio- and cultural diversity in its thirty-five years, public policies do not protect this un-traditional "lake"—a truly special place considering that the large state of Texas has only one naturally occurring lake within its borders; SCS#16 was treated by government institutions as a technology limited to its original objective of flood control, not as the natural, social, cultural resource it had become. For example, students involved in Klaver's Philosophy of Water Project revealed a United States Department of Agriculture Natural Resources Conservation Service (NRCS) guide for landowners, which outlines "What Living Near a Flood Prevention Site Means to You." In this document, the NRCS articulates the management benefits of sites like SCS#16 but is unable to explain how a body of flowing water also exceeds its scientific uses besides a cursory mention of "scenic beauty": "Texas watershed projects provide more than $118 million in annual benefits, which include flood prevention, sediment retention, wetland creation or enhancement, and other social benefits." Such a statement highlights, in many ways, why the humanities must be a part of the environmental debate. The roles of "social benefits" and aesthetic beauty here are undefined: undefined, indeterminable, they become the disregard-able aftereffects of the scientific management of nature. They fall into the environmental margins. Perhaps this is why, when describing "landowner responsibilities" in relation to "floodwater retarding structure[s]," the NRCS warns only that "your land may be covered by an easement." No mention of environmental protection, natural resources, or ecological-cultural commons. It seems that unless a body of water is naturally wild, it does not enter into the imagination of environmental protection. SCS#16's interconnectedness with local cultures, social structures, and biological creatures (human and nonhuman) disappeared from the scientific, governmental, and private-property record.

Prof. Klaver and her Water Project team informed us that approval had been given for the construction of a Walmart across the street. The Project's overriding concern was the parking lot that the company would construct for customers' vehicles. Because of its impermeable asphalt construction, the oil and gasoline that drips from cars to the ground would drain not into the underlying soil, where it would undergo some natural filtration, but rather into holding tanks specially designed to capture runoff. Any overflow would be channeled into pipes draining into SCS#16. In other words, concentrated solutions of oil and gasoline would pour directly into SCS#16's growing environment, endangering the biological and cultural diversity that had developed there for almost forty years. We wondered how we could use performance art and community happenings to activate the public imagination of SCS#16's "wildness," of its unique, unpredicted, always-changing qualities that make it a peaceful refuge, a sanctuary for human and nonhuman animal life, interconnected with the developed landscape. If the experience of wilderness is located "somewhere else," in specially designated safety zones, or if it is recognizable only in the form of extreme natural beauty, the places where we actually live suffer for not attaining such sublimity. As William Cronon wrote, in his groundbreaking critique of U.S. environmentalism, "Idealizing a distant wilderness too often means not idealizing the environment in which we actually live, the landscape that for better or worse we call home. Most of our most serious environmental problems start right here, at home, and if we are to solve those problems, we need an environmental ethic that will tell us as much about using nature as about not using it" (85). How to inspire a sense of ecological wonder about a water body named after a governmental agency, Soil Conservation Services, and designated by such an unlovely descriptor as the number 16? How to turn the "retarding pond" into a "lake"? And would this create the public discussion about ecology that Latour argues is the prerequisite for contemporary democracy? Although we did not conduct Indeterminate Hikes at the SCS#16 retardation pond, we interacted with and investigated the site as if it were a nature preserve, looking for moments of surprise and wildness, setting the tone for the app's development in the future.

Klaver's philosophical essay "Wild: Rhythm of Appearing and Disappearing," a text that in many ways was born of SCS#16, was inspirational for us in this effort. Rather than positing the wild as some faraway place, set off from human enterprises, Klaver sees it everywhere, in "the interstices of wildness in the grass of our backyard," in a retardation pond, and as a state of mind. That is, the undomesticated is not only the quality of the beyond- or extra-human, of nature untouched by the human hand; it can be experienced "in our everyday existence," and Klaver calls for "active everyday engagement with the world around us by affording space for the presence of otherness" and by "fostering a mentality that takes otherness, including nature, seriously and affords it a place to co-exist with and in human culture" (486) Cronon closed "Trouble with Wilderness" with a similar suggestion: "We need to honor the Other within and the Other next door as much as we do the exotic Other that lives far away" (89). With an openness attentive to what is wild nearby, Klaver writes that it is possible "to enhance and intensify our everyday life, to experience that there is always more to the here and now, and that this more is always already here" (498). This is like Debord's "renovated cartography," bringing the wilderness usually relegated to a hiking guide to the seemingly ordinary, bringing a sense of wonder to a retarding pond on the side of a highway.

For Klaver, this perspective makes life richer; for Cronon, it creates an environmental ethics more attentive to the ways we use nature in our daily lives:

> if we acknowledge the autonomy and otherness of the things and crea-tures around us—an autonomy our culture has taught us to label with the word "wild"—then we will at least think carefully about the uses to which we put them, and even ask if we should use them at all . . . wild-ness (as opposed to wilderness) can be found anywhere: in the seem-ingly tame fields and woodlots of Massachusetts, in the cracks of a Manhattan sidewalk, even in the cells of our own bodies... Learning to honor the wild—learning to remember and acknowledge the autonomy of the other—means striving for critical self-consciousness in all of our actions. (89)

The dissolution of the boundaries between the wild and the domestic, between otherness and the everyday, parallels happenings' collapse of the distinction between life and art. Hierarchies are rearranged into dem-ocratic relationships that do not privilege one entity or space over anoth-er. In his chance-driven sound performances, Fluxus musician John Cage eschewed formal compositions and adopted a Buddhist-inspired mind-fulness to attune his ear to the beauty of sounds playing out all around him, the "music" of silence or car alarms. In a special 1965 issue of *Tulane Drama Review* on the emergent movement of Fluxus happenings, Michael Kirby described how Cage's *4'33"* literally puts silence's aes-thetics on the musical stage by having an orchestra put down its instru-ments for four minutes and thirty-three seconds: "The non-playing . . . allows any 'incidental' sounds—perhaps traffic noises or crickets outside the auditorium, the creak of seats, coughing and whispering in the audi-ence—to become "music" (34). Whereas ordinary life is revealed to be art and music in the work of Kaprow and Cage, backyards and parking lots become spaces of unexpected happenings in Klaver's philosophy of environmental ethics. Everyday-ness turned extraordinary; daily rituals and noise pollution becoming art; dismissed environments treated with the sanctity afforded national parks. Influenced by Fluxus performances and Klaver's environmental philosophy, ecoarttech created a series of public outdoors and online events, collected under the title Center for Wildness and the Everyday, which performed the wild ecological diversity, both cultural and biological, of this mechanical-sounding, man-made, technological place. We would like to describe two of them here because they form the conceptual precursors for *Indeterminate Hikes+*, demonstrating how "environmental happenings" can democratize and dehierarchize ecological relationships, making way for the experience of "wilderness" in seemingly un-wild spaces.

The first work is "Untitled Algae for Portable Media Players," a mixed-media installation created with assistance from UNT graduate students Jordan Sloop and Amanda Turley. Installed at the center of the UNT Art Gallery, Untitled Algae was comprised of a "live" stock-tank full of SCS#16 water and algae, lit up by fluorescent grow lights. Sloop and Turely had grown the algae in the laboratory from a sample taken from the lake. In the gallery they carefully maintained its oxygen and temperature levels. The water filter filled the gallery with a vibrating hum, the sound of mechanical life. Also floating in the tank were mobile media players that exhibited videos comprised of SCS#16 scenery, including its "natural" retreat-like environment, Walmart's new holding pools, and microscopic images, provided by Sloop, of the algae showing the beautiful and complicated organisms in all their simplicity.[4] All the while, the algae mass drifted around the tank, a mesmerizing and beautiful cloud of shapeless green, chlorophyll without roots, stems, or leaves. This beautiful yet simplistic organism, hardly what one thinks of when pondering wilderness, is precisely what was under threat by drainage from Walmart's new parking lot into the SCS retarding pond; its life reflects the health of the fish, mammals (including humans), and exotic birds inhabiting the same waters. Although Untitled Algae was not a performance, it informed *Indeterminate Hikes+*'s attempt to dissolve the boundaries between sublime, spectacular "nature" and the environmental margins repressed out of eco-consciousness and outside the narrative frame of outdoor recreation. Untitled Algae demonstrated the wildness and the exotic beauty of a man-made reservoir—not only in its ability to attract exotic great blue herons and yellow-crowned night heron, which you might glimpse if you are lucky, but everyday, all the time, in the thriving green algae, beautiful and mysterious in its own right yet invisible to the eye trained to see only certain ecological occurrences—much like the gang of pigeons living in the AC unit is lost to the camera lens focused on the High Line's more aesthetically proper wildflowers.

One of the conditions of our UNT commission required that we "leave behind" an Internet-based artwork on the University's server. Our goal was to create a website continuing our investigation into the wildness—the appearance and disappearance, to use Klaver's definition—of water, so we constructed the networked texts of Center for the Wildness and the Everyday to be undisciplined, fluctuating, and diffuse. They appear and disappear, reflecting water's tendency to do the same. Texts fade until they are unreadable, disappearing, as water does as it soaks into the earth; images refuse to display stably and instead expand and diminish in size, as in a flash flood. When you reload a page, you never know what you will get—a chance-driven performative website appropriating the qualities of water.

One particular text within the Center for the Wildness and the Everyday (CWE) site visually documents the Trinity River. Yet ecoarttech did not want to provide more photographic images of the rambling river, flowing through cities and woodland areas. These picturesque scenes were already available all over the internet; an excellent project had already been undertaken by KERA/Public Media for North Texas, which launched a site, "Living with the Trinity: A River's Story."[5] Rather than repeat such efforts, ecoarttech attempted to interrupt popular conceptions of what a river looks like, to perform a "renovated cartography" of its flow so it would be experienced anew.[6] During our research trips and discussions with UNT faculty, we heard repeatedly that, in the water-scarce environment of North Texas, "flushing toilets keeps the Trinity River flowing." Rather than provide images of the river as it moves through naturalized areas, CWE provides a Google map of downtown instances of water flow. (See Image D.) Just as *Indeterminate Hikes+* transposes the concept of waterfall to city drips and drains, CWE identifies the Trinity River not in naturalized settings such as forests and protected sites but rather through a Google map of geo-tagged drains and faucets in the kitchen sink at the Jupiter Coffee shop, the garden hose at the Village Church, the flooded lot near the UNT campus, the grated street drain at Avenue A, the produce spray at Cupboard Natural Foods, the ancient water fountain at the used bookstore at the Opera House, and the Styrofoam cup of water enjoyed by a salesgirl at a clothing boutique.

Mapping the movement of water through downtown businesses, its over-flowing into puddles, Center for Wildness and the Everyday performs wilderness and brings the environmental margins into the representation-al mainstream.

INTERACTIVITY, PERFORMANCE, AND COUNTER-FOCALIZATION

With these performances, our aim has been to inspire participants' "counter-focalization." Coined by narrative theorist Gerard Genette, the term "focalization" refers to the point of view through which a narrative is told, which determines how and what the reader sees. More recently Gayatri Chakravorty Spivak used "counter-focalization" to describe the rhetorical effect in which the reader's questioning imagination is activat-ed. The narrator focalizes from a certain perspective, but sometimes, "the reader is provoked" to talk back, to question the intentions of the narrator (Spivak 22). Counter-focalization is not passive observation: e.g., what's going to happen? Rather, it is a process in which the reader or participant is called to exert creative effort to come to terms with an unanswerable question: e.g., What is going on here? Why does this happen this way? What do I think of this? One could say that counter-focalization is also a central part of happenings. Rather than sitting in the dark as a drama re-peats onstage, the audience is implicated during a Fluxus-inspired per-formance's chance operations. As Kaprow wrote, "You come in as a spectator and maybe you discover you're caught in it after all" ("Hap-penings in NY" 15). The results are unpredictable. This counter-focalization is also integral to the democratization of environmental dis-cussions. As long as the green movement remains preoccupied with deep ecological ideas of "nature" or natural wilderness, Latour warns, public life is divided into the human and the nonhuman with only science able to move between the two spheres. This division "render[s] all democracy impossible by neutralizing it," paralyzing discussions of the environmen-tal future to a small number of invisible authorities. "Political ecology has to let go of nature," Latour argues. While "'nature' . . . makes it pos-sible to recapitulate the hierarchy of beings in a single ordered series," political ecology "disrupts the ordering of classes of beings by multiply-ing unforeseen connections and by brutally varying their relative im-portance (14, 25, 27). Ecoarttech's performative works attempt to con-

tribute to the democratic project of political ecology by involving participants in a collective imaginative enterprise of the modern condition of
life amidst digital, biological, social, and cultural networks. In a sense,
the "readers" or participants of our works must fill in a blank that our
artworks cannot answer. That is, interactivity does not entail participants
fulfilling a pre-existing course of action or agenda; rather, our works
seek to inspire others to ask the same questions we struggle with everyday: If Nature does not exist, how can we still experience the wild otherness of our ecological environment? As Félix Guattari writes, "It is not
only species that are becoming extinct but also the words, phrases, and
gestures." Therefore, "no one is exempt from playing the game of the
ecology of the imaginary" (29, 57). This work of imagination is just as
crucial as the work of creating a just and sustainable future.

Notes

1. Please visit the *Indeterminate Hikes+* website for complete project documentation and download information for iPhone/Android: <http://ecoarttech.
org/projects/indeterminate-hike>.

2. The environmental justice movement, through its highlighting of the
disproportionate distribution of toxicity onto poor and of-color populations, has
also done significant work to disrupt the idea of the environment as a collection
of pretty landscapes.

3. Fluid Frontier is an annual exhibition and symposium produced by the
UNT's College of Visual Arts and Design and staged in collaboration with the
Philosophy Department's annual WaterWays conference.

4. These videos are included on the *Center of Wildness and the Everyday*
website produced as part of our commission. For two direct links, visit:
<http://art.unt.edu/cwetexas/algae3.html> or <http://art.unt.edu/cwetexas/algae4
.html>.

5. See <http://trinityrivertexas.org>.

6. "The Trinity River Flowing through Downtown Denton, Texas":
<http://art.unt.edu/cwetexas/map.html>.

Works Cited

Berry, Wendell. "Preserving Wildness." In *Home Economics: Fourteen Essays.*
Berkeley: Counterpoint, 2009. 137-51.

Cronon, William. "The Trouble with Wilderness; or, Getting Back to the Wrong Nature." In *Uncommon Ground: Rethinking the Human Place in Nature.* Ed. William Cronon. NY: W.W. Norton, 1996. 69-90. Print.

Debord, Guy-Ernest. "Introduction to a Critique of Urban Geography." 1955. In *Situationist International Anthology.* Ed. and trans. Ken Knabb. Berkeley: Bureau of Public Secrets, 1981. 5-7. Print.

Guattari, Félix. *The Three Ecologies.* 1989. Trans. I. Pindar & P. Sutton. Lodon: Athlone Press, 2000. Print.

Latour, Bruno. *Politics of Nature: How to Bring the Sciences Into Democracy.* Trans. Catherine Porter. Cambridge: Harvard UP, 2004. Print.

Kaprow, Allan. "Happenings in the New York Scene." 1961. In *Essays on the Blurring of Art and Life.* Ed. Jeff Kelley. Berkeley: U of California P, 2003. 15-26. Print.

———. "Pinpointing Happenings." In *Essays on the Blurring of Art and Life.* Ed. Jeff Kelley. Berkeley: U of California P, 2003. 84-9. Print.

———. "Happenings are Dead: Long Live the Happenings!" In *Essays on the Blurring of Art and Life.* Ed. Jeff Kelley. Berkeley: U of California P, 2003. 59-65. Print.

Kirby, Michael. "The New Theatre." *The Tulane Drama Review* 10.2 (Winter 1965): 23-43. Print.

Klaver, Irene. "Wild: Rhythm of Appearing and Disappearing." In *The Wilderness Debate Rages On: Continuing the Great New Wilderness Debate.* Eds. Michael P. Nelson and J. Baird Callicott. Athens: U of Georgia P, 2008. 485-99. Print.

Living with the Trinity. <http://trinityrivertexas.org>. Living with the Trinity, n.d. Web.

Morton, Timothy. "Ecologocentrism: Unworking Animals." *SubStance* 37.3 (2008): 73-96. Print.

———. *Ecology without Nature: Rethinking Environmental Aesthetics.* Cambridge: Harvard UP, 2007. Print.

Oravec, Christine. "John Muir, Yosemite, and the Sublime Response." *Quarterly Journal of Speech* 67 (1981): 250-8. Print.

Spivak, Gayatri Chakravorty. "Ethics and Politics in Tagore, Coetzee, and Certain Scenes of Teaching." *Diacritics* 32.3-4: 17-31. Print.

Wardrip-Fruin, Noah. "Introduction to 'Happenings in the New York Art Scene.'" In *The New Media Reader.* Eds. Noah Wardrip-Fuin and Nick Monfort, 2003. 83. Print.

Part III

MATERIALS AND PROCESSES

Chapter Ten

Indigenous Theatre in Global Times: Situated Knowledge and Ecological Communities in *Salmon Is Everything* and *Burning Vision*

Theresa J. May

Stories are ecological forces. Like a hurricane or a drought, they shape the land around us. We don't have to look very far to see that the material consequences of stories are inscribed in bodies and the land. Everywhere that environmental degradation exists it seems injustice has also left its mark. For this reason efforts toward sustainability must include social and environmental justice and recognition of the central importance of cultural (as well as biological) diversity. A story is a product of connection that maintains a field of contact not only among people but also between people and place. Stories create a matrix of belonging, a living tissue between past and present, and between human and nonhuman communities; and in this way, stories help heal the earth and ourselves.[1] In this chapter I show how two indigenous plays— *Burning Vision* and *Salmon Is Everything*—exercise the power of story to effect ecological healing.

In the theatre, stories *take place*, conjured before us by living performers and materials which were (and are) part of a living environment. Audiences attend in the flesh, bearing witness to actions that happen before them. As an ephemeral, embodied art, theatre reminds us that—no matter how abstracted, destabilized, or virtualized—our existence is always in situ. Ecocriticism, like gender, postcolonial, or multicultural theories, must address injustices felt in the body—the body of experience, of community, of land. Latina poets Cherríe Moraga and Gloria Anzaldúa have articulated this "theory in the flesh" as one that arises from "the physical realities of our lives—our skin color, the land or concrete we grew up on, our sexual longings [which] all fuse to create a politic born out of necessity" (23). Both plays I discuss below deal with land/body wounds in which the ecological impact of rapacious resource use is felt in the human and nonhuman communities. In both plays indigenous intellectual and artistic traditions show how situated knowledge—knowledge specific to culture and place—can help heal ecological wounds.

Examples of what I call "ecodramaturgy", *Burning Vision* and *Salmon Is Everything* suggest we think of our planet as a neighborhood—a place of ecological as well as social relations.[2] Neighborhood, as these plays demonstrate, is a visceral, embodied, familiar sense of belonging and being known. The experience of "neighborhood" escapes many of us much of the time in this post-local, post-place world. Theatre can conjure the embodied experience of neighborhood—at least for a few hours at a time—while simultaneously redefining what we mean by neighborhood. In *Burning Vision*, neighborhood is wrought by the use and misuse of a rock; in *Salmon Is Everything*, neighborhood is a river of relationships touched by salmon.

You have probably seen the bumper sticker, "think globally, act locally." When we are acting locally, however, we are also acting globally (or "glocally"). The two plays I discuss below make this catchphrase palpable by theatricalizing what sustainability discourse sometimes refers to as the life cycle of things. One of the keys to sustainability is to live with the cognizance of the life cycle of the myriad products we use every day.[3] Each thing—this pencil, this keyboard—has a life cycle that begins as some natural resource (wood, graphite, petroleum) and passes through many human hands before it reaches mine. In this way, I am connected (as in touch) to all those others who shaped this thing. This material connection links me to the places as well as the people that have been part of the life cycle of this product. The material world asserts our interdependence even as it demonstrates our ethics with regard to that world. We touch others and are touched by them in every moment of each day through the products and goods that we change and exchange. Both plays demonstrate how such stories of "vibrant matter" can be brought into the light and *material presence* of the stage, illuminating a web of ecological consequences.[4]

Burning Vision: A Quantum Neighborhood

Certain events (political and ecological) are of such a magnitude that the human interconnectivity they signal cannot be ignored. Surely the droughts, storms, and heat waves of climate change are such events. The detonation of the first atomic bomb over Hiroshima, Japan, on August 6, 1945, was another. Like these events, theatre can call us to the same table. In *Burning Vision*, Marie Clements weaves spatial and temporal images to tell an untold story of the making of the first atomic bomb, beginning with a countdown, followed by the "sound of a long, far-reaching explosion that explodes over a long, far-reaching time" (19). The arc of the play then transpires in the split second between that first flash of light and its reign/rain of sudden death. In this time-outside-of-time the play makes visible a web of human agency that binds together places, people, and creatures across the globe. But it does so while simultaneously calling attention to local places, individual experience, diverse and specific cultural perspectives.

Burning Vision is written in four "movements," like an orchestral score. Giving new meaning to "nonlinear," it lacks the predictable dramatic structures of beginning/exposition, middle/action, end/resolution. The whole play is about being in the middle. Like an Escher painting, the middle moment is a site of intersection, what Gloria Anzaldúa has called "the borderlands/*la frontera.*" Being in-between is a place of deep wounding: a crisis. The current ecological crisis has surely thrust society into such a middle moment, one that, like Escher's paintings, requires transformation.

Reading Clements reminds us that drama is not merely a genre of literature, but an imagined event that is meant to be realized in a community space and time. Too often in literary ecocriticism of drama, plays are treated solely as texts, with little analysis paid to their performative aspects, which have as much or more to do with meaning-making than the words on the page! Clements's play does not lay nicely on the page, offering up its meaning to literary logic. Rather, like an orchestral score, it is meant to be seen, heard, felt, *played.*

The voices and images of each movement emerge, overlap, intersect, and collide. Between each movement, the sound of caribou hooves on tundra seems to drive us deeper into the play's vision of connection. Traditional Dene communities follow the migration of caribou around Great Bear Lake; and so, through the sounds of hooves and the voice of the Dene elder and prophet, the action of the play proceeds and comes round to where it began: the moment of "now," the middle moment, in which time and space split open in the detonation of the first atomic bomb.[5]

In 2010, I directed Marie Clements's *Burning Vision* for the University of Oregon. Clements is from Vancouver, B.C., and many of her plays have been staged in Toronto, Montreal, and elsewhere in Canada. Our production was the first staging of *Burning Vision* in the United States. Members of my production team complained that Clements's play was "too postmodern." Time does not pass as the action unfolds. Instead, the play insists on another kind of time: an intersecting, simultaneous time that bends upon and within itself, defying rational chronology in favor of a transcendent now. Similarly, the play blurs the boundaries of space/place and ruptures any sense of geographic logic, as characters in Japan emerge from the bottom of a lake in Northern Canada, or a factory worker from Pittsburgh descends into the belly of the earth. Once the written text is played onstage, conventional boundaries of time and space evaporate, and different historical moments collapse in on one another in a kind of double and triple exposure. After reading the script, one team member exclaimed, "It's as if she wrote several narratives and then cut them up with a pair of scissors and pasted them together again in some random fashion!" *Burning Vision*'s dramaturgy is not postmodern; rather, it is indigenous, grounded and expressing First Nations' intellectual traditions and worldviews. In "The Ceremonial Motion of Indian Time: Long Ago, So Far," Paula Gunn Allen explains "achronology" as that "tribal concept of time [that is] timelessness." Similarly, a tribal concept of space is multidimensional. Indigenous understandings of time and space are similar, she observes, to those of contemporary physics, in that the self is conceived "as a moving event within a moving universe" (Allen 69). Clements's play moves beyond magical realism into a laser-focused *contemplative realism*—a dreamtime. The play's achronological structure allows a searing vision to blow our minds—and here I mean mind as the set of habitual mental frames through which we view the world—to rupture the hegemonic assumption that we are separate from one another, the planet, or our collective history.

Burning Vision grew out of Clements's desire to trace her family's history in the Northwest Territory. "I had taken a trip to the Great Bear Lake region with my mother. I wanted to tell this story of my family's genetic connection to the history of the land up there, and to the running of uranium."[6] The play follows the route of the "black rock," from which both radium and uranium are harvested and plutonium is made. From the first decision to unearth it, through the laboring of the miners and "sandwich girls," the Dene ore carriers, and the captains and stevedores that worked along its watery passage across Great Bear Lake and down the Mackenzie River to Fort McMurray, where it was loaded on trains bound for Ontario refineries and, eventually, the labs and test sites of the Manhattan Project.[7] Clements maps the intersections of indigenous Dene culture, extractive capitalism, global ideological conflicts and the military-industrial juggernaut to presence a global neighborhood of very local lives onstage. Weaving together the stories of those who worked on and in the mine with the stories of Japanese characters in Hiroshima, Clements challenges how we remember and whom we remember, creating a transnational "countergeography" that makes previously invisible relationships both explicit and meaningful.[8]

The cast of characters in this trans-national, trans-temporal, trans-species, inter-cultural neighborhood include: the LaBine brothers (who started El Dorado Mine at Port Radium); a Miner; an Icelandic Riverboat Captain; Dene stevedores; a Dene Widow; Dene radio announcers; a Japanese fisherman and his Grandmother in Hiroshima; a Radium Dial Painter; Tokyo Rose (a fictional radio personality of World War II); Lorene Greene (a Canadian radio host during WWII); Fat Man, a "test dummy" who lives in a mock home in Nevada's Jornada del Muerto; and Little Boy, the personification of the rock itself. Movement by movement, these individuals collide with one another like atoms in a nuclear explosion. In the midst of this diverse and metaphorically resonant community, Rose, a young Métis woman, makes bread.

"What was extraordinary to me," Clements said, is that "one person's decision not only impacts that person and their community, but has an effect beyond, in this case, an effect that encompasses the whole world." The "money rock," as the Dene called it, was claimed by white prospectors and mined on Dene land at Great Bear Lake, Port Radium. "The decision to unearth is an extraordinary event. You can't go back," Clements claimed, and so began her play with that moment of so-called discovery.[9] The LaBine Brothers, as the prospectors who laid "claim" to the ore and founded El Dorado Mine, thrash about in the dark of the theatre, collide with walls and objects, and discuss what to "trade" for their claim. "What's an Indian gonna do with money? We'll give him some lard and baking powder and he can bake some bread. Sure! What the hell! What the hell is an Indian going to do with a rock anyways, at least he can eat the bread" (37). According to the oral account of Dene elders (which carry the same authority as written eyewitness accounts under Canadian law), the whites traded sacks of flour for the ore: "They say it was . . . Beyonnie, who first found the money rock at Port Radium. Beyonnie gave it to the white man, for which he received a bag of flour, baking powder and lard about four times" (Gilday 108). Bread is payment for the ore from which the bomb is made.

As the play follows the life-cycle of two products—bread and bomb—it draws our attention to things made by human hands. Clements's play is about making: making bread, making bombs, making enemies, making love, making family, and about taking responsibility for what we have made. Calling attention to the flesh of our bodies and that of the plants and animals we take for sustenance, Rose describes herself as a "perfect loaf of bread" that "is plump with a rounded body and straight sides. I have a tender, golden brown crust which can be crisp, or delicate. This grain is fine and even, with slightly elongated cells; the flesh of this bread is multi-grained" (58). Each of us is just such a grainy substance of self. We make ourselves, Rose suggests, by the way we engage the elements of the earth.

A function of relationship, *making* infers transaction, invokes connectivity, and results in a transformation of substance. Environmental historian Richard White has observed in his treatise on nature and work "Are You an Environmentalist? Or Do You Work for a Living?", that our labor is the very *site* of our kinship with the things of the earth. He argues that "our work—all our work—inevitably embeds us in nature" (185). Work, then, is a way of knowing, an expression of our intimacy with the environment. Rose mixes the ingredients for her bread throughout the four Movements, "substances meeting like magic" she says (39) "Flour, yeast, salt, sugar, lard, liquid. Bread" (59). Eventually the sacks of flour become indistinguishable from the sacks of ore. The wind mixes the white flour leaking from Rose's sack with the black dust that infects the environment. "The wind's blowing it everywhere," Rose observes, "The kids are playin' in sandboxes of it, the caribou are eating it off the plants, and we're drinkin' the water where they bury it . . . I guess there's no harm if a bit gets in my dough" (103). Both bread and ore are *material* aspects of the earth's body and become our bodies.

Similarly, Clements personifies the two atomic bombs dropped by the United States on Hiroshima and Nagasaki, mapping the life cycle of the ore from mine to transport to factory to test site.[10] In Dene worldview the ore is a living being, personified in the play as "Little Boy" a "beautiful Native boy . . . the darkest uranium found at the center of the earth." Little Boy is "discovered," chased, captured; then escapes and runs. He is desperate to "go home," back to his place in the earth, but once loose upon the earth he cannot go back. The character of Fat Man is a "test dummy" from the 1940s and 1950s aboveground tests in Nevada, in which mock homes came complete with foodstuffs, canned goods, appliances, and mannequins that represented the stereotypical 1950s nuclear family. Fat Man animates the mindset that made the bomb. He is ideology incarnate: an all-American male, a "living room soldier" (94). As a manikin, he is a thing made, like a loaf of bread (34). The characterizations materialize two indigenous ideas: that the stuff of the earth is alive and must be treated with respect and discretion, and that ideas and stories (like that of Fat Man, 1950s xenophobia, the nuclear family) have power to shape and reshape the world.

Like the play's four movements, the four primary elements of earth, air, water, and fire call attention not only to how we use (what we make with) the material substance of the earth, but how we are commingled with the land around us. The Dene Widow, lamenting the loss of her husband to cancer caused by exposure to the radioactive ore, knows that the land resides in the fabric of our bodies: "I miss the smell of sweat on his clothes after a long day hunting. I miss how the land stayed in the fabric even when he got inside the cabin" (44-45). In a dream, she pulls him to her, calling on their kinship with the earth, and resisting the doomsday change that her waking hours struggle to comprehend. "There are plenty of trout and caribou to last us till we die" (70).

Even as the Widow prays that nothing will change, the bodies of workers who came in contact with the ore are changed, transfigured. In the 1920s and '30s radium dial painters, mostly women aged sixteen to twenty, painted clock dials with radium paint so that military personnel could read time in the dark.[11] Encouraged to lick their brushes to produce a fine tip for painting, many radium painters developed disfiguring cancers like radium jaw.[12] The bodies of the Radium Painter and the Miner (coughing with disease) carry the markers of human intimacy with the earth. When she turns to him, their dance is cut short: "half her face . . . missing and her beautiful hair is entirely gone" (117). One of the strategies of ecodrama, seen here, is to show that what we do to and on the land is writ in our bodies. Like the land, we are living archives of human action.

Richard White argues that we must "pursue the implications of our labor and our bodies in the natural world" (185). The moral implication of our capacity to take and to make becomes clear when the Widow chides Rose, whose face is white with flour from making bread: "you gonna get rich like those LaBine Brothers wanna be. They should be prospecting bread, instead of putting their hands on things that shouldn't be touched" (55). The Dene Widow questions economic gain for its own sake, but she also, by implication, asks what else might have been done with the billions of dollars and thousands of human work-hours spent on making a weapon that endangered the whole planetary community, and points to the moral uncertainty that would later haunt Manhattan Project workers, most of whom were not aware of the products of their labor (see Fermi and Samra).

Great Bear Lake is one of the largest and deepest freshwater lakes in the world, and its presence percolates through the soundscape of *Burning Vision*. The lake is the center of life for traditional Dene who depend on it for sustenance (Gilday; Abel). Dene villages fished for trout and followed the seasonal migration of caribou herds around the lake.[13] Linking actions with consequences, *Burning Vision* connects Koji, a Japanese fisherman who has just caught a trout at the edge of the sea in Hiroshima, with the source-site of the ore. In a Dene legend a medicine man journeys to the heart of Great Bear Lake. After a "trout steals the medicine man's hook . . . he dives deep into the lake's abyss" to retrieve his hook. He "takes on the spirit of the loche" and there he finds "a living, breathing heart, called the Tudzé" that gives life to the world of plants, animals and human beings.[14] In Clements's play, Eldorado's wet-mine tunnels become liminal passageways that, as the Miner says, "go all the way to China [or Japan]." At the moment of the atomic blast in Hiroshima, Koji, his exclamation resonating with the Dene story of Tudze, cries "Pika!"–the Japanese word for the brilliant flash of atomic detonation–meaning "the light of two suns." Letting go of the cherry tree where his Obachan (grandmother) told him to wait, Koji falls into darkness, journeys through the tunnels, and surfaces, trout-like, in Great Bear Lake where two stevedores on the Radium Prince haul him out of the water, and where Rose gives him dry clothing and the possibility of new life.

Soundscape and lighting effects carry the memory of the fireball that swept out from ground zero in Hiroshima, vaporizing flesh and turning sand to glass. But there is another fire, too. The Widow keeps a vigil fire kindled by her grief, where she conjures the young Dene husband she lost to the ore. She tends the fire, but is also trapped by it. Traditional Dene practice is to burn the earthly possessions of those who die so that they may cross over,[15] but the Widow cannot let go of her lover's clothes, especially a jacket that she made and beaded.[16] "It is always the little things of his that take my breath away. The real things like a strand of his hair lying on the collar of a caribou hide jacket he loved . . . the real things like the handle of his hunting knife worn down from his beautiful hands that loved me. The real things . . ." (87).

Koji also sites/sights the real, the "little things," as his spirit roams the post-blast "landscape of notes." "There are notes left on anything that still exists. On pieces of houses, on stones shivering on the ground, on anything that did not perish . . . hope remains nailed to what has survived . . . a tin box of pictures, a rock wall, a rice bowl . . . a chair, a typewriter, a neighbor, a woman" (51). As Fat Man, the nuclear "test dummy," realizes that, like the ore, the lake, and the air itself, he is being used as an instrument of war, even Fat Man is radicalized (13). Finally aware of his connection to the others, he cries out in rage and realization: "This is my neighborhood!" (115). Mapping the making of ore into bomb, Clements points to a new trans-local neighborhood. It demonstrates indigenous understandings of the interplay of self, community, land, and spirit. It insists on a radical, familial connectivity between and among people, and between people and the more-than-human world. Theatre is a place where these kinds of neighborhoods can be made real, palpable— for they are no less material than any other.

Now I want to turn to a play that is more local, but no less global in its resonance, as indigenous people everywhere are struggling to maintain the integrity of both cultures and places. In this discussion my emphasis is equally on the process of writing/making the play and performance, and I argue that the quality of process demonstrates an indigenous way of working—what a Karuk elder called working "in a good way."[17]

Salmon Is Everything: **Theatre of Place**

In September 2002 an estimated 70,000 salmon died on the banks of the Lower Klamath River. At the time I was assistant professor at Humboldt State University, located about forty minutes south of the mouth of the Klamath, on California's north coast. The fish kill, as locals called the event, impacted Native fisheries, as well as commercial fishing, in ways that are still being studied. Shortly after the fish kill, I attended a kind of emergency meeting of scientists, fish and wildlife officials, and water policy folks. I noticed two things at this meeting that stayed with me into the weeks that followed: 1) the room was electric with antagonisms, perceptible even through the veil of academic presentations; and 2) the back of the room was crowded with people from the tribal communities, for whom the catastrophe was not only economically measurable, but profoundly painful. The loss of the salmon signified an ongoing loss of traditional cultural ways of life for the Karuk, Hupu, and Yurok communities who live in the lower Klamath watershed. This loss, however, was not a topic in the room. The several elders sitting in the back were silent even as policy wonks and government officials presented theories about the causes of the fish kill and suggested potential directions for watershed management.

The salmon crisis on the Klamath produced bitter polarization between the Native people downriver, and the farmers and ranchers in the
upper valley. (Several dozen dams on the river regulate water flow to
provide irrigation for the farmers.) As scientists and politicians became
increasingly ineffectual, local civic groups hired professional mediators.
As an artist living in a community facing such a situation I asked, "what
can theatre do?" Initiating the Klamath Theatre Project I hoped to tap
theatre's power to touch the human heart by developing a performance in
collaboration with the people who are directly affected by the salmon
crisis—Yurok, Karuk, and Hupa communities. The project's aim was to
open dialogue, grow compassion, and build consensus around the complex issues that plague the watershed. Over two years I worked with Native students, staff and faculty, as well as community members, to write a
play that expressed the experiences and viewpoints of Native people,
whose relationship with the salmon seemed to be going unacknowledged
in national media.

The play was developed from interviews with Lower Klamath tribal
members, as well as reflective and creative writing done by students. Research and stakeholder meeting transcripts allowed us to weave in the
voices of farmers, ranchers, and other constituents of the Klamath watershed. Over two years, we read various versions of the script at community meetings and then listened to and gathered suggestions from the community on how to develop the play further. The final script, *Salmon Is
Everything* (the title taken from an elder's description of the salmon's
central place in Klamath culture) premiered in spring 2006, performed by
a cast of twelve Native and five non-Native actors (most of whom had
never acted before). In the community discussions held after every performance an audience of the real-world counterparts of the fictional
characters of tribal families, scientists, farmers, ranchers, and others
commented that what had been contentious and impossible in mediation
rooms and courtrooms became possible in the theatre: people found
themselves listening to one another's stories.

Elders remarked that the play spoke about their experience in the
manner of traditional storytelling, and young people said "this is the only
way we're going to solve these issues, by listening to one another's stories; not through governments and lawyers, but through people." As a
record of collective memory, *Salmon Is Everything* serves to locate the
fish kill of 2002 as a turning point in the politics of the watershed, to
mark and call attention to the grief experienced by members of the Lower Klamath tribal communities, and to illuminate the current and ongoing

debates about dam removal, species preservation, indigenous rights, and the sustainable use of resources.

The story of the 2002 fish kill is part of a larger story, and a larger healing. The Klamath Theatre Project and the process of developing *Salmon Is Everything* provides a model for the ways in which theatre's methodology can voice collective memory and contribute to healing historical trauma. At the heart of community-based theatre is the knowledge that the land holds stories, and like layers of sediment, these stories deserve to be told not only to know our local and regional histories, but also to *allow the past to participate in our decisions about the future.*

We faced questions and problems about how to develop a work with non-actors whose cultural traditions do not necessarily include theatre. Whose story is being told? Is it enough to tell the story of the marginalized community? Who "owns" the stories? The question of authority is very important in community-based theatre, and it's not an easy one. Certainly another significant issue for me, as an outsider, was how to engage and empower my Native students, while getting myself increasingly out of the way. The depth of the grief around the fish kill was such that elders were reluctant to talk about it and Native young people were angry, distrustful. This tenderness in the community was a constant reminder that community-based theatre is not merely about making a performance, it's about the process; what happens in the process is perhaps even more significant than the final product.

Our development process was committed to ongoing dialogue with community members about the work, about the story being told, about the final product, and its audience address. As Native students conducted interviews in the community, word of the project spread. In *Native American Drama*, Christy Stanlake presents Choctaw writer LeeAnne Howe's idea of "story bundles" as the process by which the empathic space created by storytelling gives rise to shared feelings and new stories in response (109). In this way, after each reading of our script-in-process, discussions brought forth more stories and perspectives that made their way into the script.

From the beginning, we wanted the play to make the distinction that for indigenous people of the Klamath River, the salmon is more than food, more than an environmental problem; it contains and carries a sense of self, a community identity, and spirituality. The following scene between the character of Julie, a young Yurok/Karuk student and mother, and Kate, her non-Native co-worker, captures a crucial difference between indigenous perspectives and non-Natives:

JULIE: But for us the threat of extermination is immediate, just like it is for the fish. You come here doing your research that will eventually get you some good agency job. You care, sure, but if the salmon go extinct, you'll find some other species to save. For my family, if the salmon don't survive my grandmother will die of a broken spirit. You called that fish "brother"—
KATE: When?
JULIE: —a couple minutes ago—but it's a metaphor for you. It's *not a metaphor* for us! My people have lived here for 10,000 years or more. (*increasingly angry as if something unstoppable is welling up from within her*) My people live here, they die here. They are the trees, the water, the fish. That the salmon are brothers is not some kind of myth; the salmon are not symbols of life, they are life. We have maintained a healthy balance with the river and the salmon and everything else because it's all one body, one family. If the salmon die, we break apart; the salmon make life make sense!

When a person has lived on the land, taken sustenance from it, buried the dead within it, and maintained a long-standing, generational relationship of mutual care with it and the creatures that dwell there, that land is not only home, it is kin: familial flesh.

We also wanted the play to demonstrate the profound intimacy that indigenous people traditionally share with the more-than-human world. In the following excerpt, the character of Will, Julie's partner, a subsistence Karuk fisherman, speaks to Tim, an Upper Klamath rancher:

WILL: I've lived in the Klamath River system my entire life. The river is part of me, the life-blood of my people . . . The Klamath is my home, my church, garden, highway, counselor, friend, brother—hell, provider . . . . The carnage I've seen over the weeks is so utterly disgusting I can't sleep. I close my eyes and the images of dead, rotting fish— maybe you've seen photographs . . . but you cannot begin to imagine the smell. The smell of death and decay messes with my mind. I can't eat because food, no matter what it is, reminds me of the smell. Come walk along the banks of the river with me . . . I dare you . . . Come and walk with me and cut open the bellies of rotten salmon to detect their sex . . . Come and walk with me . . . count with me . . . hack their tails so they won't be recounted. You can't escape the smell. This is a real life situation. It's not a book; it's not pretend. It's not something you read about that happened a hundred years ago. It's happening right now, today. To people in my life. Maybe all your rancher and farmer friends up there don't understand that. You tell them to get the hell down here and help us clean up this mess that they helped make.[18]

Theatre, unlike town hall meetings and city council meetings, embraces rage and grief. The pivotal convention of theatre—the "willing suspension of disbelief"—can also mean that people are more apt to suspend their beliefs about one another, including their enemies. It gives human emotions space to be. Theatre can be a place where we listen from the heart and give one another the benefit of the doubt.

Salmon Is Everything provided a forum for acknowledging pluralism, for giving voice to stories that represented distinct knowledge, which, while not shared by all members of a community, nonetheless enriched all members. In the imaginary world of the play that was eventually created, those groups and individuals who held so much ill will toward one another spoke to one another through representation, as if in a dream. We were surprised and heartened by tribal members who came long distances to see the performance. Each night the theatre was full, and with many people who had never been to our campus before. In this way, the concrete results of the process occurred onstage, in the moment of performance, as well as in the discussions and interactions following the performances. Tribal members invited us to take the show on tour through the Klamath Watershed, offering their homes and help. They called it the "take it home tour" in honor of the elders who came to see the performance and said to us afterward, "This is a good thing that you have done. You have told the story. Now we have to take it home. We have to share it with all the people in the watershed who are represented here."[19] Community-based theatre is more than a preamble to social justice activism, it *is* civic action. Transcending the town hall, theatre functions as a site of collective dreaming where a seemingly impossible future might be envisioned.

The process embodied Iris Marion Young's notion of "communicative democracy," in which situated knowledge is recognized and valued over so-called common ground. The performance development process raised complex questions of authority and ownership of stories, as well as of the politics of representation, and of the collision of so-called "Western" theatre conventions and Native storytelling. The project's resonance and implications go beyond the local, mapping the global connections that are implicit in, and complicit with, local land and water use and indigenous rights. As a local expression of the politics of water rights, environmental restoration, and social justice, *Salmon Is Everything* resonates trans-locally, serving as an example of how grassroots theatre might participate in social justice advocacy and in community healing.

Conclusion

Indigenous perspectives call forth a simultaneous past, present, and future. The spirit world coexists with the embodied world in which nothing of the earth or made by human hands is inanimate. The land is filled with ancestral stories. Community (neighborhood) includes the rocks, trees, streams, and animal others of that place. The invitation of both *Burning Vision* and *Salmon Is Everything* is to contemplate how we are always/already touching others who are out of sight and out of mind.[20] Clements's play makes use of the space of possibility that is theatre to suggest that each object, each material, each thing that we interact with in our contemporary lives can tell a story of how we are connected. The uranium rock, the sack of flour, a trout, a fire, a caribou hide jacket, a work boot, a cherry tree: everything is spirit-filled, alive with presence.

The indigenous perspective in both these plays asks us to perceive our material interconnectivity even across the divides of space and time. In *Burning Vision*, Clements has conjured a transnational neighborhood. In *Salmon Is Everything*, local experience speaks out of its specific time and place to endangered watersheds around the world. In both plays the idea of "neighborhood" carries implications for what environmentalists mean by "sustainability" and what activists mean by "community." If we are to have the former, we must be centrally concerned with the latter. On stage, neighborhood is a web of interdependent, reciprocal, local-yet-global relationships—both ecological and cultural—that fuse the concerns of justice and cultural identity with those of ecological sustainability.

Theatre has an important role to play in ecological survival and healing not only because we can tell stories that inspire change or get people thinking in new ways, but also because stories are actually part of our ecology: they have a material impact on the land, on our communities, even on our bodies. Stories are all around us, layered in the land like geologic sediment, and built into our towns and villages and cities. The choices we make about the stories we tell are crucial. We've seen the damage that stories can create. The story of the American frontier, for example, sanctioned genocide, the near extinction of certain animal species, and rapacious use of resources. The story of the garden paradise propelled vast hydroelectric projects intended to "tame" wild rivers of the West. Artists must remember and ask: Are we buying into and recycling stories that have already done damage? Or are we encouraging and nurturing stories that heal—perhaps ones that have been silenced and need to be told, or ones that we have not yet dared to dream?

Notes

1. I have written similarly about the ecological force of stories and story-making in other publications over the past fifteen years. See, for example, "Beyond Bambi" and "Consequences Unforeseen."

2. "Ecodramaturgy," as I coined it in "Kneading Marie Clements' *Burning Vision*" (*Canadian Theatre Review*) is "play-making (both script development and production) that puts ecological reciprocity and community at the center of its theatrical and thematic intent." However, I have been discussing this approach to theatre making in publications since 1994.

3. This idea is much discussed in sustainability discourse. See, for example, work by Durning and Braungart.

4. See, for example, *Vibrant Matter: A Political Ecology of Things* by Hope Franklin

5. See *Drum Songs: Glimpses of Dene History* by Kerry Abel, 23-27.

6. Dene communities are still coping with the health and environmental impact of the radium mining; however, scientific study of long-term health effects on Dene communities has yet to be conducted. See, for example, Abel.

7. The array of Manhattan Project locations spanned the United States, and included Chicago, Illinois; Berkeley, California; Oak Ridge, Tennessee; Hanford, Washington; Los Alamos, New Mexico; and Nevada's test site at Jornada del Muerto. See Rachel Fermi and Esther Samra or Anthony Cave Brown and Charles B. MacDonald.

8. "Countergeography" is a term drawn from the discourse of critical globalization studies referring to the strategic re-mapping of people, places, and the effects of globalization. See, for example, *Critical Globalization Studies*, Richard P. Appelbaum and William I. Robinson, eds., 155-166.

9. In preparation for directing *Burning Vision*, I spoke with Marie Clements on 12 November 2009. The connection between her family history and the play is also discussed by Nelson Gray in his paper "Canadian Theatre and the Ecopolitics of Place" in *Readings in Performance and Ecology*, Wendy Arons and Theresa J. May, eds.

10. I use the term "personify" here because it will be familiar to readers. However, it is important to understand that what non-Native people understand as a figure of speech, a technique of text and stage, is actual for First Nations

and Native Americans: that is, things have spirit and power. See, for example, Paula Gunn Allen.

11. See, for example, Ross Mullner, *A Deadly Glow: The Radium Dial Worker Tragedy.*

12. Radium, like calcium, attaches to the bone, and poisoning typically produced malformations of bone tissue, particularly in the face and jaw. See Mullner.

13. See, for example, Olive Patricia Dickason, *A Concise History of Canada's First Nations*, and Abel.

14. The legend can be found on the website of the Canadian Broadcast Company (CBC) North as part of a story about the making of a documentary entitled "Waterheart: The Deline Project" in which Dene elders tell their stories about the uranium mining on their land. See http/www.cbc.ca/north/features/ waterheart 1/11/2010.

15. See Abel, 23.

16. Dene clothing design is often intricately beaded and highly ornamented. See, for example, Thompson.

17. Karuk elder Susanne Burcell. Personal conversation, 2006.

18. This monologue was adapted from an essay entitled "For My People Salmon Is Everything" by Barry McCovey, Jr., and published in *Yurok News* shortly after the 2002 fish kill.

19. Ron Reed, Karuk Cultural Resources Director. 7 May, 2006.

20. Paula Gunn Allen, Jaye T. Darby and others discuss the holistic worldview and multidimensionality of space and time in indigenous drama in *American Indian Theater and Performance: A Reader*, Hanay Geiogmah and Jaye T. Darby, eds. See also, Christy Stanlake, *Native American Drama: A Critical Perspective*, especially Chapter 4.

Works Cited

Abel, Kerry. *Drum Songs: Glimpses of Dene History*. Montreal: McGill Queen's UP, 2005.

Allen, Paula Gunn. "The Sacred Hoop: A Contemporary Perspective" in *American Indian Theater in Performance: A Reader*. Hanay Geiogmah and Jaye T. Darby, eds. Los Angeles: UCLA American Indian Studies Center, 2000.

Anzaldúa, Gloria. *Borderlands/La Frontera: The New Mestiza*. 3rd Edition, San Francisco: Aunt Lute Books, 2008.

Appelbaum, Richard P., and William I. Robinson, eds. *Critical Globalization Studies*. New York: Routledge, 2005.

Artaud, Antonin. *The Theatre and Its Double*. Mary Caroline Richards, Trans. New York: Grove, 1958.

Bielawski, Ellen. *Rogue Diamonds: Northern Riches on Dene Land*. Seattle: U of Washington P, 2003.

Braungart, Michael. *Cradle to Cradle: Remaking the Way We Make Things.* New York: North Point, 2002.

Brown, Anthony Cave, and Charles B. MacDonald, eds. *The Secret History of the Atomic Bomb.* New York: Dial, 1977.

Clements, Marie. *Burning Vision.* Vancouver: Talon, 2003.

Dickason, Olive Patricia. *A Concise History of Canada's First Nations.* Oxford/New York: Oxford UP, 2006.

Durning, Alan Thein. *Stuff: The Secret Life of Things.* Northwest Environmental Watch, 1997.

Fermi, Rachel, and Esther Samra. *Picturing the Bomb: Photographs from the Secret World of the Manhattan Project.* New York: Harry N. Abrams, Inc., 1995.

Franklin, Hope. *Vibrant Matter: A Political Ecology of Things.* Durham: Duke UP, 2010.

Geiogamah, Hanay, and Jaye T. Darby. *American Indian Theater and Performance: A Reader.* Los Angeles: American Indian Studies Center, 2000.

Gilday, Cindy Kenny. "A Village of Widows" in *Peace, Justice and Freedom: Human Rights Challenges for the New Millennium.* Gurcharan S. Bhatia, et al, eds. Edmonton: Alberta, 2000: 107-18.

Harrison, Julia D. *Métis: People between Two Worlds.* Vancouver: Douglas and McIntyre, 1985.

May, Theresa J. "Beyond Bambi: Toward a Dangerous Ecocriticism in Theatre Studies." *Theatre Topics* 17.2 (2007): 95–110.

_____. "Consequences Unforeseen . . . in *Raisin in the Sun* and *Caroline, or Change.*" *Journal of Dramatic Theory and Criticism* 20.2 (2006): 127–44.

_____. "Greening the Theatre: Taking Ecocriticism from Page to Stage." *Interdisciplinary Literary Studies: A Journal of Criticism and Theory* 7.1 (2005): 84–103.

May, Theresa, and the Klamath Theatre Project. *Salmon Is Everything.* Unpublished, 2006; revised 2011.

Mullner, Ross. *Deadly Glow: The Radium Dial Worker Tragedy.* Washington, DC: American Public Health Association, 1999.

Sealy, Bruce D., and Antoine S. Lussier. *The Métis: Canada's Forgotten People.* Winnipeg: Pemmican, 1975.

Shorter Oxford English Dictionary on Historical Principles (Sixth Edition) Vol. 1. Oxford UP: Oxford 2007.

Stanlake, Christy. *Native American Drama: A Critical Perspective.* Cambridge: Cambridge UP, 2009.

Thompson, Judy. *From the Land: Two Hundred Years of Dene Clothing.* Hull, QC: Canadian Museum of Civilization, 1994.

White, Richard. "Are You an Environmentalist? Or Do You Work for a Living?" in *Uncommon Ground: Rethinking the Human Place in Nature*, William Cronon, ed. New York: Norton, 1996: 171-85.

Chapter Eleven

Staging Sustainable Shakespeare: "Greening" the Bard While Advancing Institutional Mission

Ray Schultz and Jess Larson

Introduction: Environmental Concern as Institutional Mission

In April 2010, the theatre discipline of the University of Minnesota, Morris, mounted a production of Shakespeare's *As You Like It* in its 160-seat Black Box Theatre. It was directed by Associate Professor of Theatre Ray Schultz, and his design team was led by Associate Professor of Studio Art Jess Larson, who designed costumes and also functioned as informal sceneographer to the production's overall look. Although this was the third play of Shakespeare's directed by Schultz since he began teaching at UMM in 2000, *As You Like It* differed in one notable respect: even before a specific title was chosen, Schultz envisioned a "Green Production," one which would strive to keep both its costs low and carbon footprint shallow.

In recent years, there has been growing interest in the issue of "greening" theatre and theatrical practices. Understandably, much of this interest primarily focuses on the environmental benefits and cost savings of sustainable practices, and these factors certainly had a strong influence on the theatre discipline's decision to pursue a green production. However, just as in the politics of ecology, a fundamental axiom is to "think globally, and act locally," what most crucially served as the catalyst for Schultz was his home institution. Since about 2001, the University of Minnesota, Morris, had begun to engage in sustainability-based projects and subsequently to develop a series of environmental initiatives that have led to UMM's "fairly dramatic transformation in the way the institution views itself and in the way it serves and is viewed by the surrounding region" (Goodnough 1138).

The Morris campus, one of five in the University of Minnesota system, is a small, public, liberal arts college of less than 2,000 students in a town of slightly more than 5,000 people. Situated on the prairie of rural west central Minnesota, Morris's flat terrain causes it, depending on how one chooses to view it, either to enjoy or suffer significant wind. Indeed, UMM's location led to the development of the centerpiece of its sustainability initiatives, namely the building of a 1.65 MW Vestas wind turbine in March 2005, "the first large-scale research turbine at any U.S. public university" (Goodnough, 1139). Current expectations for the wind turbine, in combination with a second one built in 2011, allow for 70 percent of UMM's annual electrical load to be off the grid. In the wake of the wind turbine, other initiatives and environmental projects followed, including a "green dorm" currently in the planning phase; and a biomass gasification plant, which began operations in 2008 and takes advantage of large supplies of local feedstock to heat and cool campus buildings (again, it is expected in the next few years that 70-80 percent of fossil fuels used for these purposes will be displaced). Additionally, the campus has partnered with local groups and agencies to champion local foods initiatives and to provide educational outreach through service learning opportunities, workshops, and conferences. Faculty and students also routinely engage with environmental issues both in the classroom and in their research; indeed, besides the wind turbine, arguably one of the most significant components of UMM's sustainability initiative was the 2007 approval of an environmental studies major. With its first tenure-line faculty housed in the Division of Social Science, the major began serving students in 2008 and offers an interdisciplinary curriculum, also drawing heavily from science-based courses, as well as a smattering of humanities. Moreover, because many of these courses are part of UMM's general education offerings, this new discipline "should help to shape the environmental sensibilities of a wide swath of the undergraduates passing through the institution" (Goodnough 1140).

It is fair to say, then, that issues of sustainability and concern for the environment at the University of Minnesota, Morris, have permeated a large part of campus culture. This extends even to marketing and recruitment where sustainability has essentially become the primary way in which UMM self-identifies, thus "branding" itself as "green" to the outside world. The most vivid and visible example of this "green" branding is available online at UMM's home page (www.morris.umn.edu). There one may discover a slogan prominently displayed directly under UMM's name: "a renewable, sustainable education." This webpage, too, invites prospective students to enter a "green" world with the following tagline: "This is your world. Where the skies are big, the classes are small, and living green is second nature."

During the time the institution was developing these sustainability initiatives and identifying itself as a campus nurturing environmental responsibility, the major activity and interest in these issues sprang overwhelmingly from disciplines based in the sciences and social sciences. Faculty research, for example, focuses on ecosystem changes, local, organic dairies, and renewable energy regulations; much institutional and individual grant monies are also generated by these concerns. Perhaps not surprisingly, the arts are not generally thought of as a major locus of environmental practice or inquiry and certainly not in the same breath as the sciences or social sciences. Such was the case on the UMM campus; the arts simply did not figure heavily or naturally as exemplars of sustainability initiatives. For example, the environmental studies major requires several humanities courses, in English and philosophy, but no specific arts courses; and Goodnough's 2009 case study of UMM's sustainability initiatives mentions only a local arts organization as tangentially figuring into the mix through exhibits that are thematically linked to general environmental issues.

Teaching and directing in this "green world" of "renewable, sustainable education," Schultz began to ponder how someone in the arts might engage in and contribute to the dialogue advancing the sustainability mission that seemed to be in full bloom on other parts of campus. What would or could happen if one consciously tried to link theatre production to environmental mission?

Genesis: Shakespeare, an Eco-conscious Artist

The seeds of a "green" theatre production at the University of Minnesota, Morris began germinating with the previously discussed institutional mission of sustainability and how the arts might significantly contribute to that mission. The decision to embark on the project was an impulsive, instinctive, and relatively quick one in that it represented one of those artistic and collaborative occasions that felt "right." The particulars of how precisely the collaborators as theatre and fine artists might contribute substantively to that mission in the form of a cohesive theatrical production developed more slowly and underwent considerable evolution.

In April of 2009, Larson, together with one of her studio art colleagues, Jenny Nellis, taught sections of a 3-D design course that culminated in a public presentation of student work. Dubbed "Fashion Trashion" by Larson, the presentation featured examples of clothing that students constructed entirely from recycled and repurposed materials, such as pop cans, plastic bags, compact discs, etc. (see photo 11.1). Drawing some inspiration for the assignment from the popular television reality program *Project Runaway*, whose contestants engage in similarly themed challenges, Larson further devised the public presentation as a runway show in the UMM art gallery, complete with "celebrity" judges comprised of faculty and staff, including Schultz. The event, wherein students displayed their work as "art" in a gallery setting and simultaneously "performed" as models before a large audience of peers, family, and teachers contained elements of both artistic enterprise and theatrical performance—something not lost on Schultz or Larson. "Fashion Trashion" was such a success that it has since become an annual event, with subsequent presentations housed in one of the theatre spaces in order to accommodate demand for seating.

From his position as a judge of the students' "art," Schultz was impressed not only by the level of student ingenuity vis-à-vis the use of recycled and repurposed materials, but was also struck by the skill and artistry with which some of the students elevated these seemingly mundane materials into clothing, the best of which emulated haute couture. The liners of Capri juice, for example, were stitched together to become an impeccably tailored, silver cocktail dress; one student constructed a "chain mail" vest out of pop can tabs that was the epitome of trompe l'oeil craftsmanship; and the fashion show climaxed, fittingly enough, with a spectacular bridal gown, the train of which consisted of used, sheer plastic shower curtains and Dasani water bottles.

Moreover, Schultz began to mull the possibilities of incorporating these kinds of materials in a theatrical context. As part of a small theatre department that is perennially strapped for cash, he was quite accustomed to the concept of "recycling" as a matter of economic reality: the UMM theatre discipline, like many college theatre departments, routinely recycles costume and set pieces to keep production costs low. However, such recycling is, more often than not, primarily motivated by economic considerations, with sustainability benefits sometimes materializing as a happy by-product. Sadly, aesthetic considerations are all too rarely a deciding factor in such choices; if anything, a production's design is, to the contrary, often compromised in that one is forced to make do with departmental stock rather than realizing one's ideal vision from scratch. Thinking about the deliberately artful way in which recycled and repurposed materials were reimagined in "Fashion Trashion," Schultz became intrigued by the prospect of a production concept based on a foundation of sustainability that not only advanced his institution's green initiatives, but also, perhaps more important, shifted its priorities: what if aesthetics, and not economics, dictated the course of a "green" theatrical design and its execution? Although there were obviously practical issues to be considered—some of the student garments, for example, were too delicate or unwieldy to withstand the rigors of theatrical performance—Schultz felt that the idea held enough potential to approach Larson about collaborating on a theatre design for the following academic year. Larson quickly agreed and as soon the semester ended, they began meeting in earnest to develop a concept and subsequent design for a production that would perform in April 2010.

From the very beginning the collaborators agreed on several key points: this project would be interdisciplinary in nature, while also giving focus to undergraduate research by actively involving students from both the studio art and theatre disciplines in part of the design and execution processes. Additionally, because a goal was to investigate the aesthetic uses of recycled and repurposed materials, the selection of precisely what play to produce and what materials to employ became crucial considerations. Ideally, the chosen play's thematic and narrative cores would complement the green initiatives of the university, while also supporting and stimulating such a design concept.

Because of UMM's status as a public liberal arts college, its theatre discipline maintains that it should offer students—both majors and non-majors, participants and audience—a broad spectrum of plays drawn from the classical and modern repertory. During a student's career, he or she would, ideally, have the opportunity to experience musicals, contemporary drama, Greek tragedy, children's theatre, etc. During a four-year cycle, the UMM theatre repertoire typically includes a play by Shakespeare, and for the 2009-10 academic year it was again time to produce Shakespeare, since his work was last represented on campus in 2005 with *The Merchant of Venice.* Although the choice of Shakespeare was to some extent a practical and popular one (theatre students had been lobbying for Shakespeare), it also had the potential to support and stimulate the design concept; indeed, past UMM Shakespearean productions directed by Schultz employed a nontraditional approach in design and staging; the aforementioned *Merchant,* for example, was given a 1980s Wall Street setting. The question that remained was which of Shakespeare's work might best suit a "green" treatment.

Schultz gravitated towards and settled on *As You Like It* for a variety of reasons. First and foremost, the play is an example of the pastoral genre, a literary tradition wherein Nature, the countryside, and the virtues of rustic living are generally celebrated in an idealized manner. Such nostalgia for a simpler environmental model can still be relevant to a frenetically paced and technologically advanced society, especially one challenged by such issues as climate change: "*As You Like It* goes to the heart of the dream of simple country life, which still remains potent in Western industrialized society of the twenty-first century. Our contemporary vision of rustic retreat is part of Shakespeare's play" (Dusinberre, 97).

Moreover, as part of its core mission statement, the University of Minnesota, Morris, views "environmental stewardship" as a matter of civic responsibility, and Schultz found a similar respect and concern for the environment in a key speech of Duke Senior, the usurped ruler who, fleeing the machinations of his evil brother, sets up an alternative court in the Forest of Arden. In this speech, Duke Senior idealizes the countryside as a source of unblemished innocence and native wisdom, in marked contrast to the politics of a jaded and morally polluted urban society:

> Now, my co-mates and brothers in exile,
> Hath not old custom made this life more sweet
> Than that of painted pomp? Are not these woods
> More free from peril than the envious court?
> Here feel we not the penalty of Adam,
> The seasons' difference, as the icy fang
> And churlish chiding of the winter's wind,
> Which when it bites and blows upon my body
> Even til I shrink with cold, I smile and say:
> 'This is no flattery. These are counselors
> That feelingly persuade me what I am.'
> Sweet are the uses of adversity,
> Which, like the toad, ugly and venomous,
> Wears yet a precious jewel in his head.
> And this our life, exempt from public haunt,
> Finds tongues in trees, books in the running brooks,
> Sermons in stones, and good in everything. (2.1, 1-17)

Indeed, besides celebrating Nature, Shakespeare's play epitomizes a classic comic trope inherent in the tension of the manners and mores between city and country lifestyles, a dichotomy which is "as old as Theocritus" and "took on special significance for the Renaissance in relation to the examination of political morality" (Brissenden 45). Nowhere does Shakespeare present this contrast more vividly than in the encounter between Touchstone, the quick-witted jester—who, as a visitor to the Forest of Arden, is decidedly "a fish out of water," dismissing country life as "tedious"—and Corin, a humble shepherd, who matches Touchstone's sophisticated wit with plain common sense:

> Touchstone: Why, if thou never wast at court, thou never saw'st good manners . . . If thou never saw'st good manners, then thy manners must be wicked, and wickedness is sin, and sin is damnation. Thou art in a parlous state, shepherd.

> Corin: Not a whit, Touchstone. Those that are good manners at the court are as ridiculous in the country as the behavior of the country is most mockable at the court. You told me you salute not at the court but you kiss your hands. That courtesy would be uncleanly if courtiers were shepherds. (3.2, 40-50)

And even though Duke Senior and his followers, along with Rosalind and Celia, all follow the tradition of the pastoral wherein they are depicted as "asylum seekers," fleeing the court because it has been "dangerous" (Dunisberre 101), Shakespeare presents their colonization of this Eden-like Arden to bear some ironic consequences from the perspective of ecology that might resonate with modern audiences. For example, Rosalind, Touchstone, and Celia may upset the emotional balance of Arden when they come into contact with its human inhabitants, yet Duke Senior, even as he professes his love and respect for Arden's environment, may be responsible for disturbing the balance of the Forest's food chain, since the presence of his men necessitate that they must kill its wildlife to ensure their survival. Indeed, such a reading is in line with contemporary Shakespearean ecocriticism, which seeks to draw attention to the playwright's work as it relates to "anthropocentrism, living systems, environmental degradation . . . and an investment in expunging the notion that humans exist apart from other life forms" (Bruckner and Brayton 3).

Inherent in *As You Like It*'s classic city/country dichotomy, Schultz saw, too, metatheatrical resonances peculiar to UMM's geographic location and institutional demographic. As a small college located in a town of just over 5,000 people and 160 miles from a major metropolitan center, UMM is, for all intents and purposes, "the country," yet its rural landscape is, like Shakespeare's Arden, also inhabited by many "city" dwellers, since many of its faculty and staff hail from urban centers from across the United States. Even more to the point, along with students from rural locales, UMM's student population consists of a large proportion of transplanted "city" folk from the greater Minneapolis—St. Paul area. Schultz could see that these natural tensions and juxtapositions in the play might complement and play off of the same tensions and juxtapositions present on campus.

Ultimately, what made *As You Like It* seem an appropriate choice for this "green" design experiment was that the play's clash of city and country sensibilities provided a worthy vehicle, capable of inspiring a similar clash of visual and textural sensibilities through the choice of what recycled, reused, and repurposed materials would comprise the manufactured, synthetic world of the urban court and which would make up the natural, and, arguably, more environmentally friendly world of the country. Schultz and Larson subsequently went to work on envisioning these worlds, engaging in, what they affectionately referred to, from an aesthetic perspective, as "the Game."

Rules of "the Game": Playing with Green

With past productions, rather than entering a design process hampered by UMM budgetary pressures, Schultz had opted to view monetary limitations more positively, as part of "rules" in the game of theatre production, a source of lively challenge rather than numbing dread. At the beginning of this project, the collaborators similarly found themselves formulating rules, although in this case these rules had little to do with economic constraints. To the contrary, the aesthetic aims for *As You Like It* created parameters that allowed for the development of a production process that was, ironically, both fiscally and environmentally responsible.

The sole economic consideration that remained constant was one of human resources, something in common with all UMM theatre discipline productions. With the exception of Larson and Schultz and the assistance of three part-time staff members who functioned in supervisory and/or design capacities (Merlin Peterson, Stagecraft Instructor; Liz Spohr, Costume Shop Supervisor; and Jason Rasinowich, Scene Shop Supervisor and Set Designer), the entire workforce executing the design would be composed of undergraduate students. Student labor broke down into four subgroups: a small number (6—8) of paid, work-study students; about 6—8 theatre and studio art students assisting in the design and execution as part of a directed study, supervised by Larson; about thirty-five Stagecraft students were employed, often in the most manual tasks, as part of their class practicum supervised by Peterson; and roughly twenty theatre majors, many of whom were part of the cast and crew, also volunteered their services throughout the process. In many cases these groups over-lapped considerably: for example, some work-study students were also in the cast or crew; certain Stagecraft students might also be part of Lar-son's directed study, etc.

The foremost rule that was formulated in initial design meetings, which began in the summer of 2009, was that, to the best of everyone's abilities and what was logistically possible, there would be no purchasing of new materials for costumes, set, or props. Instead, this project's cos-tumes and set would be built from an amalgam of stock or previously used or purchased items (sourced from theatre, art, or individuals), or recycled materials foraged or acquired from local sources (recycling cen-ters, businesses, and individuals); all materials would then be subject to repurposing and revisioning as dictated by the needs and tenets of the design. What's more, early on it was envisioned this foraging process would not only serve as a source of materials, but also as a means to en-gage the community in this eco-conscious arts project. For example, as the design process progressed, multiple lists of desired materials, such as used cds, and denim jeans, pieces of discarded wood, magazines, and plastic bags, etc. were created; these lists were then disseminated cam-pus-wide via email. In this way, the entire campus community was, sim-ultaneously, apprised of this artistic enterprise and invited to participate in and contribute to its design.

As previously discussed, *As You Like It* presents a bifurcated mise-en-scène of urban and rural landscapes, on which the collaborators planned to anchor their choice of materials. One of the first exercises during initial meetings was to draw up lists of words associated with "city" or "urban" and those associated with "rural" or "country"; one such list read as follows:

urban =	synthetic	country =	natural
	gray		green
	hard edges		soft
	gritty		swirling lines
	metallic		light
	concrete		water
	excess		foliage
	polluted		simple
			comfort

Meditating on these associations, it was decided, befitting these land-scapes, to similarly bifurcate, as much as logistically possible, specific material choices to each locale, roughly limiting the production to natural objects and fibers for the Forest of Arden and its inhabitants and synthetic, man-made materials for the cityscape. Additionally, as discussions deepened, Schultz and Larson took the play's characters and experimented with placing them on a spectrum from the most "citified" to the most "countrified." This exercise resulted in identifying the gossipy courtier Le Beau as the epitome of all the court's excesses and the humble shepherd Corin as the character in Arden literally and figuratively closest to the land. The rest of the cast would eventually fall somewhere on a continuum between these extremes.

In the quest to emphasize the visual and spiritual dichotomy of city and country, Schultz saw a theatrical way of melding or presenting the two milieus on the body of one actor. In keeping with the Elizabethan tradition of doubling actors, it was decided that a single actor would play both the good Duke Senior (country) and his evil brother Duke Frederick (city). Larson envisioned that the characters' quick changes might be best effected from the waist up, giving each doublets of varying materials that would evoke the appropriate environment. Also in keeping with Shakespearean tradition, they decided that summer, even though a set designer had not yet come onboard to actively participate in preliminary discussions, they would emulate principles of Elizabethan staging and utilize the basic framework of a thrust stage, complete with tiring house wall and minimal set pieces. In this way two very important goals might be achieved: such minimalism would allow for fluid and rapid movement, not only from scene to scene, but also from city to country (from the start they envisioned the back wall as rotating or morphing in some way from city to country); a stark scenic look would also provide a neutral setting in which best to highlight both the actors and what were shaping up to be very elaborate costumes that would function on a certain level as scenery.

Indeed, this notion of "walking scenery" played into the development of select costumes for both the court and forest that would certainly fall on the extreme end of the aforementioned city/country spectrum. For the city, the collaborators began to envision stressing the excess and corruption of the urban court in the female fashions by exploring ideas that would make Rosalind and Celia's dresses, along with those of their two waiting women, "walking heaps of conspicuous consumption." Such extreme clothing would also provide a dramatic contrast to the more, natural and relaxed fashions of their country disguises as Ganymede and Aliena. For the country, Schultz saw the possibility of suggesting subtle shifts in the topography of Arden by having actors play the "Forest," costumed as trees or bushes, which the other characters could directly and materially relate to by hiding behind them, leaning against them or using them as shade—or, as Orlando does in one of their more comical uses, tacking love letters to them. How the "Forest" would precisely look and what specific natural materials would be used to create them would require a long gestation period. At this juncture, it was agreed upon that one rule would be that Arden would "move" and that costumed actors would provide said movement.

Because the decision to create costumes and scenery exclusively from recycled or reused materials would, perforce, cause the design to be drawn from an eclectic, yet focused, range of objects and materials, Schultz and Larson allowed themselves to consider, from the beginning of the design process, a wide and eclectic range of silhouettes and periods in order to fully realize the final vision of *As You Like It*'s city and country worlds. Schultz brought to the process his experience of Shakespearean performance, which combined postmodern and Elizabethan sensibilities; he lobbied early for having the costumes retain vestiges of an Elizabethan silhouette, while at the same time dispensing with any constricting demands for period accuracy. Larson brought both her personal artistic identity, with an emphasis on the use of textiles and clothing as art, as well as her affinity for some of the edgier practitioners of high fashion, such as Christian Lacroix and Alexander McQueen. Additionally, both began to see possible parallels between the Seattle grunge movement of the 1990s, which sought an alternate lifestyle to the urban, corporate grind of the post-Reagan 1990s and which also popularized a layered, relaxed, and eclectic style of fashion that might be appropriated for the Forest of Arden's clothing.

For the court, their historic scope was widened to allow exploration of female fashion of eighteenth-century Versailles, with its dripping excess and elevation of fashion to a form of high art. This, in turn, led to musings about the inherent political nature of clothing and fashion as markers of class, gender, and personality, and how the politics of clothing and the self in it were manifested in such actions as a lord presenting himself at Elizabeth's or Louis's court or a model strutting a contemporary Paris catwalk. Such musings would certainly prove helpful in developing appropriate clothing for Shakespeare's characters. However, these discussions also proved to be a catalyst for the development of certain staging ideas that might showcase the politics of Duke Frederick's court in that the collaborators envisioned the opening moments of the show as a prologue wherein the characters would present themselves to the Duke and, by extension, the audience in the style of a modern fashion show. Because Schultz predicted that the audience might be distracted by the outlandishness of some of the fashions, this "fashion show" opening served not only an aesthetic purpose, but also a practical one in that it allowed an audience to take in the clothing and acclimate themselves to the more extreme fashions before any of the actors ever spoke. It was one way to avoid the visual detracting from Shakespeare's language.

As preliminary talks continued, Larson introduced Schultz to the work of the artist Nick Cave, a sculptor, dancer, and performance artist. Cave's signature pieces are what he calls "Soundsuits," pieces that may be viewed as either sculpture when displayed, or as performance art when models, wearing them, move or dance through space:

> By intention the Soundsuits can be worn and displayed and each has been constructed to fit the artist himself. Performance is not fundamental to their meaning, but the suggestion that each piece functions as a costume from some private or public ritual is nonetheless pervasive. In other words, there is both an autonomous existence to the suits, and a context-dependent existence, either one of which could be brought to the foreground at any moment. (Cameron qtd. in Cave 22)

Cave's Soundsuits are composed of both natural materials like twigs, feathers, or dyed, human hair and synthetic materials, such as plastic buttons, beads, and sequins. Schultz drew inspiration from Cave's Soundsuits, particularly from the ones using organic materials, such as his suit made entirely of twigs, and ones incorporating found objects, like a suit of children's toy tops and one that resembled a tree with "birds" made of porcelain figurines nesting in them. Perhaps more than any other source, these inherently theatrical Soundsuits helped the collaborators to see the possibilities of making some of the costumes "walking scenery," from both functional and artistic perspectives. Most intriguingly, the range of materials that Cave employed in his art meshed very nicely with the list of recycled, reused, and found objects that was being compiled for the UMM production.

What Schultz saw in Cave's work reminded him of what he had seen in the "Fashion Trashion" experiment: basing his art largely in everyday objects Cave, by his won admission attempts to "reconcile[e] low art as opposed to high art and what might be considered crafty" by "taking the discarded and claiming, repurposing, and recycling it," just as similar materials had been transformed by UMM students into examples of "high fashion" (Harvey). For UMM's *As You Like It*, Shakespeare's nobility might be dressed like nobility but with materials decidedly not associated with nobility; for example, through similar manipulation and repurposing, from a semiotics perspective or at least what Davis refers to as the "quasi-code" of clothing (5), an audience might be led to "read" discarded black plastic as distressed black leather, when it is specifically worn by Duke Frederick. As preliminary design ideas started to crystallize, Schultz and Larson realized that they would be attempting to create their version of haute couture garments, singular, one-of-a-kind creations that are notable for their construction from materials that are often, rare, luxurious, and costly; these fashions are traditionally designed with little thought given to whether their materials are sustainable or environmentally conscious. Ironically, although Schultz and Larson's version of haute couture aimed to create unique garments, the materials used to create them would run counter to the spirit of such clothing in that the production's garments would be made with materials that were common, plentiful, and striving to be environmentally responsible.

And just as a haute couture collection essentially strives to create and present a unique microcosm, so, too, it was decided that, for UMM's *As You Like It*, the court's nobility and forest dwellers should be their own unique microcosms, beholden to no particular period or style for its sense of fashion, but worlds of the collaborators' imagination, defined by their numerous aesthetic influences and the limits of what agreed upon materials could be gathered and harnessed for artistic purposes. Schultz and Larson would, in a sense, be emulating the kind of process that Caroline Evans suggests is the basis of high fashion in a postmodern world:

> In the process, the distinction between past and present is almost imploded . . . . The modern fashion designer rummages in the historical wardrobe, scavenging images for re-use just as the nineteenth-century ragpicker scavenged materials for recycling. (13)

Furthermore, Schultz began to realize that this process would need to be atypical to that of the more traditional theatre set and costume design process wherein, due to the constraints of time and economics, director and designers conference, develop a concept and renderings, and subsequently execute them, usually with minimal deviation from the final renderings. In this case there were several factors that seemed to cry out for

an atypical approach that allowed for a process that blurred the line between design and execution. For one, Larson was approaching the process from a fine arts background, as well as someone interested in fashion. Generally speaking, the creation of fashion and especially art tends
to involve processes that undergo considerable evolution and transformation in the execution phase; more often than in theatre design, a work
may deviate from an initial artistic impulse or plan and continue to
change and transform itself until it is deemed "finished." Additionally,
the choice of actors themselves—their personalities and body types—
held the potential to influence the design in all sorts of interesting ways.
Schultz had found it odd that on occasion theatre costumes might even be
designed and rendered before the casting process occurred. Most important, the variable nature of the foraging process would likely produce
surprising finds of materials that a traditional theatre design process
could neither anticipate, nor adjust to, nor take full advantage of. In a
pivotal way, the collaborators wanted to acknowledge that the mission to
create with recycled and reused materials was an aesthetic mission, as
well as an environmental one: therefore, the result of the communal foraging should at least partially dictate the course of the designs themselves. That they would allow what they were able to find influence how
the final costumes evolved was perhaps their ultimate "rule": constricting, yet also potentially liberating.

Execution: Making Shakespeare Green

In late fall of 2009, set designer Jason Rasinowich joined the production
team and began developing a design for *As You Like It* in collaboration
with Schultz and Larson. Seeking to continue in the vein of a city-
country dichotomy, the team explored several approaches, many contrasting the mechanistic, hard-edged aspect of urban living with the more
natural, soft edges of Shakespeare's green world. First attempts tended
toward more literal renderings of urban skylines and country forests,
complete with foliage, which would be assembled from stock and foraged materials. Rasinowich also experimented with more abstract patterns of cogs for the city and vines for the country, which he proposed to
construct on a frame of wooden pallets that were available for the taking
from a local, recently closed grocery store; the wooden cogs would be
painted to appear metallic (city) and recycled rope might be repurposed
as vines (country). Here was a prime example where availability of exist-

ing materials influenced design ideas. However, this approach was ultimately rejected for two reasons: the design became so elaborate that it threatened to potentially overwhelm the actors, especially given the equally elaborate costumes, and the pallet design in execution would almost certainly prove too heavy and cumbersome to effect a fluid transition from city to country.

Opting to remain true to the simplicity of the traditional Elizabethan tiring house wall, the team finally settled on simple, gray walls for city, with corresponding green ones for country. Moreover, the final choice of material proved not only practical and environmentally conscious, but also aesthetically apt. The final design's walls were reversible panels that were constructed out of previously used cardboard, obtained in plentiful supply from the campus recycling center and local businesses. The city panels were left in their smooth, finished state and painted grey to evoke concrete; they were also given a black tinge in places to suggest urban grime and pollution. For the reverse side, the cardboard was distressed to give the country a more natural, textured, and corrugated feel and was additionally treated to a green wash to evoke the forest. The essence of "city" and "country" was further abstracted by appropriating words from the city-country lists that had been free-associated during initial brainstorming meetings, along with others contributed by students of a creative writing class, and placing them randomly on the walls. Words such as "strip mall," "smog," and "gridlock" were stenciled in crisp, san serif black lettering to emphasize the oppressive nature of the court, while words like "green," "streams," and "breezes" were hand painted in swirling, curvilinear lettering amidst the textured cardboard of the forest.

Additionally, for each locale the center back wall, flanked by entryways, was dominated by a set piece that sought to encapsulate the essence of each environment. The city look featured a large throne for Duke Frederick that the design team imagined towering over the rest of the court. The centerpiece of the design was an automobile's bucket seat, recovered from a local salvage yard. To it were welded foraged scrap metals and other objects like discarded "exit" signs and computer monitors; all this was sprayed with metallic paint and the throne's base was embellished with mosaic "tile" made from bottle caps (a local bar happily supplied them by the bucketful) and shredded cds. Behind the throne was attached the duke's crest, a mosaic created entirely of metal from cut-up recycled pop cans. Solely making use of the materials at hand, the team purposefully strove in its design and execution to follow an environmental aesthetic that emulated the process and effect of sculpture made from found objects, essentially elevating the common to the royal, the mundane to the artful. Similarly, the Forest of Arden was anchored visually by a large fountain that was constructed almost entirely from scrap wood found in the shop; it, too, featured a crest of the banished Duke Senior that aimed for a sculptural effect, but was made from natural materials: in this case a wooden household blind, with a bas-relief tree pattern fashioned from rope.

Meantime, final designs and execution on the costumes began in earnest. As previously mentioned, throughout the fall the Theatre Discipline had been accumulating recycled and previously used or purchased objects, many of which were donations from people across campus and the greater Morris community, to serve as the primary source of materials from which to create. In the costume shop were bags and boxes filled with a wide and sundry range of items: used audio- and videotapes, old ribbon and wrapping paper, denim and corduroy pants, curtains and drapes, stock fabric from people's attics, plastic grocery bags, vintage men's ties, plastic and paper flowers, rope, flannel shirts and pajamas, costume jewelry, shoes, tchotchkes of all stripes, etc.

In keeping with her studio art background, Larson continued to eschew traditional drawings and began this phase by creating design boards for various silhouettes and characters. Many of these were composed of images culled from high fashion, historical, and fine art and industrial design sources. Essentially collages, the team hoped to replicate the look and feel of the design boards by assembling and creating living collages on the actors' bodies with the materials at hand. Through a process of a kind of "eco-invention," our cache of disparate found materials would need not only to embody character but also to evoke and represent properties not always intrinsic to the objects themselves (see photo 11.2).

The team began by making prototypes of basic Elizabethan silhouettes: men's "pumpkin" pants and doublet and women's skirt with farthingale. After a basic pattern was cut, the experimentation came primarily in the choice and manipulation of the fabric and embellishing materials. While some of the first examples of the pumpkin pant and doublet leaned towards the "crafty"—for example, outfits for the good Duke's men were constructed almost entirely of denim with lots of felt "leaves" and real sticks appliqued to suggest embroidery—the team eventually began to hit their stride in the design for Duke Senior's musicians. Denim, for example, was mixed with vintage stock fabrics to lend the pants and jackets that "slashed" fabric look typical to Elizabethan menswear. Grunge was added to the mix through the use of modern Henley and tee shirts on top, with flannel shirts tied at the waist; tights were combined in some instances with legwarmers or oversized socks and Chuck Taylor sneakers; various hats, scarves, and handkerchiefs were circulated on the various bodies to complete the look. As the process evolved, the Duke's musicians began to resemble a sort of Elizabethan grunge "house band"; the lead singer even wore a thermal shirt, taken from stock, and embroidered with the a picture of Shakespeare and the words "the Bard Unplugged," along with the years of his birth and death.

After the basic male silhouette had been arrived at, details of character and class began to emerge through the use of specific materials. The Dukes' doublets emphasized both their characters and environments: a "studded, leather" jacket made of plastic, duct tape, and pop can tabs for the urban ruler, a natural wool cardigan sweater trimmed with vintage stock fur for the country one. The old servant Adam's essential role as laborer was evident in a pumpkin pant "coverall" with work boots and a simple, muslin full-sleeved shirt. The misanthropic Jaques, the sole member of the banished Duke's entourage unhappy in the forest, was devised as an Elizabethan country club snob, with khaki pumpkin pants slashed with loud plaid fabric reminiscent of a Burberry raincoat and a pink polo shirt with a sweater draped like a cape on his neck. Orlando's rebel status was evidenced by a donated olive drab army jacket that was cut and repurposed as an Elizabethan doublet, its upturned collar providing a naturally defiant "ruff." Moreover, Larson, whose own fine art work often incorporates computer-generated embroidery, embellished the back of this doublet with an elaborate design that featured a logo of an "upstart crow," the notorious nickname one of Shakespeare's jealous rivals conferred upon him; this helped to reflect Orlando's outsider status, while also allowing for a postmodern wink at the audience. And for Touchstone the jester, traditional Elizabethan "motley" was given a contemporary interpretation: a doublet made entirely of stock zippers of all colors, with fringe of vintage tags, and pants boasting stripes of synthetic velvet pompoms originally intended as fringe for kitchen curtains. A series of embroidered tee shirts with sayings such as "Go Prithee Thyself" and "Compost Doth Happen" helped to underscore the jester's role as verbal wit.

Two of the production's more eco-inventive pieces of male attire employed materials that not only evoked character, but also some of the play's central thematic concerns. For Rosalind's disguise as the saucy boy, Ganymede, Larson combed through a stash of stock, vintage neckties and selected some to create the slashes in his/her pants; it was both an artful way of achieving the effect and a sly commentary on the female character's assumption of the male role. Ironically, the necktie, often viewed from a modern perspective as a societally imposed fashion restraint on the male, became in this instance an article of potential liberation for the newly "male" and empowered Rosalind. Additionally, the shepherd Corin's jacket epitomized the pastoral theme of Shakespeare's play. Taking stock muslin and hundreds of used tea bags, Larson constructed a garment that under stage lights, caused the jacket alternately to resemble tree bark or sheepskin; to this was added an old tie-dyed tee shirt, bandana, and love beads, giving him the air of a faded hippie, thus, suggesting—in both a literal and figurative sense—that he was a creature of, and at one with, his pastoral environment.

On the distaff side, the female court garments, with their wide Elizabethan silhouettes, gave the team a broad canvas on which to create. Largely designed and executed by students, as instructed by Larson to emphasize urban excess, the garments were constructed on a fabric base and stock corsets and were an extreme example of eco-collage and assemblage in that they were heavily layered with an eclectic melange of recycled and found materials, such as cds, plastic garbage bags of varying colors, costume jewelry, bubble wrap, plastic Coke bottle fringe painted to look as if "the real thing" was still inside, and other items of kitsch ephemera; for example, Celia's petticoat was even trimmed with used, yellow caution tape from a campus construction site (see photo 11.3). The women's look was further designed to lend their outfits corresponding vertical excess with the addition of videotape and pop can headdresses, a flourish intended to suggest a sort of postmodern periwig. Indeed, accessories and embellishments led to some of the more inspired touches of eco-inventiveness. Two such examples were ruffs of plastic six-pack rings and sleeves trimmed with video tape "lace." Even more striking were hats and leggings for Duke Frederick and his men; "crocheted" from hundred of yards of repurposed audiotape, they were as pliable as natural fiber but also noticeably shimmered under the stage lights. These hats were a notable testament to the high level of craftsmanship evidenced by Larson and her team and the team's original aim to elevate mundane materials into couture; many audience members who admired them admitted having no idea from what material these hats and legwear were made.

Perhaps most emblematic of both the fluid process of the production's design and its intent to blend sustainability and aesthetics was the final design and execution of the costumes for the two actors who would play the "trees" representing the Forest of Arden. Early on Schultz and Larson envisioned these figures literally as moving scenery. Primarily drawing from artist Nick Cave and his "sound suits" for inspiration, the team developed a clear vision for the trees' "foliage"; it would be evoked through the creation of elaborate headdresses made from yarn, twine, old sacks, real tree branches and leaves, pinecones, grasses, and shrubs, as well as porcelain bird figurines obtained from stock. As the production period went on, the question of what to dress the "trees" in became a regular topic of conversation in design and production meetings. The idea of dressing them in camouflage fatigues was seriously considered and rejected because this would be a major violation of the "no pur-chase" rule; other ideas like dressing the actors in plain brown pants and shirts were rejected on the grounds that they were not connected strongly enough to the eco-aesthetic of repurposing to elevate.

One member of the production team was an army veteran, who jok-ingly suggested dressing them in ghillie suits. While the team all found the idea intriguing, after some initial research, the idea was similarly re-jected for being another costly violation of the no-purchase rule; it was further thought that merely "pulling" a costume without repurposing it would be aesthetically "cheating." The team finally settled on trying to create its own version of a ghillie suit. Using actual grasses, leaves, and branches was considered and rejected as too unwieldy and uncomfortable for fluid actor movement and potentially too fragile to survive the per-formance period intact. It was then decided to make the suits of fabric. Using two stock costumes that were worn in a children's show as a base, the costume shop literally cleaned house, taking scores of old costumes and stashes of old unwanted fabric, and putting them through a meta-phoric wood chipper or paper shredder, cutting them down to thousands of pieces of small strips and squares of material, which were subsequent-ly sewn to the base garments. These recycled costumes and fabrics, some unused for decades, found new life and purpose not in a landfill but back on the stage in a new incarnation. In much the same way that recycled plastic and paper are recycled in the manufacture of many household green products, these materials were transformed to function as "bark" for the trees of this green world. Like so much of the design for UMM's *As You Like It*, this last accomplishment was notable for its creative in-novation but, most importantly, this aesthetic choice strove to imbue the-atrical production in general and Shakespeare in particular with the no-tion of "green" that resonated on a variety of levels and with multiple meanings.

Conclusion: Art as Environmental Mission

In his essay "From Readymade to Manufractured: Some Assembly Required," Steven Holt writes about objects that are, what he coins, "manufractured," that is man-made, everyday objects that are transformed artistically though human thought and innovation:

> Manufractured objects highlight an important response to the riches of an overabundant culture. By adopting a strategy of material and cultural salvaging, artists, craftspeople, and designers are literally creating something from nothing—that is, from nothing of perceived worth. (36)

Holt hastens to add that "creativity provides the added value" and that his aesthetic contention enjoys connectivity to issues of sustainability:

> This tendency to become twenty-first century hunter-gatherers of discarded, under-appreciated materials has led to new ways of thinking about the conservation of resources and how art, craft, and design might fit more critically into the larger cultural ecology. (36)

Viewing UMM's *As You Like It* in this light, it could be considered successful on a number of levels. The production's design team indeed effected a theatrical world that created something from nothing and did so in an eco-economically and eco-aesthetically conscious manner. Schultz initiated the project as a "green" production rooted in aesthetic principles, prescribed by certain "rules of the game." And, for the most part, the team was able to produce a set and costumes whose design and construction choices could be aesthetically justified and realized with little bending or morphing of said rules. Admittedly, in a few instances some creative latitude was granted in order to achieve desired effects: for example, while Schultz and Larson originally formulated a "no purchase" rule, they gave themselves license to allow for the purchasing of previously owned or used materials from sources such as garage sales or the Salvation Army and for purchasing a certain amount of new wood and hardware in order to insure the set's durability and safety; and while they originally attempted to follow a strict synthetic/natural dichotomy for the city/country environments, the collaborators bended this rule to allow for exceptions if a particular synthetic material could be manipulated to appear natural and vice versa (a "wooden" household blind, for instance, was actually plastic that had the appearance of wood). Yet even these allowances were to a large extent justified; the rules were changed solely to ensure that the best aesthetic results would be achieved through the least use of new consumable materials and the maximum utilization of recycled or used materials. Moreover, this initiative extended beyond the production's costumes and set to include even publicity: the production substantially reduced its carbon footprint by printing programs on recycled paper, and tickets were literally recycled, made from a cache of unsold tickets from previous theatre discipline productions, with a customized "*As You Like It*" stamp printed on the back side for a total cost of less than twenty dollars. Ultimately, across the board attempts at reducing carbon footprint and costs were extremely successful: approximately 85-90 percent of the entire production was constructed of recycled or previously owned materials, and the final cost of the production—including set, costumes, lights, sound, and publicity—came to approximately $850. These statistics were especially lauded across campus, since reducing waste and material conservation are such a part of UMM's individual institutional identity and fiscal conservation is, as across all higher education in these economically challenged times, a matter of the highest priority.

Besides the natural artistic impulse to strive to improve on one's work, if there was an area where the team could have made greater strides, it was not in the design's execution that the greatest improvements could be made, but rather in the production's post-performance phase. While the majority of the materials were disposed of responsibly and returned to recycling centers, given back to the Salvation Army, and retained for stock, there were still some lapses: due to miscommunication in the scene shop and the fact that the production ended its run so near the end of the academic year, a few set pieces wound up being tossed in the conventional trash without thought to minimizing the environmental impact of their disposal. These lapses are lessons to be applied for future productions.

Indeed, from the perspective of an educational experience, *As You Like It* proved effective in that it not only fulfilled UMM's liberal arts mission to allow students to intermittently practice Shakespeare as part of a wide spectrum of theatrical diversity, but they were further able to engage with Shakespeare in particular and theatre in general within the wider liberal arts context of interdisciplinary collaborations and nontraditional creative approaches. Faculty and students were able to combine theatre, art, and ecology in a relatively ambitious and sophisticated example of undergraduate research. Just as their spiritual regional forbearers had to struggle to tame and understand their harsh, prairie environment UMM students were able, in a metaphoric sense, to wrestle with the artistic, consumeristic, and ecological contradictions that Holt suggests are part of contemporary culture, with its wide disparity of want and waste:

> For the better part of human history, the struggle has been to survive. To make do with little in the face of an often unforgiving environment . . . . But the current problems of material society are fundamentally different. How do we respond to the fullness, abundance, satiety and consumer choice occurring in our lives at every level? How do the best and brightest minds, the most creative thinkers of our time respond to prosperity, to the possibilities of enough and even "too much"? (27)

Both "Fashion Trashion" and *As You Like It*, far from educational ends in themselves, provided artistic and theatrical experiences that can further be viewed as attempts to develop a model of artistic engagement with environmental issues. Though far from perfect models, these projects developed ideas and set some basic standards that may be perceived as the foundation or rough template for future theatrical and art projects at UMM. Indeed, since *As You Like It*, the theatre discipline has produced an original children's play focusing on environmental themes and employing many design techniques developed by Schultz, Larson, and their student team. Because of these experiences, it's likely that in a student's four-year tenure, some combination of eco-themed content or eco-design techniques will be part of the theatre's repertoire and student learning, thus reinforcing UMM's wider educational goals with respect to environmental issues.

It is fair to say that both *As You Like It* and the "Fashion Trashion" art project have also played a large part in the arts claiming more of an active institutional voice in the continuing dialogue of sustainability. This is perhaps best evidenced by the fact that the University of Minnesota, Morris, has begun to cite these artistic projects as components of its institutional identity of "a renewable, sustainable education"; the university's "Green Education" web page prominently features both with links to more information, including a feature story on the play's eco-design broadcast by a regional news program.[1] A recent sustainability conference, hosted by UMM, also featured Larson and Schultz's work in one of the sessions. Indeed, the perception of the arts as locus for environmental innovation on the UMM campus has continued to spread within the university system, as well as regionally: for example, several alumni, now teachers at other schools, have produced their versions of "Fashion Trashion"; an exhibit of Larson's art in the fall of 2011 at the Dairy Center in Boulder, Colorado, featured a talk by her on the process of creating repurposed clothing for the theatre; and costumes from *As You Like It* have been displayed at the Kaddatz Galleries in Fergus Falls, Minnesota, and in a fashion show called "Bodies of Water," produced at the Surface Design Association's 2011 conference in Minneapolis, as well as featured as part of an exhibit at the Institute for the Environment on the university system's main campus. Furthermore, a recent issue of *Mnpls/St. Paul* magazine published an article profiling Minnesota's colleges that lauded UMM's "Green cred," calling it a "[n]ational leader in campus sustainability" (Cicero 99). Interestingly enough, the magazine chose to cite two examples to explain this assessment: UMM's in-house wind and biomass energy production and "Fashion Trashion" and *As You Like It*.

Much like the people who first pioneered the prairie that is now Morris, UMM has pioneered its green initiative from a certain pluck and fortitude, taking an "odd inventory of initial institutional assets," which Goodnough contends, came about through "bootstrapp[ing] some tangible assets which . . . have come to anchor the entire project (1139). Following in these footsteps, Schultz and Larson have bootstrapped certain aspects of their creative processes to position the arts as part of that anchor. With the UMM production of *As You Like It*, theatrical practitioners may have materially "invad[ed] Shakespearean texts—treading heavily on the delicate workings of the plays" in much the same way that ecocritical scholars do from a literary perspective, yet, like these literary efforts, these theatrical efforts "may also carry a real benefit for the health of the planet" (Bruckner and Brayton 9). Indeed, the production aimed to achieve, like Nick Cave's art, which on the surface possesses, according to the artist, a "fun" and "whimsical" nature, but also asks people to "to consider the underlying tragedy we are perpetrating . . . . We have invaded the natural world and now have to figure out how to change our behavior" (Cave 232). Similarly, this "green" production of Shakespeare, both in its aesthetic and sustainability practices, asked the University of Minnesota, Morris, campus to look beyond the whimsy of art and to embrace the politics of environmental responsibility.

Note

1.   See <http://www.morris.umn.edu/sustainability/greeneducation>.

Works Cited

Brissenden, Allan. "Introduction to Oxford World's Classics Edition." In *As You Like It* by William Shakespeare. Oxford: Oxford UP, 1998. 1-86. Print.

Bruckner, Lynne and Dan Brayton. "Introduction: Warbling Invaders." In *Eco-Critical Shakespeare*. Eds. Bruckner and Brayton. Surrey, England: Ashgate, 2011. 1-9. Print.

Cave, Nick, Dan Cameron, Kate Eilertsen, et al. *Nick Cave: Meet Me at the Center of the Earth*. San Francisco: Yerba Buena Center for the Arts, 2009. Print.

Cicero, Kolina. "The Big Guide to Minnesota Colleges and Universities." *Mpls. St. Paul* Feb. 2011: 92-99. Print.

Davis, Fred. *Fashion, Culture and Identity*. Chicago: U of Chicago P, 1994. Print.

Dusinberre, Juliet. "Introduction to Arden Shakespeare Edition." In *As You Like It* by William Shakespeare. London: Thomson Learning, 2006. 1-142. Print.

Evans, Caroline. *Fashion at the Edge: Spectacle, Modernity, and Deathliness*. New Haven: Yale UP, 2003. Print.

Goodnough, Troy, Arne Kildegaard, et al. "Leveraging Assets: A Case Study of the Sustainability Initiative at the University of Minnesota, Morris." *Journal of Cleaner Production* 17(2009): 1138-42. Print.

Harvey, Holly. "Artist in Residence Nick Cave's Newest Soundsuits go on Display." *NTDaily.com* 28 Feb. 2012. Web. 21 June 2012. <http://www.ntdaily.com/?p=63049>.

Holt, Steven Skov. "From Readymade to Manufractured: Some Assembly Required." In *Manufractured: The Conspicuous Transformation of Everyday Objects*. Eds. Steven Skov Holt and Mara Holt Skov. San Francisco: Chronicle Books, 2008. Print.

Chapter Twelve

Puppet Planets and Spirit Soldiers: Staging Ecological Representations in *Baby Universe* and *Forgotten World*

Courtney Ryan

This chapter considers the representation of nature in two recent pieces of ecotheater. Beginning with the nature/culture binary, as well as the debates surrounding it, it asks if all human representations of nonhumans inevitably anthropomorphize, assimilate, or consume what they claim to represent. The essay briefly considers the effectiveness of various forms of ecotheater, like site-specific theater and realism, before focusing on two plays that utilize magical realism to attempt to connect the human and nonhuman world. While critical of universalizing narratives that exclude, minimize, or mistranslate nonhuman agency, this paper nonetheless considers the possibility that humanistic representations of nonhumans might still critique exclusively humanistic theater frameworks. Although the question of how humans can fairly represent a biodiverse world is not necessarily new, this chapter adds new representational strategies and limitations to the ecological conversation.

Natureculture[1]: Culturenature

One of the greatest challenges of ecotheater is to represent the biodiverse world in innovative ways that do not simply reinforce humanism and, with it, the constructed divide between nature and culture. As Una Chaudhuri argues,

> Along with other discourses born of the age of industrialization, nineteenth-century humanism located its shaky foundations on the growing gap between the social and natural worlds, constructing a fragile edifice that could sustain itself only at the cost of actively ignoring the claims of the nonhuman. ("There" 23)

In particular, realism's very "aesthetic and ideology," rooted as it is in humanism, continues to be "programmatically anti-ecological" ("There"

24). Foregrounding human interests, it casts nature as a scenic backdrop to human conflicts; represented as remote, fixed, and passive, nature is the setting which reinforces and highlights the "realness" of the human action. Thus, even so-called environmental plays, which intend to bring ecological issues to the fore, can unwittingly obscure, appropriate, or falsely universalize their subject matter when they use realism to convey their message. Universalism, akin to humanism, can be more harmful than beneficial to ecotheater both when the nonhuman is excluded from the "universalist" narrative *and* when the nonhuman is included and thereby assimilated into a humanist framework. Chaudhuri's solution to this humanist drive is to resist the metaphoricalization of nature through a "turn towards the literal" ("There" 28). However, as Baz Kershaw points out, such an act—even if possible—would be highly paradoxical since theaters "are defined by their power to produce metaphors through the creation of spectators" (311). The theater building, as a designated place of entertainment, and the performance itself, which is inherently representational, combine to abstract any literal ecology. This abstraction is only exacerbated by the audience which mediates the performance and, thus, further distances theater from literalness.

Rather than attempt to concretize nature or continue to normalize the nature/culture binary, theater must acknowledge its role in the construction of *both* culture and nature, thereby undermining the dualistic representation of nature as natural, stable, passive and culture as artificial, instable, active. By denaturalizing nature, theater reveals the fact that nature is both a place—"in the sense of a rhetorician's place or topic for consideration of common themes"—and a trope (Haraway, "Otherworldly" 66). As Donna Haraway elaborates, "It is figure, construction, artifact, movement, displacement. Nature cannot pre-exist its construction, its articulation in heterogeneous social encounters, where all of the actors are not human and all of the humans are not 'us,' however defined" (66). It is only by highlighting the semiotic slippage between nature and culture that their dualistic representation can be destabilized, and, with this destabilization can come an awareness of how nature and culture are mutually constructed and dependent. Furthermore, as Gabriella Giannachi and Nigel Stewart point out, since nature only exists through the perception of it, it "*is always performed* and can only be *appropriated* by means of performance" (20). Despite theater's complicity in the cultural domination of nature in the past, it is still an ideal site for the representation of nonhuman nature, namely because theater so blatantly displays its own construction. The very theatrical elements that prevent an ecological literality onstage—the institution itself, the framing of the stage, the audience—all serve to keep the representational quality of theater firmly visible, and this transparency can be extended to the theatrical representarepresentation of nature.

What does this visibility of construction *do*? From a poststructuralist standpoint, it makes the audience aware that what it is seeing is inherently representational, and, as such, can be well-represented or misrepresented, well-translated or mistranslated, and—especially in the case of nature—backgrounded or foregrounded. As Chaudhuri argues, "By making space on its stage for ongoing acknowledgments of the rupture it participates in—the rupture between nature and culture . . . —the theater can become the site of a much-needed ecological consciousness" ("There" 28). By metatheatrically acknowledging its perpetuation of the dualistic divide between nature and culture, theater serves to question "the *constructionist* assumption that nature and fixity go together (naturally) just as sociality and change go together (naturally)" (Fuss 6). Exposing these humanist assumptions is the first step to undoing them, and to imagining how nature might be represented as agential, social, and changeable. The detachment of nature from fixity allows for new representational possibilities in which nonhumans are not segregated from sociality but are as bound up in it as humans. Insomuch as *both* nature and culture are constructed, unstable, and representational rather than organic, stable, and actual, they cannot escape their interdependency, their inextricable connectivity. Rather than being separated by their 'natural' differences, they are joined by their mutual construction. However, awareness is not enough in and of itself. Overcoming the nature/culture binary "requires recognition of both continuity and difference; this means acknowledging the other as neither alien to and discontinuous from self nor assimilated to or an extension of self" (Plumwood 6). Thus, in addition to exposing dualistic representations of nature/culture and highlighting the limits of representation, theater must imagine the nonhuman in innovative ways that are not merely consumptive or assimilative.

Representational Strategies in Ecotheater

Since the early nineties, ecotheater scholars have posed various solutions to the conundrum of ecological representation. Bonnie Marranca, for instance, advocates avant-garde performances (like those of Peter Brook and the Living Theatre) for their emphasis on spatialization (qtd. in Kershaw 308). She argues that, since "space" is more open and nonhierarchical than "setting"—where nature has traditionally been relegated—"any elucidation of a theatre ecology begins in the understanding of performance space" (Marranca xvii). However, as Chaudhuri points out, the connection between theatrical space and ecology is, at best, tenuous and abstract ("There" 27). Baz Kershaw, meanwhile, sees potential in immersive theater that turns spectators into participants, but, as he himself warns, the immersive environments, if not created carefully, may produce their own oppressive, absolutist civilization myths (316-17). Similarly, Chaudhuri suggests that site-specific theater holds great promise for ecotheater, but, unlike Kershaw, she believes that this ecological promise can be manifested materially rather than metaphorically ("There" 24). While all of these forms of ecological representation are equally valid, the most popular form—realism—remains relatively unexplored. No doubt this is due to realism's tendency to focus on human drama and only use the nonhuman world to make a metaphoric point about human characters; as Chaudhuri observes, ecology as metaphor is so ubiquitous in realism as to be rendered invisible in its own right ("There" 24). However, considering that the majority of theater productions today are realist, particularly within American theater, it is worth reflecting on the potential benefits and drawbacks of using realism in ecological representation.

The question is: can narrative—written by and for humans—do anything other than reinforce humanist ideologies and tropes? Theresa May believes it can, suggesting that "a story is a product of connection that maintains a field of contact not only among people but also between people and place . . . . Stories create a matrix of belonging, a living tissue between past and present and between human and non-human communities" (94). For May, the communality of theater creates an ecology which can be imaginatively expanded to include nonhumans. While her recommendation to playwrights to "tell the human story within the ecological story" is troubling, in that it maintains an emphasis on the human story, it nonetheless seeks to place and contextualize human stories in a biodiverse environment far more complex and expansive than an exclusively human environment (93).

One way to represent this biodiverse ecological story, without automatically consigning it to the background, may be through magical realism. In it, "the natural and the supernatural, the explainable and the mi-

raculous, coexist side by side in a kaleidoscopic reality, whose apparent-
ly random angles are deliberately left to the audience's discretion" (Arva
60). At its most successful, magical realism hybridizes rather than di-
chotomizes the magical and the ordinary, and, through this hybridization,
the seemingly magical and seemingly realistic are reconfigured. Works
of magical realism often also use magical elements in order to disrupt the
linearity of realism, a strategy which could be used in ecotheater to upset
humanist narratives. Theater scholars have not utilized the term to the
extent that literary scholars have, and this may be because theater, particularly realism, wholeheartedly embraces Coleridge's notion of suspension of disbelief and asks that playwright, actor, and audience alike believe.[2] However, it is this very performative practice of suspension of
disbelief that makes theater an ideal site for magical realism; in theater,
human and more-than-human representations can be equally imaginable
and acceptable—if only for the performance's time span. In other words,
what can be imagined can be believed, if only temporarily.

To better explore this issue, I turn now to two ecotheater performances, both of which deploy elements of magical realism. The first,
Baby Universe: A Puppet Odyssey, is an ecofable which imagines how
nonhuman and human characters would respond to an apocalypse. The
second, *Forgotten World*, is a memory play that draws on the spirit world
in order to give dead child soldiers the opportunity to tell their stories. I
have chosen these particular plays because both attempt to represent the
human and nonhuman world in innovative ways, the former representing
planets and the latter representing the spirits of child soldiers. On the surface, the plays could not be more different from each other: one disem-
bodies while the other re-embodies, one looks to cyborgs for environmental restoration while the other looks to spirits, one imagines the
future while the other imagines the past. However, the plays' very dis-
similarities speak to each other and reveal commonality across topical
differences. For instance, both plays utilize magical realism in order to
affect socio-environmental change in the present, even though they use
vastly different representational means to do so. Both also consider how
the human and nonhuman other have been mutually exploited. The
plays' divergences from each other, though, demonstrate the many different ways to represent, and at times misrepresent, the biodiverse world.
While neither play fully escapes its humanist overtones, both plays—
sometimes intentionally and other times unintentionally—critique humanist frameworks that exclude or appropriate nonhuman others. They
provoke questions about representation, the nonhuman other, and specta-

torship, asking, "What does representation—the fact itself of mimesis, of mediation—do to the meaning of nature?" (Chaudhuri, "There" 29). Can nonhuman organisms be represented by humans without being entirely consumed or assimilated? How does human spectatorship affect and complicate nonhuman representation?

Cybernetic and Disembodied Representations in *Baby Universe*

Baby Universe: A Puppet Odyssey is the creation of the New York-based collective WakkaWakka in collaboration with the Norwegian company Nordland Visual Theater. A self-professed ecofable, the play imagines an apocalyptic future in which the Sun and its neighboring planets—Mercury, Venus, and Earth—are all dying. Earth's oceans have already dried up and its toxic atmosphere has made it uninhabitable, but an unknown number of humans continue to survive in a space station. Earth's scientists, represented by four white, male puppets, frantically attempt to manufacture a new solar system, humanity's last hope for survival. They create "baby universes" which hatch and (theoretically) grow entire solar systems; however, most of the babies malfunction and die with malformed, enlarged, or underdeveloped planets inside them. After sundry failures, the scientists find success with their 7000 series of baby universes, when 7001, nurtured by a loving caretaker, manages to grow a whole solar system. Before the humans can move to new Earth, though, the Moon abducts 7001 and brings him[3] to the Sun, who attempts to kill the young universe, and, thus, prevent humanity from escaping the annihilation that the rest of the solar system will soon suffer. Strengthened by the Sun, however, 7001 is able to flee and, out of love for his mother, allows the remaining humans to fly into the new Earth, tellingly located in his heart.

There is no question that *Baby Universe: A Puppet Odyssey* operates within a humanist framework. The very first word of the title—"baby"—infantilizes and humanizes the term "universe,"[4] while the "odyssey" taken leaves nonhumans behind. Indeed, at the end of the play it is only humanity that survives, thanks to 7001 who, despite being created in a laboratory, is the ideal nonhuman human, willing to sacrifice himself for the sake of humanity. However, by emphasizing the gross inequality between humans and nonhumans, the ecofable calls human superiority into question. For example, once the humans have landed in 7001, a minia-ture, illuminated globe levitates, representing their new home. Holistic images of Earth, such as this one, have been soundly criticized for objec-tifying the planet as available for human consumption and appropriation. As Noël Sturgeon, drawing on Yaakov Garb's criticism of the very first photograph of Earth from space, writes, "The whole Earth image allows us to universalize the environmental dangers to the Earth without having to understand the way in which differential power and privilege means that responsibility for environmental devastation is not equally shared" (42). This inequality is certainly prevalent in the play's narrative, where countless organisms die, except for a privileged human group that es-capes to a new solar system. However, as a piece of self-reflexive thea-ter, *Baby Universe* exposes rather than normalizes the environmental injustices it stages. Whereas the images of the Earth that Sturgeon and Garb critique fill the entire photographic frame, suggesting that Earth is the only planet of importance, the globe in the play is dwarfed in a theat-rical frame that encompasses not only the stage but the entire theater space. The miniature Earth, contextualized within the scope of the play, is diminutive and diminished; its significance pales in comparison to the representative dimensions of the old planets, which are three to five feet tall and to the Sun which, at over eight feet tall, towers over planets and humans alike. Rather than signifying a totality and perfection, the play's Earth image recalls all that has been lost—an entire solar system—and the cost of such a loss.

Although *Baby Universe* seems to be yet another fairy tale that privi-leges human survival against all odds—even scientific ones[5]—it is, in fact, an actual fable, a cautionary tale that warns of the dangers of con-tinuing to pretend that human interests are separate from and superior to nonhuman interests. While many of the play's human characters fail to experience the full consequences of their actions, rescued as they are in the eleventh hour, the audience is left with a far more ominous message. The final moment of the play occurs in near dark, as an announcer from "Apocalypse Radio" warns listeners that "outside it's another sunny day;" his sinister, knowing laughter is the last sound the audience hears. Even though a brand-new solar system has just been manufactured, a shadow of impending doom already looms over it. *Baby Universe*'s dis-turbing final note implies that if humans do not acknowledge and act on their interconnectivity with other organisms, they will suffer an actual apocalypse which they more than likely will not survive. Hence, a distant reality is manifested through magical means; by imagining a fantastically bleak future, the play urges the audience to take action in the present.

The play's human salvation narrative is therefore foreshadowed by the threat of future, cyclical devastation, a surety if people fail to recognize the interconnectedness of the human and nonhuman world. As May points out, "Not only is 'nature' a cultural construction, ecology is everywhere bound up with culture" and this shared "artifice is not proof of independence from, but evidence of interconnection with, the natural world" (86). Certainly this mutually shared artifice is at work in the fable, particularly with regard to the natureculture amalgam 7001, who, though created in a laboratory and raised as a human, is still able to self-generate an entire solar system. Neither strictly biological organism nor strictly machine, 7001 defies singular categorization; he is a cyborg, "a cybernetic organism, a hybrid of machine and organism, a creature of social reality as well as a creature of fiction" (Haraway, "Cyborg" 117). While high-tech, science fiction creations like 7001 may seem to widen the constructed gap between nature and culture, suggesting that the latter can replace the former altogether through scientific progress, Haraway argues that cyborg hybridity can disrupt Western dualisms such as culture/nature, self/other, and agent/resource. As she writes, "To be One is to be autonomous, to be powerful, to be God; but to be One is to be an illusion, and so to be involved in a dialectic of apocalypse with the other. Yet to be other is to be multiple, without clear boundary, frayed, insubstantial" ("Cyborg" 143). While both the humans and the solar system in the play act out an "us or them" apocalyptic dialectic, it is the cyborg 7001 who crosses these boundaries as a machine and a biological organism. He is made by the scientists, but is also the maker of his own constellations, an imprecise fusion of the technical and organic. When the surviving humans fly their spaceships *into* the heart of 7001, they too are unwittingly cybernetic, further imbricated in the organic and cybernetic world. While this interrelatedness is lost on the play's scientists, who are determined to maintain their illusion of godlike superiority, it need not be lost on the audience, distanced as they are from the marionettes' actions. As a piece of scientific fantasy, *Baby Universe* foregrounds how, to borrow from Haraway again, "we have never been human," but have always been interconnected with other organisms and machines (*When* 1).

Alongside the cybernetic representation of 7001, the representation of the other human and planetary characters also seeks to deconstruct a nature/culture dualism and, with it, an illusion of human dominion. For example, although all of the characters, including the planets, display human emotions and tendencies, the fact that they are almost all played by puppets serves to deemphasize the human body and to somewhat equalize the humans and planets. Since the scientists and the planets are both represented by puppets, neither can be said to be more material nor more embodied than the other. Although their mentalities are unfairly humanized, their corporealities, at least, are equally abstracted. While Chaudhuri and May both stress the importance of a material ecology that is not merely metaphorical, their criticism seems to be leveled at theater that metaphorizes ecology in order to bolster the materiality of the human actors. In the case of *Baby Universe*, all of the characters are visually disembodied, and, as puppets, are equally one-dimensional and archetypical. Their lack of complexity oversimplifies the ecological crisis—turning a complicated issue into a battle between humans and nonhumans—but it is nonetheless a shared fundamentalism. The Sun's single-minded goal, for instance, is to thwart the humans' attempts to abandon the dying solar system for a new one; for the duration of the play, the Sun is in the final stages of death and is only represented as furious and vengeful. However, the human characters are equally as simplistic and their motivations just as transparent. The loving mother figure, for example, is juxtaposed with the clinically detached figures of the scientists, thus reinforcing a dichotomous representation of women as emotional and maternal and men as rational and uncaring, an essentialism that is frequently criticized by ecofeminists.[6] The scientists' ruthlessness and resourcism[7] is also exaggerated for comedic effect and shock value, but this hyperbolism—particularly of the scientists' imperialism—serves to expose species inequality and injustice, even if it uses humanist tropes to do so.

Perhaps, though, *Baby Universe*'s most valuable contribution to the still nascent ecotheater canon is its imaginative representation of the solar system. The Sun, Moon, and planets are, indeed, humanized to varying degrees; facing extinction, they carouse and make jokes about seeing stars and falling off their axes. Importantly, though, they also combat their replacement, actively thwarting the humans' agenda. Considering how often nature is depicted as a passive and, at times, even willing participant in its own destruction, such a representation, flawed though it may be, makes a crucial intervention in the dualistic construction of human as agent and nature as non-agent. As ecofeminist Val Plumwood argues, historically, *nature* is to be defined as a *terra nullius*, a resource empty of its own purposes or meanings, and hence available to be annexed for the purposes of those supposedly identified with reason or intellect . . . . It means being seen as part of a sharply, separate, even alien lower realm, whose domination is simply "natural," flowing from nature itself and the nature(s) of things. (4)

Baby Universe thus disrupts and denaturalizes this misrepresentation through the planets' active resistance to their own demise. Although the planets are problematically humanized—speaking in English, displaying human reactions, and retaliating with human methods—they nonetheless fight against humanity's agenda to abandon them for a newer universe. As the Sun bellows to 7001 after capturing him, "Do you think you can replace me? Do you think the humans will save you? . . . They're supposed to die and so are you." Such a statement questions the humanist assumption that Homo sapiens must survive, regardless of what happens to other species, and it highlights the scientists' mistreatment of the solar system as a limitless resource instead of something that is greater than humanity. Thus, although *Baby Universe*'s magical realism is limited to imagining nonhumans in human terms, it nonetheless productively uses this limitation to challenge the humanist assertion of species superiority.

May has argued that the Earth has the ability to voice itself via ecological consequences of human interference (95). While the Sun, Moon, and planets in *Baby Universe* use human rather than biological methods to retaliate against humanity's pollution and misuse, they nonetheless act as agents actively resistant to their own domination. Take, for example, the following exchange which occurs while the planets, Earth in particular, are inebriated:

MARS. Earth, wake up. Your people made a copy of you.
EARTH. Oh, I don't care about my people. I've been trying to kill them for years.
MARS. Well, they don't care about you either!

All of the planets laugh raucously at this quip, amused by the mutual disregard Earth and humans have for each other. This representation is not unproblematic: the Earth's (and the Sun's) mode of retaliation is expressed almost wholly in human terms rather than planetary ones, and, thus, fails to emphasize how human and planetary actions are biologically and materially interrelated. Furthermore, it puts the Earth and people at direct odds with each other, thereby reinforcing rather than subverting a "man versus nature" plot conflict. However, as Greg Garrard observes, "In striving to avoid anthropomorphism, it seems difficult to say anything about it [the Earth] whatsoever" (90). By representing the Earth as an exhausted, but active, fighter of human appropriation, the play at least makes a critical intervention in the "Mother Earth" stereotype, deconstructing the misrepresentation of Earth as a warm, noble, feminized entity that welcomes its own consumption.

In *Baby Universe*, the human and planet puppets are not only pitted against each other through characterization but also through the genre of apocalyptic fable. Garrard cautions, "Apocalypse provides an emotionally charged frame of reference within which complex, long-term issues are reduced to monocausal crises involving conflicts between recognizably opposed groups" (105). While apocalyptic metaphors are often highly imaginative and have the potential to spur people to take ecological action, they also tend to obscure sociohistorical and sociopolitical factors in their singular focus on ecological catastrophe. Indeed, postcolonial ecocritics have long critiqued deep ecologists for their singled-minded emphasis on the environment to the detriment of disenfranchised peoples who are themselves victims of colonization.[8] Both the fable and apocalypse genres that *Baby Universe* borrows from have a tendency to privilege master narratives at the expense of spatiotemporal specificity, and, as a result, the play, though highly innovative, still falls into the representational trap of false universalism and ahistoricity. Take, for instance, the promotional blurb for the production: "Sometime in the future, a government program to save the population of an unnamed, dying planet in a dying universe is furiously underway." While the notion that environmental catastrophe can occur anywhere, at any time, certainly imbues the play's message with a sense of urgency, it also prevents *Baby Universe* from resonating with actual, particular ecologies, and, as Cara Cilano and Elizabeth DeLoughrey argue, "a refined ecocriticism is all about location, location, location: geographic, historical, and 'geopsychic'" (77).[9] Devoid of any location or contextualization, the nonhuman and human characters become homogenized and truncated from their environments. Lacking the biological, geographic, and historical particularities that make each species unique, the characters—particularly the Sun, Moon, and planets—are thus generically humanized. So, while the magical realism in *Baby Universe* offers a creative, phantasmagoric vision of the future, which may very well produce environmental change in the present, it nonetheless could go further in imagining the nonhuman

characters and their environment in biodiverse—rather than universal—
terms. It is for this reason that I turn now to Deborah Asiimwe's *Forgotten World* which, in contrast to the egalitarian disembodiment of *Baby
Universe*, offers a re-embodiment of deceased child soldiers whose history proves to be very much interconnected with that of their environment.

Multiple Modes of Representation in *Forgotten World*

In *Forgotten World*, Deborah Asiimwe stages an imagined encounter
between the spirits of deceased child soldiers and a Western war photographer. The play opens and closes at an art auction at which the unnamed
photographer is selling images of the children as well as those of African
warlords, many of whom were likely responsible for the children's capture. While the photographer attempts to pragmatically describe her images, she is repeatedly interrupted and distracted by memories of the
children. Although "their spirits appear as seen on the mind of the photographer," they are corporeally present, and, with the assistance of a
mediary, Mother Spiritual, they metaphorically transport the photographer (and the theater audience) into the past (Asiimwe 2). This past, in
which the children were all alive, consists of several nonlinear vignettes—some are of the children's war games and practices, others are
of their initial interactions with the photographer, and still others are of
their individual stories of life before and at the moment of their abduction. The play is ultimately a multilayered battle for representation, as it
cuts back and forth between the photographer's present, in which she
represents the children through images and hard facts, and the children's
past, in which they reenact their personal life experiences.

Whereas the apocalyptic *Baby Universe* reveals the ways in which
nature and culture are mutually constructed, the ritualistic *Forgotten
World* reveals the way in which nonhuman and human life are ecologically intertwined. The former offers a cybernetic hybrid in the shape of
7001, while the latter offers a liminal hybrid in the shape of spirits, who
simultaneously occupy the material world and the spirit world. As such,
these spirits, formerly child soldiers, are now reanimated only through
memory. In reliving and reimaging moments from their former lives, the
spirits find some degree of peace; the rupture that war created between
them and their environment begins to heal as the children connect with

each other and with the Earth. Through the liminal spirits, *Forgotten World*, like *Baby Universe*, seeks to expose the exploitation of nonhuman and human others; however, whereas WakkaWakka uses hyperbole to accomplish this task, Asiimwe uses meta-representation. By critiquing a Western photographer's depiction of child soldiers and offering her own counter-representation, she foregrounds the fallibility of representation. Metatheatrically, Asiimwe employs direct address to embroil the audience in the photographer's commodified misrepresentation, thereby fostering an awareness of the fact that the experiences of nonhuman and human others are not fully translatable. While *Baby Universe* has moments of metatheatricality, it is *Forgotten World* that pointedly considers the danger, challenge, and complexity of representing anyone but oneself.

What makes *Forgotten World* an ideal companion to *Baby Universe* is its similar use of multiple modes of representation—spatial, artistic, and ecological. The first is evident early on when Mother Spiritual invades the space of the art gallery and, by ritualistically cleansing it, summons the children: "Come children, play. Play in the space . . . play on our mind" (Asiimwe 14). The art gallery—uncomfortably similar to the theater space itself—is established as a Western place of privilege, complete with champagne, clinking glass, and classical music. In contrast, the space to which Mother Spiritual and the children take the photographer is a liminal other-space that is neither the art gallery setting nor a specific, war-torn country. This liminality imagines a recuperative space inaccessible through nonliterary means, and it emphasizes the children's perspectives over geographical specificities. Caught between the physical world and the spiritual world, the children repetitively play out their pasts. In this other-space prepared for them by Mother Spiritual, the children's play gradually shifts from war games to healing rituals. Whereas the Western photographer only states facts—countries, names, dates, etc—the children only tell stories, stories which reveal their intimate familiarity with the violence and horror of war but do not convey an understanding of the political and geographical reasons for war. Thus, seen from the children's viewpoint, the effects of war eclipse the causes of war; fights over borders, resources, and power pale in comparison to the emotional and environmental damage they cause.

At the same time, the play's spatial lack of specificity is problematic from an ecological standpoint, since, as Chaudhuri recognizes, "Who one is and who one can be are . . . a function of *where* one is and how one experiences that place" (*Staging* xii). While *Forgotten World* is not ahistorical or asocial to the extent that *Baby Universe* is, its unwillingness to focus on one particular country, which has its own unique ecosocial concerns, prevents the play from being as environmentally specific as it could be. That said, the ambiguity surrounding the children's homelands is, in fact, deliberate. In an email response to this author, Asiimwe writes, "Uganda [the playwright's home country] and particularly the northern part of Uganda informed the play hugely, but I was also looking at the world of the twenty-first century and how children have become objects globally and more so in the so called 'third world' countries." Indeed, while the past to which the children's spirits transport the photographer is vaguely African, particularly in its use of Swahili phrases and lullabies, it is also intercontinental. For instance, at one point the children all sing in different languages—Runyankore, Korean, Spanish, Hindi, French, Mandarin, and English—and thereby displace any one particular sense of location. Considering that over nineteen countries contained child soldiers between 2004 and 2007,[10] Asiimwe's implementation of diverse languages and regions highlights the severity and pervasiveness of child soldier use. It also emphasizes the fact that "using child soldiers is not, for example, 'an African thing,' nor is it to be found where genocides have recently occurred" (Gates and Reich 9). It is, however, mostly to be found in postcolonial countries,[11] which suggests that the use of child soldiers is not only a transnational concern but is also deeply connected to imperialistic histories of colonization. Thus, although Asiimwe deemphasizes unique postcolonial differences—all of which bear influence on each country's current conflicts and use of child soldiers—she nonetheless foregrounds the endemic, transnational abuse of children in war zones.

Despite the fact that the playwright does not situate the children in a particular postcolonial country, she still demonstrates that people and place are inextricably connected, a key tenet of ecocriticism across disciplines. Postcolonial ecocriticism, in particular, examines the ways in which the colonization of people and land are interrelated, and how this shared colonization has caused a rupture between the two. As DeLoughrey and Handley argue, "an ecological frame is vital to understanding how geography has been and still is radically altered by colonialism, including resource use, stewardship, and sovereignty" (24). Whereas the children's environment is excluded from the photographer's narrative as well as her photographs, which are only of people, the spirits are unavoidably tied to the land. When they speak of the violence they have encountered and perpetuated, they unwittingly always include environmental elements, whether it be the rivulets of blood running through the river (Asiimwe 18), the mango tree under which one child's whole family was slaughtered (Asiimwe 20), or the flowers which get splattered with blood during battle (Asiimwe 44). While the photographer—homogenously focusing on human politics and drama—fails to consider how an ecological lens might expand and enhance her humanistic frame, the children do not have the luxury of ignoring their ecological ties. Through bloodshed, death, and violence they witness the reciprocity of human and environmental suffering; they are not just *in* the environment but the environment is *in them*. As the spirits collectively admit, "I never rest. I never sleep. I keep roaming. My ears keep discharging particles of flesh, bones and sand and my body aches . . . I keep moving. To stop the discharges from my ears, the aching in my body . . ." (Asiimwe 66). Blood, skin, bones, and earth mingle and lodge in the children's ears, demonstrating the ways in which, as May succinctly observes, "Place and person are permeable" (94). In *Forgotten World*, it is the spirits—in flux between life and death—who must help the photographer and the audience alike remember their shared permeability.

Sadly, children and their environment are largely interlinked through a shared subjugation: while the land is mined for diamonds and oil, the children are exploited for their labor. It is important, though, not to prioritize one dominated group at the expense of the other, but rather to highlight how "biotic and political ecologies are materially and imaginatively intertwined" (DeLoughrey and Handley 13). *Forgotten World* imagines a liminal space in which the biotic environment and the spirit figures are both metaphorized *and* materialized. In May's words, "Always an immediate, communal and material encounter among embodied performer, audience and place, theatre is ecological even as it is representational" (86). Theater itself is an ecology of different performances, places, and perspectives, which is magnified in Asiimwe's play, where spirits are re-embodied in a transitional space of memory that is neither fully here nor there. Rather, it is an imagined place of ecological and emotional recuperation, where the children's spirits may create new ties with the land that are not based solely on their mutual oppression. The figure of Mother Spiritual is, according to the playwright, based both on the sundry mothers whose children were abducted as well as the Ugandan goddess Nyabingi, who is known to possess select women as her medium.[12] As such in the play, she searches for the children and attempts to restore them to peace through healing rituals. An intermediary between the hu-

man and the spirit world, she creates an ecological and spiritual haven
wherein the children can imagine games of peace rather than war: "The
space is prepared. Air cleansed. Incenses burnt. Come play. Play games
of joy. Games of laughter" (Asiimwe 27). At first, though, the spirits
cannot remember how to play children's games; they are too full of violence to play anything other than war games.

This question of how to physically and emotionally restore former
child soldiers is one which continues to plague all those who work in this
area.[13] Indeed, a recent ten-year study of former child soldiers in Sierra
Leone found that "the long-term mental health of former child soldiers
was associated with war experiences and postconflict risk factors," such
as community stigmatization (Betancourt 606). While children who were
reaccepted in the community fared better than those who were not, all of
the children continued to suffer long-term effects. However, Kathleen
Kostelny cautions against using Western psychological models which
emphasize trauma and mental illness without considering well-being and
social ecology, particularly the importance of ritual in the healing process (23). Just as biotic and political ecologies are interconnected in devastation, so too are they in recuperation. For instance, when one child
spirit in *Forgotten World* attempts to relate her story of abduction, it is so
traumatic that she begins to hallucinate, trapped in a cyclical repetition of
horror. In order to rescue her, the other children improvise a chant: "Get
up, move, touch the plants, touch that one, and that one and the other
one. Come over here, touch the earth, smell the clay, now lie down, use
both your hands as a pillow. Close your eyes" (Asiimwe 62). Through a
sensory reconnection to the healthy parts of the environment, the girl is
awoken from her catatonic state. In her abduction story, she complained
of smelling dead, bloody chicken, but, after the children's chant, she
claims only to smell ginger, lemongrass, and eucalyptus leaves (all of
which, in herbal medicine, are known to have healing properties) (62). It
is the communal and ritualistic engagement with the earth and plants—an
engagement that is tactile, olfactory, as well as imaginative—that re-
stores the girl to a communicative state.

Within the magical realism of *Forgotten World*, the children's spirits
are reconnected to their ecological community through the performative
practice of playful rituals. As Richard Schechner has famously noted,
performance is "twice-behaved behavior," and, thus, is intricately connected to ritual (1). In his working definition of "play," Schechner notes
that it collaborates with ritual to create "its own (permeable) boundaries

and realms: multiple realities that are slippery, porous, and full of creative lying and deceit" (26). He points out that the very ubiquity of play means that its enactment is often overlooked and, hence, differences between violent, involuntary play and healthy, voluntary play often go unarticulated (27). However, these differences are emphasized in *Forgotten World*, where the children's games begin with war and violence but gradually give way to peace and restoration. The war lords' "creative lying and deceit" is abundantly apparent in the children's games of torture and battle, particularly when the spirits, as one voice and body, recite and march to the unforgiving rules of war. It is Mother Spiritual's cleansing ritual that creates a liminal space of healing and improvised play, in contrast to the dogmatic *non*play of the war games. Guided by Mother Spiritual, the spirits perform recuperative rather than destructive rituals, and thus begin to imagine the land as a place of healing rather than one of devastation.

It is extremely difficult for exploited people, like the spirit children, to imagine a relationship with the environment not based on mutual subjugation and violence. As Édouard Glissant asks, how can postcolonial subjects, impoverished by ecological and social disaster, imagine an "aesthetics of the earth," imagine an "idea of love of the earth—so ridiculously inadequate or else frequently the basis for such sectarian violence"? (151). DeLoughrey and Handley suggest that Glissant's ecological recuperation is at first only possible through imagination, because postcolonial land has been so entirely appropriated and misused (4). It is only through literary imagination that an "aesthetics of rupture and connection"—rupture from territorialization and connection to the land itself—is first conceivable (Glissant 151; DeLoughrey and Handley 28). For the children in *Forgotten World*, who are the greatest victims of sectarian violence and whose grandparents were more than likely colonized subjects, the only way to recuperate any love of their land is through imagination. Hence, despite the fact that all the children seem to share with their surroundings is a mutual suffering, they still dream of a peaceful, reciprocal propitiation with the environment. Although Glissant focuses on the imaginative possibilities of *literature*, theater's communal and material imaginativeness makes it equally suited, and perhaps better situated, for an ecological articulation of human and environmental interdependency. Thus, while performance lacks the global reaches of printed literature, it brings people together in one shared space, and, as demonstrated in Asiimwe's play, has the potential not only to imagine but also to *stage* meetings between the human and nonhuman.

As with literature, theater is inescapably representational, and this is only intensified by spectatorship. In the words of Barbara Kirshenblatt-Gimblett, "What we observe is changed by virtue of being observed" (49). Unacknowledged, this mediatization can result in a perceived assimilation of the human and nonhuman other, a misrepresentation of the other as just like oneself. This consumptive impulse may produce a humanistic representation of the biodiverse world or an over-identification with the human and nonhuman other. However, "one way to avoid this is to emphasize the limitations of representation and translation, and to highlight the local and often inassimilable aspects of culture and history" (Cilano and DeLoughrey 77). Furthermore, a "heightened self-awareness" of representational frames and individual complicity in them can disrupt the consumptive drive toward universalism and assimilation (Cilano and DeLoughrey 77). Asiimwe effectively deploys this strategy in *Forgotten World* by meta-theatrically implicating not only the photographer and art buyers but also herself and the theater audience, as both photographer and playwright use their media to represent others, and both art and theater audiences have come to view their representations.

Metatheatricality—and with it, complicity—is evident in the very first scene in which the audience, doubling as theater and art house audience, is directly addressed by the photographer and is welcomed to look at the child soldier photographs lining the walls and to begin bidding on the photos. The opening scene, entitled "Vaudeville," is a theatrical spectacle of human commodification, and the hyperbolic representation of the photographer as appropriating the suffering of others immediately conveys the grave dangers that misrepresentation can present. However, as a paying audience who has come to the theater to watch a play about child soldiers, the audience is made uncomfortably aware of its own complicity in the children's commodification. The photographer's open invitation to spectate and purchase is frighteningly similar to the playwright's invitation—once issued in the prologue of many a classical drama—to purchase and spectate.

In her desire to package her photographs as holistic, the photographer admits that she has put fragmentary images and stories together "to make the whole" and "complete the story" (Asiimwe 4). By critiquing the photographer's misrepresentation of the children, and juxtaposing it with the spirits' "own" representation, Asiimwe stages a battle for representation, in which the photographer performs one narrative, but her memories perform another. As Joseph Roach posits, genealogies of performance "attend to '*counter-memories*,' or the disparities between history as it is discursively transmitted and memory as it is publicly enacted by the bodies that bear its consequences" (emphasis added 26). The children's improvisational games, played out repetitively in the photographer's mind, therefore contest and counteract a historical representation that seeks to erase the materiality and individuality of each child. Likewise, the personal stories of abduction, inculcation, and violence act as performative counter-memories to a realist narrative that would imagine the children in terms of statistics. Although the photographer asserts a grand narrative, her own memory is overwhelmed with disjointed stories that clamor to be told, and these fragments act as necessary disruptions to holistic, hermetic representations that suggest that any ecology can be completely known or captured—be it through a photographic or a theatrical lens.

Conclusion

Utilizing magical realism, both *Baby Universe: A Puppet Odyssey* and *Forgotten World* imaginatively represent the biodiverse world. Perhaps more important, they pose provoking questions about environmental exploitation and, meta-theatrically, about theater's representation of exploitation. While *Baby Universe* critiques human consumption, *Forgotten World* critiques commodifying misrepresentations. While the former urges the audience to consider the solar system as more than a resource, the latter urges the audience to consider child soldiers as more than statistics. Both plays use varying degrees of universalism to accomplish these goals: in the case of *Baby Universe*, the solar system is humanized, ironically, to combat humanism, and, in the case of *Forgotten World*, the emotional and environmental effects of war are universalized in order to combat representations that exclude these concerns. Through magical realism, the two plays creatively represent what could not be represented in realism alone, and this, in itself, is a step in the right direction for ecotheater.

The next step, though, is imagining the nonhuman and human other as related to *but not as* oneself; thus, the question remains, how can theater represent the human and nonhuman without assimilating the latter? For *Baby Universe*, this might mean imagining how planets would express themselves and contest their consumption in nonhuman, rather than human, terms. For *Forgotten World*, this might mean imagining how spirits, who are no longer human, can be both human and more-than-human. Certainly this suggestion poses its own potential danger; if the more-than-human is represented as entirely unfamiliar, it may be fetishized, alienated, or exoticized, which is just as problematic as when it is assimilated, universalized, or consumed. Thus, while still acknowledging the limits of representation, ecotheater must strive for representational balance and find innovative ways to imagine the other as relational without being relatable, connected without being cohesive, conceivable without being (fully) comprehensible.

Notes

1. This concept was first formulated by Donna Haraway.

2. Although Coleridge coined the phrase "willing suspension of disbelief," it was popularized in the theater by Stanislavski who, in *An Actor Prepares*, urged actors and audiences alike to suspend their disbelief.

3. I use the male pronoun for 7001, because, despite the fact that he does not have a human anatomy, the other characters consider him to be male.

4. I am grateful to Annika Speer for this suggestion.

5. As scientists K.-P. Schröder and Robert Connon Smith write: "It seems clear that the HZ [habitable zone] will move out past the Earth long before the Sun has expanded very much, even if the figure of one billion years is a rather rough estimate of how long we have before the Earth is uninhabitable" (5). While Mercury, Venus, and the Earth will eventually be engulfed by the Sun as it evolves into its final stage as a white dwarf star, this will occur several billion years after the Earth is uninhabitable (1).

6. Ecofeminism focuses on how women and indigenous people have been (mis)aligned with nature and represented as both nature's equal (and man's inferior) and its protector. For more on this, see Noël Sturgeon's *Ecofeminist Natures: Race, Gender, Feminist Theory and Political Action* and Greta Gaard's *Ecofeminism: Women, Animals, Nature*.

7. Resourcism, or shallow ecology, is the myth that "nature is an eco-machine, a virtual factory pouring out a stream of raw materials to be transformed into commodities" (Chaudhuri, "There" 25).

8. For more on the field of postcolonial ecocriticism and its concerns with deep ecology, see Rob Nixon's "Environmentalism and Postcolonialism" and Cara Cilano and Elizabeth DeLoughrey's "Against Authenticity: Global Knowledges and Postcolonial Ecocriticism."

9. Cilano and DeLoughrey draw on Patrick D. Murphy's *Farther Afield in the Study of Nature-Oriented Literature* in order to make this point.

10. According to the 2008 Coalition to Stop the Use of Child Soldiers (CSUCS) Global Report, "Children were actively involved in armed conflict in

government forces or non-state armed groups in nineteen countries or territories between April 2004 and October 2007."

11. Fifteen of the nineteen countries mentioned in the CSUCS report are postcolonial countries, while the remaining four have been or are still occupied: Chad, Central African Republic, Cote d'Ivoire, Sri Lanka, Uganda, India, Israel, Sudan, Somalia, Myanmar, Indonesia, Burundi, Democratic Republic of Congo, Colombia, and the Philippines are all postcolonial countries, while Nepal and Thailand have been occupied in the past and Afghanistan and the Occupied Palestine Territory continue to be occupied.

12. For more information on the Nyabingi religion and its role in anticolonialism, see Elizabeth Hopkin's "The Nyabingi Cult of Southwestern Uganda."

13. See Radhika Coomaraswamy's "Child Soldiers and Small Arms: the Link" and Scott Gates and Simon Reich's *Child Soldiers in the Age of Fractured States.*

Works Cited

Arva, Eugene L. "Writing the Vanishing Real: Hyperreality and Magical Realism." *Journal of Narrative Theory* 38.1 (2008): 60-85. Web. 10 June 2011.

Asiimwe, Deborah. *Forgotten World*. Kampala, Uganda: Masterly Book and Stationary Point, 2009. Print.

———. *"Forgotten World."* Message to the author. 23 March 2011. Email.

———. *"Forgotten World* Questions." Message to the author. 6 July 2011. E-mail.

Baby Universe: A Puppet Odyssey. By WakkaWakka Productions. Baruch Performing Arts Center, New York. 17 December 2010. Performance.

Betancourt, Theresa S., Robert T. Brennan, Julia Rubin-Smith, et al. "Sierra Leone's Former Child Soldiers: A Longitudinal Study of Risk, Protective Factors, and Mental Health." *Journal of the American Academy of Child & Adolescent Psychiatry* 49.6 (2010): 606-15. Web. 15 July 2011.

Chaudhuri, Una. *Staging Place: The Geography of Modern Drama*. Ann Arbor: U of Michigan P, 1997. Print.

———. " 'There Must Be a Lot of Fish in that Lake': Toward an Ecological Theater." *Theater* 25.1 (1994): 23-31. Print.

Cilano, Cara, and Elizabeth DeLoughrey. "Against Authenticity: Global Knowledges and Postcolonial Ecocriticism." *ISLE* 14.1 (2007): 71-87. Print.

Coalition to Stop the Use of Child Soldiers. *Child Soldiers Global Report 2008.* Web. 27 June 2011.

Coleridge, Samuel Taylor. *Biographia Literaria*. New York, 1834. The Literature Network. Web. 30 July 2011.

Coomaraswamy, Radhika. "Child Soldiers and Small Arms: The Link." *United Nations Office for Disarmament Affairs Occasional Papers No. 14, July 15,*

2008: Conflict of Interests: Children and Guns in Zones of Instability. New York: United Nations Publication, 2009. 1-4. Web. 10 June 2011.

DeLoughrey, Elizabeth, and George B. Handley, eds. "Introduction: Towards an Aesthetics of the Earth." *Postcolonial Ecologies: Literatures of the Environment.* Oxford: Oxford UP, 2011. 3-42. Print.

Fuss, Diana. *Essentially Speaking.* London: Routledge, 1989. Print.

Gaard, Greta, ed. *Ecofeminism: Women, Animals, Nature.* Philadelphia: Temple UP, 1993. Print.

Garb, Yaakov. "Perspectives or Escape? Ecofeminist Musings on Contemporary Earth Imagery." *Reweaving the World.* Ed. Irene Diamond and Gloria Orenstein. San Francisco: Sierra Club, 1990. 264-78. Print.

Garrard, Greg. *Ecocriticism.* London: Routledge, 2004. Print.

Gates, Scott, and Simon Reich, ed. "Introduction." *Child Soldiers in the Age of Fractured States.* Pittsburgh: U of Pittsburgh P, 2010. 3-13. Print.

Glissant, Édouard. *Poetics of Relation.* Trans. Betsy Wing. Michigan: U of Michigan P, 1997. Print.

Haraway, Donna. "Chapter Four: A Cyborg Manifesto: Science, Technology, and Socialist-Feminism in the Late 20th Century." *The International Handbook of Virtual LearningEnvironments,* 2006. 117-58.

———. "Otherworldly Conversations: Terrain Topics, Local Terms." *Science as Culture* 3.1 (1991): 64-98. Print.

———. *When Species Meet.* Posthumanities: Vol. 3. Minneapolis: U of Minnesota P, 2008. Print.

Hopkin, Elizabeth. "The Nyabingi Cult of Southwestern Uganda." *Protest and Power in Black Africa.* New York: Oxford UP, 1970. 258-336.

Kershaw, Baz. *Theatre Ecology: Environments and Performance Events.* Cambridge: Cambridge UP, 2007. Print.

Kirshenblatt-Gimblett, Barbara. *Destination Culture: Tourism, Museums, and Heritage.* Berkeley: U of California P, 1998. Print.

Kostelny, Kathleen. "A Culture-Based, Integrative Approach: Helping War-Affected Children." *A World Turned Upside Down: Social Ecological Approaches to Children in War Zones.* Eds. Neil Boothby, et al. Bloomfield, CT: Kumarian, 2006. 19-38. Print.

Marranca, Bonnie. *Ecologies of Theater: Essays at the Century Turning.* Baltimore: Johns Hopkins UP, 1996. Print.

May, Theresa J. "Greening the Theater: Taking Ecocriticism from Page to Stage." *Interdisciplinary Literary Studies* 7.1 (Fall 2005): 84-103. Print.

Nixon, Rob. "Environmentalism and Postcolonialism." *Postcolonial Studies and Beyond.* Ed. Ania Loomba, Suvir Kaul, et al. Durham: Duke UP, 2005. 233-51. Print.

Plumwood, Val. *Feminism and the Mastery of Nature.* New York: Routledge, 1993. Print.

Roach, Joseph. *Cities of the Dead: Circum-Atlantic Performance.* New York: Columbia UP, 1996. Print.

Schechner, Richard. *The Future of Ritual: Writings on Culture and Performance.* London: Routledge, 1993. Print.

Schröder, K.-P., and Robert Connon Smith. "Distant Future of the Sun and Earth Revisited." *MNRAS* 1.10 (2008): 1-10. Web. 10 June 2011.

Stanislavski, Constantin. *An Actor Prepares.* Trans. Elizabeth R. Hapgood. New York: Routledge, 1964. Print.

Sturgeon, Noël. *Ecofeminist Natures: Race, Gender, Feminist Theory and Political Action.* New York: Routledge, 1997. Print.

———. *Environmentalism in Popular Culture: Gender, Race, Sexuality, and the Politics of the Natural.* Tucson: the U of Arizona P, 2009. Print.

Index

Mother Nature, 57, 117, 132
Muir, John, 178
Mullner, Ross, 208n11, 208n12
Murphy, Patrick D., 254n9
Myanmar, 255n11

Nadir, Leila, 4, 175-189
Naess, Arne, 37
Nagasaki, 198
narrative, 28, 82, 125, 160, 285,
     187, 196, 215, 238, 239, 241,
     248, 252; collective, 133;
     grand, 87, 253; human
     salvation, 242; master, 245;
     realist, 253; universalist, 235,
     236
Nash, Damian, 84-85
National Communication
     Association, 2
National Public Radio, 51
Native American, 97, 128, 208n10
*Native American Drama: A Critical
     Perspective*, 203, 208n20
Natural Resources Conservation
     Service, 182
Natural Resources Defense
     Council, 63
Natural Resources Information
     Clearinghouse, 142n5
naturalization, 39
nature/culture binary, 235, 236,
     237, 242
natureculture, 235, 242
NeighborSpace, 109
Nellis, Jenny, 213
Nelson, Lisa, 173n2
Nepal, 255n11
New England, 165
new media, 175, 176, 181
The New Media Reader, 176
New York City, 150-151, 153, 165

The New York Times, 51
Newton Creek Nature Walk, 167
NGO, 125
Nixon, Rob, 254n8
No Impact Man, 87
nonhuman liberation, 27, 29-32, 35,
     37-38, 40-46
Nordland Visual Theater, 240
Northwest Territory, 196
NRCS, 182. *See also* Natural
     Resources Conservation
     Service
NYC, 179. *See also* New York City

Oak Ridge, TN, 207n7
Oakland, 20
Occupied Palestine Territory,
     255n11
Occupy Wall Street Movement, 30,
     41
ocean dead zone, 37
omnicide, 37, 44
Ontario, 63, 196
Openlands, 102
Opovoempé, 44
Oravec, Christine, 178
ownership, 79, 80
Oxbow Lake, 117, 118, 133. *See
     also* Lago Tres Chimabadas

Paroske, Marcus, 61
Peace Corps, 77
Pedal People, 162, 173n6
Pelias, Ronald J., 2, 87
Peppermint, Cary, 4, 175-189
perceptual intervention, 63, 68n1
performance, 1-257
performativity, 43, 46n8, 47n10,
     117, 176; geo-, 122
perspective by incongruity, 73, 74,
     76-77, 84, 85-87. *See also*
     Burke, Kenneth

About the Contributors

Richard D. Besel (Ph.D., University of Illinois) is an associate professor in the Communication Studies Department at California Polytechnic State University, San Luis Obispo. His primary research interests focus on rhetorical studies, environmental communication, science communication, and media studies. Dr. Besel's work has been published in a variety of books and journals, including *ANQ: A Quarterly Journal of Short Articles, Notes and Reviews; Communication Theory; Environmental Communication: A Journal of Nature and Culture; Making Connections: Interdisciplinary Approaches to Cultural Diversity;* and the *Southern Communication Journal.*

Jnan A. Blau (Ph.D., Southern Illinois University) is an associate professor in the Communication Studies Department at California Polytechnic State University, San Luis Obispo. His primary research interests focus on performance studies, performance theory, and cultural studies—especially as these relate to music and culture. His teaching has encompassed performance studies, intercultural communication, cultural studies, popular culture, and communication technology and culture. Dr. Blau's work has been published in a variety of venues, including *Cultural Studies ⇔ Critical Methodologies; Trans: Transcultural Music Review, Popular Music & Society;* the *Encyclopedia of Activism and Social Justice*; and blog essays at *HeadCount.org.*

Alison Bodkin (Ph.D., Southern Illinois University) is an interdisciplinary lecturer at James Madison University, where she teaches in Communication Studies, Environmental Studies, and Women's Studies. Alison is also the faculty advisor for the JMU EARTH Club, as well as a steering committee member of Climate Action Alliance of the Valley. Alison's primary research interests are environmental performance and environmental rhetoric. She was awarded the Dissertation Research Award in 2009 from Southern Illinois

University at Carbondale for her work on environmental comedic performance.

Jason Del Gandio (Ph.D., Southern Illinois University) is an assistant professor of public communication at Temple University. He specializes in the philosophy of communication, rhetoric, critical analysis, radical social and political theory, and to a lesser extent, performance studies. Jason's experiences with radical activism and grassroots organizing led to his first book, *Rhetoric for Radicals: A Handbook for 21st Century Activists* (New Society, 2008). He is now working on his next book, which focuses on the political relationship between desire and reality. In general, Jason is a writer, thinker, activist, and teacher dedicated to social justice. More information can be found at www.jasondelgandio.com.

Julia Handschuh is an artist and organizer who works at the intersection of dance, installation art and writing. She grew up studying improvisational movement and went on to enter the world of conceptual art. She draws dismantling buildings, lives in a cabin off the grid, plays in porcelain and paper and travels by bike and hitch. She's learning to articulate how each of these things are improvisational and site-specific in their own right. She received a BFA in performance and installation from The School of the Museum of Fine Arts, Boston and Tufts University and is currently a master's candidate in Performance Studies at New York University where she is focusing on improvisational dance, ecology and the politics of space. She is a recipient of the Jack Kent Cooke Foundation Community College and Continuing Graduate Scholar awards and has exhibited her work in New York, Boston, Key West, Oaxaca, Mexico, and Quebec, Canada.

Jess Larson is an associate professor of studio art and holds a Masters of Fine Arts in Sculpture from the University of Colorado, Boulder. Her work has been shown nationally and internationally in various group and solo shows, including the Spoletto Piccolo Festival and the Jerome Book Arts Exhibition at the Minnesota Center for the Book Arts. Her work has also been featured in *Allure* magazine and *Textiel Plus*.

Theresa J. May is assistant professor of Theatre Arts and Environmental Studies at the University of Oregon, where she is Artistic Director of Earth Matters On Stage: Ecodrama Playwrights Festival. She is co-editor of *Readings in Performance and Ecology*, forthcoming from

Palgrave/MacMillan. She has published articles on ecocriticism and feminism in *New England Theatre Journal; The Journal of Dramatic Theory and Criticism; On Stage Studies; American Drama;* and *Theatre Studies.* Chapters in edited volumes include "Remembering the Mountain: Grotowski's Deep Ecology" in *Performing Nature: Explorations in Ecology and the Arts,* Gabriella Giannachi and Stewart Nigel (eds.) Bern, Switzerland: Peter Lang (2006). She is co-author of *Greening Up Our Houses* (Drama Books, NY 1994), the first book on sustainable theatre management. Her current book project: *Earth Matters On Stage: Ecology and American Theater.* From 1989 to 2000 she was Artistic Director of Theatre in the Wild, doing site-specific and earth based theatre in Seattle, WA. In 1979 she participated in Project Mountain of Flame at the Teatr Laboratorium in Wroclaw, Poland, under direction of Jerzy Grotowski. She holds a Ph.D. in Theatre History and Criticism from University of Washington (2000), an MFA in Acting from the University of Southern California (1983), and a BA in Drama from the University of California at Irvine.

Leila Nadir is a writer, curator, artist, literary critic, and Mellon Post-Doctoral Fellow in Environmental Humanities at Wellesley College. She has a Ph.D. in English from Columbia University and is co-founder of ecoarttech, an interdisciplinary art collaborative, with new media artist Cary Peppermint. Recent exhibitions include the Whitney Museum of American Art, Exit Art Gallery, Neuberger Museum of Art, the Sonoma County Museum, and the European Media Art Festival. Leila is also at work on a book manuscript on the role of sacrifice in the imagination of modernity, sustainability, and democracy in environmental art and literature. She has published writing on eco-art, American literature, and digital studies, and was the 2008 recipient of the Society of Utopian Studies Arthur Lewis Reward and a 2009 artist fellow of the New York Foundation for the Arts.

Cary Peppermint is a new media environmental artist and co-founder of the EcoArtTech collaborative. His work is in the collection of the Whitney Museum of American Art. He has taught at Cornell University, Colgate University, and Bronx Community College, and is currently Assistant Professor of Digital Art at University of Rochester. More information about his practice can be found at www.EcoArtTech.org.

Courtney Ryan is a Ph.D. candidate in UCLA's department of Theater and Performance Studies. Her dissertation, "Ecological Encounters: Staging Women, Nature, and Aliens," examines theatrical genealogies of ecofeminism and considers the cultural interrelations between women and nature, both of whom have been (mis)represented as simultaneously earthly and otherworldly. Her work has been published in the March 2011 volume of *Theatre Journal*. Courtney presented a paper in 2009 for the ATHE Emerging Scholar Panel, and, in the summer of 2010, she attended Northwestern's Summer Institute in Performance Studies.

Ray Schultz (Ph.D., Wayne State University) is an associate professor of theatre arts at the University of Minnesota, Morris, and has published articles on Terrence McNally, Lanford Wilson, and Tony Kushner. His professional acting credits include roles in *Angels in America, Doubt*, and *Take Me Out*; directing credits include *The Laramie Project, The Little Dog Laughed* and *The Merchant of Venice*, among others.

David P. Terry (Ph.D., University of North Carolina at Chapel Hill) is an assistant professor of performance studies in the Communication Studies Department at San José State University. His work has been published in *Qualitative Inquiry*; *Theatre Annual*; and *Text and Performance Quarterly*; heard on WBEZ Chicago's Re:Sound; and audienced at stages around the country. He is currently at work on a book about heterotopic performance and alternative modes of belonging based on ethnographic research in Athens, Greece.

Anne Marie Todd (Ph.D., University of Southern California) is an associate professor of public communication in the Communication Studies Department at San José State University. Her research and teaching interests focus on environmental rhetoric, with an emphasis on popular culture, climate change and environmental activism. She has published numerous book chapters and journal articles in these areas including publications in *Environmental Communication: A Journal of Nature and Culture*; *Critical Studies in Media Communication*; and *Public Understanding of Science*. She is currently working on a study of environmental patriotism.

Barbara Willard (Ph.D., University of Iowa) is an associate professor in the College of Communication at DePaul University. Her research involves the rhetoric of landscapes as they are both read by and created by humans. Additionally, she examines how the rhetoric of popular culture and environmental rhetoric intersect, informing and influencing cultural practice. She also conducts research that assists in the development of public campaigns that foster sustainable behavior such as natural landscaping and support for restoration practices. She has published in a variety of academic journals including *Environmental Communication: A Journal of Nature and Culture*; *Rhetoric Society Quarterly*; and the *Journal of Popular Culture*.